FROM BEHIND THE SCREEN

FROM BEHIND THE SCREEN

How a Brash Young Man from Jim Crow New Orleans Became a Civil Rights Leader in Texas

Curtis M. Graves

Bartleby Press
Washington • Baltimore

ISBN 978-0-935437-61-4 (print)
ISBN 978-0-88400-402-8 (ebook)
Library Of Congress Control Number: 2023941978

Bartleby Press
JACKSON WESTGATE PUBLISHING GROUP
PO Box 858
Savage, MD 20763
800-953-9929
BartlebythePublisher.com

Printed in the United States of America

10 9 8 7 6 5 4 3 2 1

CONTENTS

A s a child you learn so much sitting at the knees of your parents. I know I learned what love was all about. They truly loved me. I learned a sense of right and wrong. They raised me with the belt so I knew early that I needed to take the right path. They gave me a since of self worth. They did what ever it took to make me feel that I was as good as anyone else. From sitting at their knees, I learned about early civil rights because being raised in segregated New Orleans I needed to know how to navigate that stream.

From sitting at the knees of my grandparents, (my mother's parents), I learned a sense of family history. We came from proud people who knew where they were going even when the times were hard and the laws were not in their favor. Being raised in the house with grandparents has lots of advantages that you don't see until you are an adult. It truly was a blessing to be the only child in a house of four adults who spoke *adult* around me. I needed to know what was happening in the world just to keep up with the dinner conversation every night. It really made me the man I grew to be.

It is said that we are all composites of our experiences and I think we can take that to another level. We are not only a blend of our experiences but also a synthesis of the actions of our ancestors.

So when looking at why and how we do what we do, we must also look at how and why our ancestors did what they did.

When I watched episodes of Dr. Henry Lewis Gates PBS series, *Finding Your Roots*, it struck me that in many cases his research shows that his subjects seem to be repeating the deeds of their ancestors in more cases then one can chart up to coincidence.

You will see in the pages of this book, many things about my ancestors in order to better understand why I took the paths that I took.

However, when I entered the political world, I needed someone else to teach me that side of things. That came from Robert (Bob) Eckhardt. In the Foreword of the book, *Eckhardt* by Gary Keith (University of Texas Press), Al Gore said this about Bob:

> "Bob Eckhardt was an intellectual giant who made an indelible mark on the work of the U.S. House of Representatives during the fourteen years he served in that great institution."

I learned so much about the world of politics and the law just flying slightly below his wings. Gary Keith said it better than I.

> "Of all the things that are Politics, one of the more obvious is that it is a never-ending battle between competing centers of   power. Politics is also biography, and these two approaches to understanding politics come together in the life of Bob Eckhardt.

> "He is a fascinating, colorful individual who spent his career fighting to wrest power from the economic centers and likewiseto use public office to empower labor unions, to strengthen Citizens against corporate power, and to invigorate environmental and consumer interests.... As a lawyer, state legislator, and Congressman, Eckhardt made a lasting mark on public policies, breathing life into progressive politics in Texas and the nation and living a legacy of lawmaking."

Throughout the years there were others, of course, but Bob was my sounding board, legal advisor and introducer to some of the political movers and shakers of the day. We often helped each other at times when the way forward was not easily seen.

ONE

THE EARLY YEARS

My earliest memory in life is of the December 7, 1941 attack on Pearl Harbor. I was a little over three years old. My mother had given me a bath, wrapped me in a towel and sat me down on the ironing board right outside of our bathroom at 3711 S. Galvez Street in New Orleans. As she dried me off, I remember someone coming in with a newspaper. I learned later that it was a *States Items* "Extra." Before twenty-four hour cable news, the newspaper would put out an "Extra" when big news happened after the morning paper was printed. I remember that there was a black picture centered on the first page. She started crying. I said to her, "Why are you crying?"

"We are going to war," she told me. "People are going to die."

I do not have many memories of the war years. However, I do remember that my dad, Fregelio Joseph Graves—he went by Buddy—was, among other things, a neighborhood Air Raid Warden. Most coastal cities had Air Raid Wardens during the war. Cities were divided into areas and all the assigned Air Raid Wardens were responsible for making sure the lights were off and everyone was indoors when the air raid siren went off in their area. Each Air Raid Warden had a white hard hat, a yellow jacket and a night stick. I would put on dad's hat when nobody was watching. I recall sitting in the living room (which we New Orleanians call the front room) before our large freestanding radio listening to President Roosevelt giving us updates on the war effort. Later, that same radio delivered the news that the war was over.

When I was about three years old, my parents sent me off to the only colored nursery school in the city. It was the Martinez Nursery School, founded in the mid-1930s by a lady whose influence must have touched the children of most of the Creole families in New Orleans at that time. Any family that could afford it sent their children to Miss Martinez's. She was a tall, light brown-skinned lady who knew every child by name and loved each and ever one. She seemed to know more about us and our families than we knew about ourselves.

As I recall her, she knew all our parents and our individual backgrounds. So I guess, at that point in my life, she really did know more about us then we knew about ourselves.

The Creole descendants of New Orleans included a mixture of French, German, Spanish, and Italian, with American Indian and African peoples thrown in. They found themselves in a place where their various cultures could mix into a "Gumbo" of people unique among the cultures of the United States. In some cases they were *gens de couleur libres*, or free people of color, and in others they were descendants of slaves. In his book *Blackcreole*, Dr. Maurice Martinez, a son of my teacher, Mrs. Martinez, talks about these free people of color needing a written license known as "Walking Papers" to navigate the streets of New Orleans in the 1800s. As you can see, the "Gumbo" that made up the New Orleans Creole population in the early 1940s was a diverse lot.

I was picked up each morning to go to Martinez Nursery

School by Mrs. Roane. She lived just around the corner from us so I got picked up first. She would have me by myself for several minutes and I would give her a detailed report on what was going on in our house. One of these reports included my dad's work during the war as a food inspector at the New Orleans Port of Embarkation.

Much of the food that was going to the troops came through New Orleans and was put on ships to feed the US fighting forces wherever they were stationed. Many years later, as an adult, I was told how the process worked. One case of whatever was being shipped would be taken off the train or ship and inspected to see if it was the quality that the government wanted. Inspection completed, the inspection team would divide up the rest of the box and take it home to their families. My dad would come home with a big can of cookies, or a ham, or other grocery items that a family normally would have needed ration stamps to be able to buy from the store. I started telling Mrs. Roane what goodies we got, but that caused problems. One day, as my mother was paying for my daily rides, she was confronted about how we were getting all this food.

Well, from that day forward the food came in the house under the cover of darkness. After my eyes were closed and I was long asleep, the extra food would make its way to our pantry. I could no longer blow the cover of our additional food supply.

I also have a lot of memories of my mother's work as a dressmaker. In many cases, dressmakers were called seamstresses. In Creole New Orleans, there were many seamstresses who worked at the clothing factories around the city. In the hierarchy of seamstresses, the dressmakers were at the top. At one time my mother had started a little business with two of her relatives to make dresses for the wealthy white folks of the city. She would

Galvez Street. New Orleans, 1942.

occasionally ask for help when she had a big job, such as a beaded wedding dress. The business did not last long, however.

For a time, she would go to white ladies' homes and do their sewing for them "on premises." "On premises" was a common term for people who worked and/or lived in a home or who would come by day to do various jobs. That ended when she went to a home on St. Charles Avenue and the lady of the house said to her, "Mabel, the cook will have your lunch on the table in the kitchen."

When lunchtime came and she went down to the kitchen, she noticed another plate of food was placed on the table. It was for the gardener. A few minutes after she was seated and eating, he came in smelling like sweat combined with the garden. Without washing his hands, he sat down and started eating. She got up quietly and determined that she would no longer eat in anyone's kitchen. She ate at her sewing machine a few times and then resolved that all her customers needed to come to her if they wanted her dresses. Because my mother was such a good dressmaker, most were willing to travel. All her customers were white.

One day a longtime customer came to see my mother to get something made. She parked her large car in our driveway and saw me playing on the sidewalk outside of the house. She called me over by name. "Here's something for you."

She attempted to give me a nickel. I dropped it on the ground. She gave me one of those looks that you always remember from someone who knows that they're doing you a big favor and you're too dumb to take it. She stormed up the stairs without saying another word to me and reported my actions to my mother.

Without hesitation, Mother told her that I had been taught not to take money from anyone. She was angry that a black child wouldn't take her money. She considered it a sign of disrespect. But my mother was firm. She must have been very good at her job, because despite the perceived disrespect, the lady kept coming for new dresses until Mother retired from dressmaking and moved from the neighborhood.

If Mother was told by one of her customers that they liked a dress displayed in a window at one of the downtown department stores, she would ask the color and what window. She would catch the bus, go to Canal Street, find the store, and make a sketch of the dress. Then she would buy the material requested and, without a pattern, make that dress. Because of her talent, all who could afford her kept coming. Today you'd call those dresses knock-offs. But back then, it was the way things got done in New Orleans.

My last memory of Martinez Nursery School was the day of

graduation. The graduation was held at Booker T. Washington High School Auditorium. I was all dressed in my little cap and gown and my dad presented me with my graduation gift before I went to sit with my class of newly-minted Martinez graduates. It was a Mickey Mouse watch with Mickey standing in the middle of the watch face with one short arm and one long arm that would point out the time. I started winding the watch as soon as he put it on my arm. By the time the graduation was over, the stem was in my hand and the watch never worked a day after that one. It sat at the bottom of my underwear drawer with the stem beside it for many years. I learned that it was unfixable, and it was a memory of that day that was unfulfilled. But, twice every day the time was right, and like most things that go back that far in your life, it dropped from sight.

The next year, when I had just turned six years old, my mother enrolled me in the second grade at St. Monica's Catholic School at First and Galvez Streets. It was a seven block walk from our house. My mother walked me to school the first two days and walked those evenings to pick me up. On the third day she said, "You are a big boy now and you can walk by yourself."

Only one street, Washington Avenue, had a lot of traffic, and at that time there was just a stop sign to control the passing cars. I was on my own crossing Washington Avenue, but after all, my mother said that I was a big boy, and I knew I just had to do it. Today, of course, a six-year-old child would be a target walking the streets of a major city. But 1943 New Orleans was a different time.

I skipped the first grade and was placed directly into second grade. The class levels were a little fluid anyway. I met a number of kids in second grade that I would never forget. A few made their musical mark on New Orleans and around the world.

Ernest Kador, known throughout his life as Ernie K-Doe, was an R&B artist who had a number one hit in 1961 with "Mother-in-Law" and was known for other popular songs.

James Booker's piano style that combined rhythm and blues with jazz became synonymous with the New Orleans sound. Flamboyant and difficult, he earned his nickname, the Piano Prince of New Orleans. A documentary called *Bayou Maharajah* was made about his legendary life.

Arthur and Charles Neville were also in the class. Along with younger brothers Aaron and Cyril, they traveled the world performing as the Neville Brothers. We stayed in touch all these years. Charles and Artie, as we called him, are gone, but Aaron and I still talk and text regularly. We've been friends for more then seventy years—a rare thing.

There were 72 students in that second grade class. I remember because many mornings I was asked to write the number on the blackboard in the upper right corner after the nun had made her count and called the roll.

After the fourth grade, my parents moved me to McDonogh #6. John McDonogh had given money to the city of New Orleans for public schools in the mid-1800s, resulting in the city naming

St. Monica School , 1945

both black and white schools after him. Number 6, as it was called, was a public school that had a reputation for excellence. My mom and dad thought that Number 6 would give me a better chance to learn. The class size was in the thirties so I did well.

After the seventh grade, the junior high school system was instituted in the black schools of New Orleans. I went to S. J. Green Jr. High. This is where I met Peter Clark. Despite his day job as a math teacher, he was a sports guy in the truest sense of the word. He was frequently on WBOK radio to call many of the local college games and some of the high school games. I became his radio engineer. I would go to the games with him and be at his 10 a.m. Sunday radio show. It was very exciting for me. After the eighth grade at Green, I went to Xavier Preparatory School. The Prep, as we called it, was one of only three Catholic high schools for colored children in the City.

James Booker playing piano in the Graves house

It was a good time in the Graves/Haydel household. My mother's father, Elphege Haydel (known by everyone as Bull), and his wife, Josephine Honore Haydel, lived with us. We had the kind of house that was welcoming to everyone. It was strange for us to have Sunday dinner without one or two guests. We frequently had family members or friends of my mother or father come over to stay a few days or just come over to eat with us. Over the years, some of these people became quite well-known. I was reminded by my father that Thurgood Marshall spent a night or two with us. In the 40s and 50s, segregation demanded that when people came to town to defend civil rights cases, for example, they were placed with a family since there were no hotels where they could stay. In the case of Marshall, he was brought over to our house by A. P. Tureaud, a local attorney who handled much of the civil rights issues in New Orleans and throughout Louisiana.

When Marshall was nominated to the Supreme Court years later, my dad called to ask if I remembered him. I said that I didn't.

"You remember him, he slept in your bed and you slept on the couch in the living room. He's a tall, light-skinned man who told a lot of jokes. He loved your mother's cooking."

Years later I was living in Washington and a neighborhood friend named Willie Branton, also a civil rights attorney, died. I went to the wake and sure enough Justice Thurgood Marshall was there. There were people around him so I waited my turn to speak to him. I introduced myself and told him that I was Buddy Graves' son from New Orleans. "You spent a few days at our house when you had cases in New Orleans," I said.

I could see from his face that he didn't recall. I added, "You were brought to our house by A. P. Tureaud. We lived in a large white house in the uptown section of the city."

I could see his face light up. "Oooh, your momma could cook."

"What do you mean *could* cook? She's cooking like that right now!"

The smile never left his face. "I got to find a time to get to New Orleans to get some more of that good cookin'."

More recently, I learned that he stayed with several families when he had business in New Orleans. I found out from Farrell Christophe that Justice Marshall also stayed at his parent's home. His father was Haidel Christophe, an insurance executive in the city and a neighbor of Dr. C. C. Haydel. In addition to being my mother's first cousin, Dr. Haydel was one of my dad's best friends. I guess they passed people like Thurgood Marshall around, depending on who had room for him to stay for a day or so.

Both my mother and father did everything they could to try to shield me from the harsh reality of growing up Colored in the south in the 40s and 50s. To be blunt, they lied a lot. They had a deception or fib for everything that would have caused me to think that I was anything but first class. They told me that we sat upstairs in the movies because you could see better than sitting downstairs. They told me that we needed to sit in the back of the bus because it was cooler. They told me that we sat in the first coach on the train because we would get off first. The glasses at the lunch counter just weren't clean at D.H. Homes, Maison Blanche, or Kress, the department stores on Canal Street, and that's why we couldn't eat there.

I remember asking my mother if I could go to tell Santa Claus what I wanted for Christmas. She replied, without missing a step, "The lines are too long."

I guess they were too long for several more years. I never did tell that Santa Claus what I wanted, but on Christmas Day the gifts came anyway. It was like the comedian Dick Gregory who said that he did not believe in Santa Claus because he knew a "white dude" would never come into his neighborhood at night.

They had a great hoax for everything to protect me. I may have gotten a lot of lies during those days, but my self-worth was intact. One could say that I was living on a little island in the middle of a segregated New Orleans. My block was all Colored but I didn't think that much of it. The blocks around me were white. I even had some white friends who lived in the neighborhood, but I didn't go into their homes and they didn't go in mine.

I really don't know how old I was when I figured it all out. However, I do remember that it was a Friday night. My mother and I had walked to the Tivoli Theater to see a movie. This was almost a weekend ritual for me at that age. I went to either the Friday or Saturday movie with my mom or dad or my two older cousins, Belmont and Byron Haydel. They had to pass my house to get to our local theater. As I remember it, the lights came up after the movie ended and I said to her, "I know why we're not sitting downstairs."

"Why?"

"We're not white," I said.

On the way back, walking the seven blocks to our home, she laid it all out for me. All those stories she and my dad had told me were not true. It was strategy designed for me to feel good about myself and not think that I was less than anyone else. As I look back at it now, that was a very important lesson that I needed to learn. It just might have given me the confidence to do whatever I thought I could in life.

New Orleans was segregated, but I still had a rich childhood. Not because we were rich, but because my parents wanted me to be exposed to as many things as they could expose me to. For instance, there were no radio stations that programmed Black music. As a matter of fact, there was only one hour a week that a Black person spoke on the radio. That was 11 a.m. on Sundays. Broadcasting from the gymnasium of the Dryades Street YMCA (the black YMCA), a local principal of one of the public schools had an hour long program. He was O.C.W. Taylor and it was called the O.C.W. Taylor Hour. It had a sponsor, Wylon Beauty Products, a Black-owned beauty products company, and he interviewed Black stars and sports personalities that were in the city. My dad took me many times to see the broadcast at the Y. What I did not know until many years later was that Mr. Taylor could not broadcast from the studios of WNOE, the station that carried the show. He had to find a location in our community for the show to be remotely broadcast.

When my parents took me to plays and music events, we were always seated in a segregated section or it was all Black folks.

One Saturday, when I was ten or twelve years old, my mother asked me to walk over the Washington Ave. and Broad Street to buy two dozen French dinner rolls from the Broadmoor Bakery. It was her turn to host the Ladies Bridge Club for their monthly gathering and before the games, the host would have dinner for the twelve or so ladies. She gave me the money and I went down the steps to make the seven block walk, but I decided to ride my bike instead of walk. I was at the bakery in no time at all. Back on the bike, I was riding while holding the dinner rolls in one hand and guiding myself with the other. The street had just been paved and the pavement did not go all the way to the curb, so there was a drop-off of about six inches from the street to the ground. I was riding facing traffic but moved too close to the edge and dropped off, losing my balance. I fell, hurt my leg, and bent the fender of my bike. But I did not drop the dinner rolls.

I could not ride, my leg was hurting so bad. So I made my

way back by walking the last block and a half to the house holding the rolls and guiding the bike.

When I delivered the rolls to my mother, she could see that I had some blood on my pants. When I took off my pants, my leg was bruised and hurting. My dad soon arrived home, looked at my leg, and said that he thought it needed to be X-rayed to see if it was broken.

So we were off to Charity Hospital to check me out. It was the only emergency room that was open to Blacks. Within a few minutes of our arrival, I was X-rayed and told that I had a fracture slightly above the knee. It wasn't bad and with a cast, it would heal in about six weeks.

My dad was asked to leave the room so the doctors could put on the cast. He stood right outside the room so he could hear everything that was said.

Charity Hospital was a teaching facility where the Tulane University doctors trained, so a medical intern and his supervisor were attending to me. As he was putting on the cast, one of them pressed on my leg and asked, "Does this hurt?"

"No," I replied.

He pressed another place and asked the same question. "A little," I responded that time.

After a few more questions, the doctor who was supervising said to me, "Boy, don't you know how to talk to white people?"

I said nothing.

He looked straight at me. "When you're talking to white people, you say 'yes sir' and 'no sir.'"

Again I didn't say anything, but I did shake my head to let him know that I understood.

When they were finished and had given me crutches, they wheeled me out. My dad took over. "I can handle it from here," he said.

I could tell that he was not happy. I thought he was going to give me a hard time about not walking and trying to balance the rolls and drive the bike.

Saying nothing, he checked me out and helped me into the car. Once inside, he cleared his throat and looked at me before starting the car.

"I was standing outside the room and heard everything that was said to you. It was all I could do to not break into the room and stop them from telling you how to talk to white people."

I thought he was mad at *me*, but it was something altogether different. It was a teaching moment. He had to get something off his chest.

"You did the right thing. You answered his questions as you should have. There are times that out of common respect you might answer older people with a 'yes sir' or 'no sir.' They were not older people. Yes and no was all they needed from you. I knew that they were helping you and I didn't want them to hurt you in any way, so I said nothing."

"Son," he went on. "Under any other conditions, I would have been in there to stop them. I wanted to let you know that you were right. But young white boys do act like that from time to time."

Yes, it was a teaching moment for me. You have to know when to hold them and when to fold them. Still, kissing a young white person's ass just because they're white is not something that I should ever do.

By the time I was in high school, I was more observant of things around me. One Friday night I was sitting on the Louisiana Avenue Bus. A mother got on with her little boy. The little boy sat right behind the driver while his mother paid the fourteen cent fare for the two of them.

The mother grabbed him by the arm and said, "You can't sit there, that seat is for white folks."

I came home that evening and kissed my mother on the cheek. Clearly surprised that her teenage son would show her that much open affection, exclaimed, "What was that for?"

I smiled. "I just want to thank you for lying to me all those years about why we sat behind the screen in the back of the bus."

I described what I had witnessed on the bus and how I really understood what she and dad were protecting me from. Each time I saw something similar, I thanked my parents for never laying that on me.

My first big train ride seems like it was just yesterday. It was from New Orleans to New York City. It was summer, and I was eight. My mother wanted to visit her cousin Lucy who lived in Brooklyn. I loved my Aunt Lucy and remembered spending many evenings with her and her family before they moved to New York. In New Orleans, they lived in a large corner house with rocking chairs and a swing on the front porch. Aunt Lucy was a big woman who talked very fast. Most of what she had to say was funny. She had two children, Lucia and Harold Jr., who we called H.S. My mother was H.S.'s godmother. Her children were much older than me but always fun to be with.

We boarded the train at the station on Canal Street. Before the train arrived, Mother prepared me for what was to happen. She said, "Now, when the train comes we're going to sit in the very first coach. We want to get to New York first before all the people on the train."

We sat in the first coach behind the engine. I thought nothing of it. We had a good seat in a coach of nice people who looked like us. By the time we were heading into Hattiesburg, Mississippi, I had figured out the process. The conductor, a tall white man with a black suit and a strange hat, would enter the coach and say, "Hattiesburg, Hattiesburg, next stop is Hattiesburg, Mississippi." By the time we got into Georgia, I was waiting for him at the back of the car so I could follow and say, "Atlanta, Atlanta, the next stop is Atlanta, Georgia."

It was great fun, all the way to New York. Mother had packed a large bag with food so I was well fed and I had a memorable adventure.

New York was just wonderful. We visited Coney Island and the Empire State Building. We took the subway and used the automat. Oh, the automat food that just came out of the wall was like magic to an eight-year-old boy. You would put your money in and open a little glass door and get your pie. We even went to a Broadway play.

When we went to Coney Island, I remember Aunt Lucy taking us on the subway. Inside the park, there was a super ferris wheel. It was the biggest ferris wheel I had ever seen. It was called the "Wonder Wheel." Not only did it have the chair seats on the outside of the three-story wheel, but it also had chairs that moved around in the middle. I remember Aunt Lucy saying to my mother, "Don't let them put you in one of those inside seats. They'll drive you crazy."

One of those moveable chairs came towards us as the wheel turned. Yep, it almost drove me crazy. I didn't know if it was going to hit us or not. Crazy was a good word for those moveable chair seats.

The other thing I never forgot was getting a hot dog on the corner outside of Coney Island. Oh, a Coney Island hot dog with all the runny stuff on it was like heaven! As we were standing on the corner wolfing down our dogs, Aunt Lucy said to my mother with her quick humor, "Mabel, you see this corner."

My mother nodded "yes" because her mouth was full of that good dog.

"You can sell anything here. You could say 'Shit on a stick, shit on a stick,' and people would buy it."

I remember my mother looking at me with her finger at her

lips. She did not want me to hear "shit on a stick." But Aunt Lucy said it and that was that. However, it was not to be repeated. Now, after all these years, I have done it, repeated for all to hear. Shit on a stick.

It was the trip back home that caught my attention. We boarded The Southerner (the train that went from New York to New Orleans daily) at Grand Central station in New York and sat just anywhere we could find a seat. That is, anywhere that wasn't first class. At Washington, D.C. everyone was made to get off the train and re-board. Washington, D.C. is where Jim Crow became reality. All the Negroes were shown to the first car. Once again, my mother explained that these were better seats than the ones we had before. And after all, we would get to New Orleans and see my dad before all the other people on the train. So I took my better seat with full knowledge that we were going to get to New Orleans first. I called out the cities behind the conductor, ate the food that Aunt Lucy had fixed for us, and enjoyed the ride back to New Orleans. I never did not put it all together until after that Friday talk on the way back from the Tivoli Theater.

It was a good time in my life. Not too long after that New York trip, one of my cousins came to live with us and became the sister that I always wanted. My mother's cousin Godfrey, who we called Bolute, came over one evening and talked to my mom and dad behind close doors. After he left, Mother said to me that a cousin named Margaret, Bolute's youngest daughter, was coming to live with us. Mother said, "She's a very nice girl and she'll be company for you."

So our household grew to six. That turned out to be one of the best things that ever happened to me. Margaret came to live with us at about twelve years old and she has been my big sister ever since. Although she had blood sisters and brothers, our relationship has remained as brother and sister to this day.

I had been taking saxophone lessons since I was seven, so I

signed up for the band when I got to Xavier Prep High School. The Prep had at least four band leaders in the four years I was there. First we had Renald Richard, who went on to become an arranger and conductor for Ray Charles and also played the trumpet in his band. Then came Ludwig Freeman, a graduate of Michigan State University. He went on to become the director of the Southern University "Marching One Hundred" band. During my senior year we had Ellis Marsalis as band director. He and I had a run-in or two but we became lifelong friends. He and his sons are one of the most talented and well-known musical families of New Orleans. Actually, I'd say that they're one of the most prominent musical families of our nation.

Between them, I was the leader of the band for a month or two. It was fun and gave me some leadership experience.

I had to catch either a street car and a bus or two to get to The Prep. That is where I encountered "The Screen"was the cause of many incidents. Too many to ever remember all of them.

The Screen was a moveable sign that set on the top of the seat and divided the coloreds from the whites. It had nice rounded edges and two metal pegs that were secured into the bottom. They would fit into two holds on the top of each seat so it would sit upright to divide the races.

In some cities they called it "The Board," but in New Orleans we called it "The Screen."

Because it could be fairly easily turned around, we would face it forward from time to time. Eventually white folks would get on, grab it, and turn it back the other way. Because it pissed them off so much, we did it when ever we got the chance. A number of times when the bus or street car was full, we would throw The Screen out the window. One cold day, as I was getting off the bus from the back door, I put a Screen under my jacket and took it home. I kept it for years: a trophy from the age of segregation. I lost track of it over the years. I wish I still had it; I would put it up in our den.

One could say that I was born behind The Screen. I lived through my teenage years behind The Screen. Although The Screen did affect my life, I was not about to let it stop me from improving my life and doing whatever I wanted to do.

The Screen was designed to keep me and all other "Colored Patrons" in their place. However, I found a way to move around it, freely doing what I needed to do and going where I needed to go. Out from behind The Screen, I have made the life I have lived. Now that I think about that with the clear vision of many years, it just must be deeper than that.

My dad once said to me that we would not know who Moses was today if it weren't for Pharaoh. "Because Mr. Pharaoh would not let Mo and his people go, we know of him today," he explained.

Who knows what I would have become if The Screen was not stuck in my face. It just might have been the obstacle that I needed to make me move around; it set me on the path I took. It was really like a neon light flashing in your face every day, designed to keep you in your place. Just where was my place? Was it in the first car on the train, or in the back of the bus, or upstairs in the movie theater, or at the very end of a lunch counter at a store, or the last seat on the left side in church? They really could not make up their mind just where to put us Colored folks.

I can still remember the priest in a Catholic Church refusing to give Black parishioners communion until all the white people had received it first. How is that a Christian thing to do? But that was the way it was in a post-Reconstruction city in the southern part of these United States. You were told to accept the way things were or life was going to be hard for you.

In the summer between my junior and senior years of high school I was invited to attend Bayou Boys State, a ten-day summer leadership camp experience held at Southern University. The

Boys State program was (and still is) sponsored by the American Legion in each state.

When segregation ruled the southern states, there were two Boys State programs. In Louisiana, Pelican Boys State, the program for white boys, was held on the campus of Louisiana State University (LSU) in Baton Rouge. One was held at the main state university for white boys and another one at the main Black university. The Black Boys State program was called Bayou Boys State and it was conducted on the campus of Southern University (SU), again in Baton Rouge. Is that not something special? White boys were Pelicans and Black boys were Bayou Boys.

Two kids between their junior and senior year were invited from every Black high school in the state. The concept is to teach students about citizenship. At that time, society in general believed that only boys needed such citizenship training. It wasn't until '59 or '60 that wiser heads decided that girls were also deserving of knowledge about being good citizens.

The boys were first divided into cities and allowed to elect their leaders. I think I was first elected as a city councilman of Pine City. The city officials were given some responsibility to run the city. Two cities were put together to make a parish. A parish would be the same as a county in any other state. They then elected parish officials. By the end of the camp, we had elected a governor, lieutenant governor, state representatives, state senators and a supreme court. I became a senator and then a member of the Bayou Boys State Supreme Court.

It was fun and a great learning experience. I must have been a standout because I was invited to come back the next summer to be a counselor. I was a counselor for the next five years. It was a nice little gig when school was out. I even served as a counselor for the first two sessions of Bayou Girls State.

Bayou Boys State was my real first involvement in the world of politics. By my second year as a counselor, I was picking the leaders and giving them some secret advice which helped them become the state leaders at the end. In two of the last years, I was the one picking the boys to be counselors.

One of the boys I picked was a second cousin who lived in Baton Rouge named John (Bill) Haydel. After college, he and his family moved to Los Angeles. He went on to get a masters degree and become a principal at several of the L.A. schools. He's told me several times that the experience he had at Bayou Boys State changed his life. In his words, "It was that early training that I needed to develop leadership skills."

Over the years, our family grew some more. My father had a son named Kenneth who was being raised by his mother's sister. They lived in Madisonville, Louisiana. He was about a month old when his mother, my father's first wife, died. She knew that she wasn't going to live so she gave him to her sister to raise. Aunt Ginny, as I called her, was a loving woman who treated Kenneth like he was her own son. She cooked some of the best food that I've ever eaten. Whenever I visited her to spend some time with my big brother, I just could not get enough to eat.

I spent many good summer weeks with her and Kenneth during my early years. Madisonville was on the other side of the lake from New Orleans. Aunt Ginny lived just across the street from her brother Charley, my dad's first brother-in-law. He and his wife, Dorothy, had no children, so they adopted me during those summers.

Uncle Charley was a man of many skills. He was a boat builder, a boat captain, an outstanding fisherman, a hunter, and many other things. He took me rabbit hunting and fishing. He had good rabbit dogs that he trained. He taught me how to shoot and let me use his single shot .410 shotgun.

Truth be told, he didn't need to teach me much about shooting because my dad was also great fisherman and hunter. Despite my mother's objections, he had me in the woods hunting before

I was eight years old. I never knew a time when my dad didn't have a boat, so we went fishing all the time. I don't remember ever playing ball with him, but did we fish and hunt.

I also spent many hours fishing with my Uncle Butsy, my mother's brother and my dad's business partner. He would take me and two of his boys, Elphege and Honore, out many times to do both freshwater and saltwater fishing.

After Kenneth came back from two years in the Army, he asked my mom and dad if he could stay with us. He had seen the big cities of Europe and the United States and did not want to move back to the little town of Madisonville, Louisiana. He and I shared a room and the conversations we had many nights helped me become the person I am today. He just happened to move in when I started dating and he became my mentor. It was rewarding to have an older brother nearby to learn from and share things with.

This was during my last years at Xavier Prep and first two years at Xavier University. After two years at Xavier University, I wanted to get away from my parents and New Orleans so I got my transcript and headed to Southern University to have a talk with Dr. Rodney Higgins, the dean of the political science department at Southern and the director of the Bayou Boys State program. I was still working summers for him as a counselor at Boys State. I told him that I wanted to move on from Xavier and change my major from Mathematics to Business Administration. I had gotten some advice that did not sit well with me from Xavier's Dean of Students.

The Dean was a Blessed Sacrament nun who advised me to drop out of school and "do something with my hands." I was making C's in math so in her mind, I was not college material. I resolved that very day to leave Xavier and attend another university. So I jumped into my 1951 Mercury that Kenneth had given me and off I sped to Baton Rouge. After spending a day with Dr. Higgins and his wife, he suggested that I go to either Texas Southern University or Tennessee State University.

Trusting his good advice, my main question was where the two universities were located. He told me that Texas Southern was in Houston and Tennessee State was in Nashville.

I had already begun deciding. "Which one is the closest?" I asked.

"Houston is the closest."

That settled it.

"What do I need to do to get into Texas Southern?"

If Higgins was at all surprised, he didn't show it. Smiling, he said that he knew the registrar and would call him for me. I headed off to Houston the next morning and two days later, I was registered at Texas Southern University (TSU).

I moved into a TSU dormitory. Crammed in a room with three other students, I was not happy. The first evening, they played cards nearly all night long at a table in the center of the room. I spent the second night listening to people in the next room playing dominoes, loudly slapping the pieces on the table. I think that in order to play dominoes in Texas, you need to slap them on the table. It must be an old Texas tradition. The *slap, slap, slap* all night kept me from getting any sleep. On the third night someone played a saxophone into the early morning hours. By then I was looking for an alternative place to live.

I found a card on the bulletin board that offered a room for rent in someone's home. By coincidence, I found a friendly face from Xavier and we rented the room together. His name was John German and the family that we rented from was the Nelsons. It didn't take any time at all to learn that John was not a good roommate. He smoked, he didn't have a car, and he was a world-class moocher. If I had something to eat, drink, or anything else he thought might work for him, he believed he was entitled to it—often, without my knowledge.

One of the most upsetting incidents was when he saw my car parked outside of a friend's house who had invited me for dinner. He and his wife were both students at TSU and they had just had a new baby. They didn't have much money but insisted that I share Sunday dinner with them. John was walking back from church when he spotted my car. He knocked on the door and took advantage of my friends' graciousness by inviting himself in, then sat down and ate my pork chop. Aghast, I knew they only had three pork chops in the pot, so I got up and left to keep the embarrassment to a minimum.

Near Christmas, I was invited to help make fruitcakes at the home of a family I had befriended at church. The Shay family were Creoles from Lafayette, Louisiana. One of their daughters had attended Xavier during the time I was there. I began calling John and Dorothy, "Momma and Poppa Shay." Their daughter was also named Dorothy and was now enrolled at Texas Southern.

John jumped in the car to go with me. Momma Shay assigned me the job of cutting up the candied fruit. The job John took on for himself was watching and licking the bowls as Momma Shay poured the batter into the cake pans. He must have licked a lot of batter that evening since Momma Shay made at least ten cakes.

After we returned to our room, the uncooked batter that he had eaten started to rise in his stomach. He was in pain. I looked on in silence. I could see his stomach was bloated and he was belching and farting like a steam engine, but I never said or did anything to help. He had done this to himself. Although neither of us got any sleep that night, I got my revenge for his eating my pork chop a few weeks earlier.

Except for learning about the kind of roommate I did *not* want, my first year at TSU was not very eventful. I got to meet a lot of people and make new friends. During my second year, things started to heat up on the campus. But before I get to the rest of my time at TSU, I have to dig a little into my family history.

TWO

THE PEOPLE I CAME FROM

B oth the Haydels and the Graves have a history that is worth talking about. Let's start with my mother's side of the family. My mother's mother was born an Honoré. The Honoré family is descended from the Destrehan family of France. This is well-documented in the book *Discovering Our Ancestral Roots* by Belmont Haydel and Gina Greenlee. The black side of the Destrehan family was named Honoré. This was the middle name of one of the Destrehan boys who had several children with an enslaved woman on his father's plantation.

The line of the Honoré family is:

1. Jean Baptiste François Honoré Destrehan (1789-1842): A Frenchman born in the colonies.
2. Jean Baptiste François Honoré (1811-1890): The first person of color in the line.
3. Joseph Martin Honoré (1833-1907)
4. Josephine Rosalie Honoré Haydel (1881-1972)
5. Mabel Haydel Graves (1908-1999): My mother

Rose Josephine Honoré Haydel (1881-1972), taken September 9, 1900, when she was about 19 years old

Rose Josephine Honoré Haydel (1881-1972), or *Tante Fifine* as she was known by everyone outside of our house, was a little lady who I loved dearly.

I called her "Ma-me" and she made the best gingerbread known to mankind. She was born in Pointe Coupée Parish, Louisiana, the seventh child of Joseph Honoré (1833-1907) and Emesie Chessé Honoré (1843-1931).

Her father Joseph is listed in the census records as a carpenter and a clerk of the Louisiana House of Representatives. We think that Joseph got this position during Reconstruction through his brother Emile Honoré. Emile was a Republican, like most Blacks in the nation at that time, and was elected to the Louisiana House during Reconstruction. We also found out that Emile was a sheriff, and, would you believe, Secretary of State of Louisiana under Governor Stephen B. Packard, who was governor for only

Curtis at about 3 or 4 years old with Ma-me

a few months in 1877. Apparently, I am not the first in my family to hold public office.

Now, when we look at the heritage of my great-grandmother Emesie (my mother's mother's mother), we find that she was the child of Alexandre Chessé and Justine Olivier. The line of the Chesse family is:

1.   Alexandre Laurent Chessé (1825-1896)

2.   Marie Emesie Chessé Honoré (August 13, 1844 - January 31, 1931)

3.   Josephine Rosalie Honoré Haydel (1881-1972)

Alexandre was a Frenchman and Justine was his common-law wife. Alexandre was born in the United States of French

Joseph Honoré (1833-1907)   *Emesie Chessé Honoré (1843-1931)*

parents. We think that Justine was a free person of color born either in Louisiana or Cuba. Because she was colored and he was white, they lived in a common-law arrangement until his death. Justine was known by everyone as Madam Chessé. She had servants and lived in what is now the Tremé section of New Orleans.

Alexandre Chessé was listed in the census records as a "Ball Keeper." I wondered what that meant for more than fifty years before I learned that he was a person who held formal balls where white men could meet colored girls. This process of white Europeans entering common-law marriages with colored girls was called *plaçage*. It was also considered a "left-handed marriage." I was always told by my Grandmother Ma-me that her grandmother was an octoroon (one-eighth black) who was "found" at a ball held by Alexandre Chessé.

Ma-me also told me that her grandparents lived together as a family and he did not have another white family living across town. That tells me that it must've been a loving arrangement.

Emile Honoré

My grandmother shared another story about Alexandre with me. One Sunday morning, Alexandre was walking with Emesie and another one of his daughters on Bourbon Street. Since they had just come from church, the girls were dressed in their Sunday best.

Another Frenchman walked up to Alexandre and asked, "Chessé, why are you promenading your *niggers*?"

Alexandre was so outraged by the insult that he challenged the man to a duel, and a few weeks later he killed him under the Dueling Oaks in what is now City Park in New Orleans. According to my grandmother, her mother was six or seven years old at the time. Emesie was born in 1843, so the duel must've happened around 1849 or 1850. That story taught me that Alexandre cared for his family. His death, on the other hand, was another story.

My grandmother told me that he found that his life savings

were missing. At the time, banks were not a place where most people kept their money. Instead, they'd keep it in what was called a strongbox. Reportedly, Alexandre kept more than $10,000 in gold coins in the box (in today's money, more than $750,000). One of his sons took all the gold from his strongbox and moved to France. When Alexandre learned of the missing gold, he called each one of his children into a room, one at a time, and shot himself after he had kissed the last one goodbye.

The New Orleans newspapers carried a story that his money was stolen by one of his servants, but that wasn't true. That son who moved to France asked one of his sisters to loan him one of her sons to serve as his valet on the train ride to New York. He wanted to pass for white, or *passe blanc* as it was called in those days, and he thought he needed a servant boy to pull it off. Many years later, his French-born great-grandson came to New Orleans on business. He was a wine salesman. Somehow he found my mother. He called and came over to visit with her to learn a bit about his New Orleans roots.

She told him the story and he shared with her his great-grandfather's story: He had married a French woman, had several children and was successful. In France, he did not have to *passe blanc*, so he told his children that he had Black ancestry. It really didn't make any difference there, so he lived his life out of the shadows. My mother said that her cousin even had pictures of his family and his grandparents to share with her. It was a good visit and my mother talked about it for years.

Now back to Madam Chessé. She died several years after Alexandre's suicide after jumping into the Mississippi River off the steamboat *Fashion*, which had caught fire. I saw a newspaper report of the sinking of the steamboat. It was carrying cotton to market from Northern Louisiana, and Justine boarded in Pointe Coupée after helping one of her daughters with the birth of a baby. My mother said that Justine's son-in-law claimed he smelled smoke when he put her on the boat. Her body was never found. However, her servant, who she was traveling with, lived and was pulled from the river. The servant said, "Madam Chessé had on a big dress with many petticoats. The big dress carried her away in the rushing current."

Alexandre and his common-law wife Justine lived together for 38 years. As I said before, it must have been a loving relationship.

● ● ●

Now let's look at my mother's father's family. My mother's father was Elphege Haydel, born in Wallace, Louisiana in 1879. I called him Poppa, but most people called him Bull. He was only 5'9" tall, but he didn't let anyone run anything over him.

He spent most of his adult life as the manager of the Haydel Brothers Plantation in Wallace, Louisiana. He and his brothers owned the plantation, and that's where my mother and her three brothers were born.

He, his wife and children lived in the big house, and his brothers lived in houses built in the backyard. Because of the living arrangements, my mother was raised with all of her first cousins like they were all brothers and sisters.

Elphege married Josephine Honoré on February 8, 1905 at a beautiful Catholic church called St. Stephen's that still stands on Napoleon Avenue in uptown New Orleans. Ma-me said it was a rainy Saturday when a white carriage pulled by two white horses picked her up from the house where she was living with her mother and sister on Annunciation Street just two blocks from the Mississippi River. (That house, which was in our family until the 1990s, still stands and has been well maintained.) She said that it's very good luck when it rains on your wedding day.

Elphege Haydel (1879-1959), taken in New Orleans around 1900 or 1901

My grandmother was a city girl, but my grandfather was a country boy. It was hard for her to move out in the country to Wallace and cook for her new husband, which involved, among other things, baking bread each day.

Elphege, my grandfather, was the son of parents who were born into slavery. He was their tenth child. His father, Victor, was the child of Antoine Haydel (1805-1857) and Anna, a slave girl who was only around 14 when Victor was born.

Victor was born on the Haydel Plantation, which is now known as the Whitney Plantation and was recently restored and opened to the public. The current owners, John and Donna Cummings of New Orleans, have done an excellent job of restoring the plantation and creating a museum for the public to see just what slavery was all about.

A picture of Victor Haydel and his dog, Scout. Victor is holding a horn he used to call his sons in from the fields. This picture hung in Curtis's room when he was a child.

Before Victor was born, Marcellin Haydel and his wife Azelie (1790-1860) ran the plantation. Marcellin was in New Orleans on business and went into the slave market where he saw a little girl. As my grandfather told me, she appeared to be just 3 or 4 years old. Her brothers were sold to another plantation and she was standing alone, crying. Marcellin and Azelie had not had any children, but Azelie desperately wanted a girl. The child at the slave market was a Mulatto. However, she was thought to have an Indian father because she didn't look African like her brothers. (We now know through my DNA that she had only European and African ancestry.)

Marcellin bought the girl as a gift for his wife. He cleaned her up, bought her a nice dress to wear, and presented her to Azelie. They named her Anna.

The Whitney Plantation

Anna was raised in the big plantation house and had my great-grandfather, Victor Haydel, when she was a young teenager by Azelie's brother, Antoine. Antoine was the third child of Alphonse Haydel and Marie Troxler Haydel. They were both of German descent. We don't know much about Anna and Antoine's relationship, but we do know from oral history that Anna never married and hated Antoine. When Victor was three or four, his

Anna is depicted here standing beside a bed in the big house on the Whitney Plantation. No real pictures of her have survived.

Aunt Azelie made Antoine take him and Anna down to St. John the Baptist Church to be baptized.

In the last few years, I've found records of another white Victor born in 1829 who was baptized at the same church. Victor must have been a name that the Haydels liked to use.

According to my grandfather and my mother, our Victor remembered being baptized. They also say the date of Victor's birth might not be 1835. The baptismal record claims he was 4 months old, but if he were 4 months old at the time he would not have remembered it.

In fact, he was probably born between 1830 and 1832. I'm led to believe this because Victor told my grandfather and his brothers along with their children, who were all gathered on the levee of the Mississippi River in 1911 to watch Halley's Comet pass by, that he had seen the comet before. The last time it was seen before 1911 was 1835. If Victor was born in 1835, he couldn't have remembered seeing Halley's Comet that same year.

But if it weren't for his baptism (and now DNA evidence), we wouldn't even be able to prove that Antoine was Victor's father. However, he admitted to the priest that he was the father and

This baptismal record is from St. John the Baptist Church in Edgard, Louisiana, where Victor Haydel was baptized in 1835.

Anna the mother. Victor's godparents were Edouard and Adele, two of Marcellin and Azelie's slaves.

The only other thing that my grandfather told me that proves some kind of positive relationship between Victor and his white father was this: When the Civil War broke out, recruiters came through the river plantations collecting male slaves to use in the war. The slaves would clean up after the white soldiers and do the dirty work of the war. The recruiters were also collecting jewelry and anything else of value to be turned into cash to help fund the southern states' war efforts. I was told that Antoine hid Victor in the well with the family jewelry until the recruiters were off their property. From that I would conclude that Antoine must have felt *some* kind of affection for his son.

When Victor was in his late teens, a marriage was arranged between him and a girl from the quarters. Her name was Marie Celeste Becnel (1833-1885). She happened to be the child of Flanestan Becnel and Françoise, a slave woman. Françoise was one of Marcellin and Azelie's slaves and Flanestan Becnel was the master of the other Haydel Plantation right next door (now known as the Evergreen Plantation).

Flanestan Becnel was not only the master of the next-door plantation but also a second cousin of Antoine and Azelie. His mother was a Haydel, so Victor and Celeste actually had the same great-grandfather through their white parents. It also turns out that Flanestan had eight children with the same slave lady alongside several children with his wife.

We think that Victor and Celeste married after 1865, but they had ten children together. There were no marriage records for slaves before 1865. We also think that at least four children were born before 1865, making them born into slavery. The rest were

Marie Celeste Becnel Haydel

born free. My grandfather didn't talk much about his mother, Celeste, because she died when he was only six, but the stories about his father came down like rain.

Through the excellent research of Dr. Ibrahim Seck, we found that Celeste was bought after Azelie's death by her white half-brother, Aimé Leo Becnel, and was moved to a plantation just south of the Evergreen owned by him and his brother, Alphonse. Aimé Leo and Alphonse were two of five white half-brothers and half-sisters Celeste had.

Celeste and Victor were listed as house servants on this plantation, so, according to all the research we can find, Celeste never served as a field slave. Additionally, because Victor was born in the big house on the Haydel Plantation and was the son of the master's brother, we think that he never served as a field slave, either. There are stories of him remembering his little playmates. They were all his white cousins. Now, I'm not pointing this out to say that he was better or worse than anyone else. (After all, he was still listed as a slave on the records of the Whitney Plantation.) I am just pointing out what he and his wife did for work.

Around 1863, Aimé Leo freed Celeste. This act of a slave owner freeing his slave is called *manumission*. She became a *gens de couleur libres*, a free person of color. Celeste was freed before Victor, who was freed by the Emancipation Proclamation (or really the 13th Amendment). After Emancipation, Victor must have joined Celeste on the Whitney Plantation and they both worked as domestic servants. Just one year earlier they would have been called house slaves.

Victor and Celeste must have saved all their money because the records found by Dr. Seck show that in 1881, Victor and Celeste had saved the grand sum of $700.00 to pay half of the $1,400.00 needed to buy a plantation less than a mile downriver from the Evergreen. In today's money this would be about $40,000, but the land has grown in value since then, so it might be worth nearly a half-million dollars today.

We think the south end of the property was owned by Aimé Leo and Alphonse, her half-brothers. Victor and Celeste paid Aimé Leo the other $700.00 in three installments. The records indicate that it was a strange parcel of land, 183 feet wide facing the Mississippi River and four miles deep.

The Evergreen Plantation, owned by Curtis's great-great-grandfather, Flanestan Becnel.

Now Victor was, among other things, somewhat of an herb doctor. He was the "go-to" man in and around Wallace for anything from a snake bite to a common cold. According to a family story, Victor would catch fish in the river and put them in a fish box tied to the dock so he could have live fresh fish whenever he wanted them. (This was obviously in the days before refrigeration.)

As the story goes, he noticed that his fish box was losing fish. He realized that someone must be stealing his fish, so he caught a water moccasin, the only venomous water snake in North America, and dropped it into the fish box. Being the herb doctor he was, Victor knew that the fish-stealer would probably have to come to him for help if the snake bit him. Well, according to Poppa, it didn't take long for a fellow to show up and say that he was bitten on the hand by a snake. The man was right-handed and the bite was on his right hand.

"Please Mr. Haydel, would you help me?" asked the man with an arm swollen nearly twice its normal size.

Victor asked, "How and where did the snake bite you?"

"I was working in the field when the snake got me," the man replied quickly.

"You're a liar and I will not help you. You've been stealing my fish," Victor responded.

"No Mr. Haydel, it wasn't me," he replied.

"I can't do anything for you," Victor said. "You're going to die."

After a long pause, the man finally admitted, "I just took one or two of your fish. Please help me."

Victor walked into his lab, which was really just a storage room filled with jars, and picked up one or two. "Give me your hand," he said to the man.

Victor wrapped the bitten hand in a cloth that contained some of whatever was molding in the jars and sent him away with a stern warning.

"If you ever steal one of my fish again, I'll let you die."

I've heard so many stories like this about my Pepere. He must've been an awfully colorful guy.

When Celeste died in 1885, six of her sons inherited her half of the plantation. In 1898, Victor sold his half to the six sons who were interested in farming. Each son had a job on the plantation. My grandfather Elphege, the youngest of Victor and Celeste's children, became the plantation's business manager.

According to my mother and her siblings, Elphege and his brothers had some 1,500 acres of land under cultivation until the mid-1920s. Because of the narrow width of the plantation, additional land was leased from the neighbors to increase the size of the rice fields. The new plantation was known as the Haydel Brothers Plantation, and it stayed in our family until the Great Depression.

My mother and her brothers as well as my grandfather's

Victor Haydel on the Haydel Brothers Plantation around the year 1910. He's thought to be in his eighties in this photograph.

brother's children were born on that land, and they all worked alongside their fathers. My mother's job was to weigh the wagons as they went into the field. She ran the scales that weighed both the mules and empty wagons going in and full wagons going out. Subtract the empty weight from the full and you had the weight of the rice harvest leaving the field. Because this was related to business management, this was a job for one of Elphege's children. My mother's cousins might've tended to the farm animals or worked on farm machinery; their jobs all depended on their fathers' roles.

As an adult, I learned that my parents raised me the way they did because of my grandfather Elphege and his position in the family. My grandfather was very prosperous as a farmer and plantation owner. He was the first person on the River Road to buy an automobile, a Ford, about 1913 or '14. This car made such a splash and became the envy of most of the farmers on the River Road.

It was such a big deal, in fact, that one night around dinnertime there was a knock on the door. My grandfather answered and found a white farmer who lived just up-river from their plantation on the doorstep. The farmer said to my grandfather, "Mr. Haydel, you own the only car I've ever seen. My daughter is getting married in about a month and it would be such an honor if she could ride up to the church in your car. Could you pick up the two of us that morning and drive us to St. John the Baptist Church? I've hired a white carriage to carry them back from the church to our house for the reception."

My grandfather agreed. Returning back to the table where his family was eating, Elphege announced that he was going to drive the neighbor and his daughter to church for her wedding. My mother, who was about five or six, asked if she could come along. "I've never seen a bride before," she stated.

"Sure you can go," Elphege responded.

Shortly before the Saturday wedding, my grandmother Rose made my mother a beautiful little white dress like a child would wear for her first Holy Communion. On the day of the wedding, Elphege dressed up in a suit and my mother, his only daughter, dressed up in her new white dress. Together, they drove the short distance to the neighbor's plantation and picked up the bride and her father. They sat in the back while my mother sat up front with her dad.

My mother said she was truly excited to see the bride all dressed up in a beautiful white dress. The bride's father thanked my grandfather for the honor of riding in his car and they arrived at St. John the Baptist Church, a grand Catholic church facing the Mississippi river that still stands in that same spot today. When they pulled up in the driveway, most of the attendees at the wedding were waiting outside to see the car that was arriving with the bride and her father.

My mother recalls people cheering to see the bride get out of the car. It was truly an exciting thing for a little six-year-old girl. The bridesmaids and groomsmen lined up to enter the church. My mother remembers pulling her dad's coat sleeve and asking, "Poppa, can I go in to see the bride walk down the aisle?"

"No, we can't go in," he responded.

"But why, Poppa? I want to see her walk down the aisle," she insisted.

"Because we're not white," he responded sadly.

She told me that she started crying then and didn't stop for a week.

Elphege and his brothers owned a pew in that church. They bought it so they could have a place to sit for Sunday mass. It was located on the left side in the back. One time, when I was an adult, my mother showed me that pew.

It could only be used for mass. Whenever there was a white wedding or funeral, Blacks weren't allowed inside.

My mother said this event made such an impact on her that by the time she was a teenager, she vowed that if she ever had a child, she would never allow that child to suffer this indignity. That's why she and my dad devised a plan for me to never to feel the pain of segregation until I was old enough to understand what it was all about. I must say that their plan worked: I never felt like I was any different than anyone else. As a matter of fact, I still feel that way today. I can remember the two of us sitting in that empty church just a few years before my mother died and her still remembering the pain of that Saturday some 80 years before.

The family line of the Haydel family is:

1. Mabel Haydel Graves (August 26, 1908–August 1999)
2. Elphege Haydel (1879–1959)
3. Victor Haydel (1835?–1924): First Black Haydel
4. Antoine Haydel (July 1805–October 1857)
5. Azilie Haydel (May 1796–October 1860): Sister of Antoine and aunt of Victor

Azilie raised Anna and Victor in the big house on the Whitney Plantation. Her German parents were Alphonse and Marie Haydel, who had 13 children. They were the third generation of German Haidels or Haydels born in what is now the United States. Victor, the first Black Haydel, was the great-great-grandson of Ambrose Haidel, the first German to make his way to what is now Louisiana.

● ● ●

Now the Graves side of my family is also interesting. After much research, I found that my grandfather Joseph Graves (1838–1908) was from the city of Pearlington, Mississippi. I learned he was a carpenter and builder of both houses and churches before stepping into more professional roles. At some point, my dad had been given a book called *The Progress of the Races* by Etienne W. Maxson. It provided more information about Joseph's time working as a Harbormaster of Ship Island in the 1870s. It also mentioned that he was elected Justice of the Peace for Pearlington in November of 1885 and appointed Postmaster of Pearlington in May of 1889. I have also found newspapers from southern Mississippi that list these accomplishments.

Around 1986 I had the good fortune to visit Ship Island with my son Christopher. There I learned that Ship Island was located eight miles off the coast of Gulfport, Mississippi. At the end of the Civil War, the North used the island to hold southern troops that were captured in the war. My Grandfather Joseph must have been appointed to this post by someone from Washington, D.C. But the question is, how did he get such an appointment after the war?

Before I visited the Mormon Temple in Hampton, Virginia, I didn't know much else about Joseph or his parents. Through a friend at the Temple, I verified that Joseph was indeed a Justice of the Peace and Postmaster for Pearlington and Harbormaster of Ship Island. I also learned that he had a family before he became involved with my grandmother. Nothing about this earlier marriage had been passed down to anyone in our family, so imagine my surprise when I found information in the census records of 1880. At the time, Joseph was married to Mary I. Graves, who was then 33 years old. In 1880 they had two sons, John (age 16) and Fred (age 8). Evidently, Mary died in 1900, soon after her will was completed on July 18th of that year. Their two sons reportedly moved north. Joseph married his second wife in 1901. His new wife was my grandmother, Fannie Cade Graves. When they married, she was in her late twenties and he was 62.

I had some difficulty finding out who Joseph's father was, but my Mormon friend told me to look for a Graves who lived near him in the census records. In the 1880 records, I found a Judge James Graves who lived two houses down from Joseph. The judge was listed as being a white 58-year-old male. He was married to Florintine Graves and they had two children, Isaac, a

31-year-old sawmill worker, and Louisa, a 21-year-old who was living at home. Now the next problem: how does one prove that this Judge James Graves was Joseph's father?

The fact that he was a Hancock County judge might explain how Joseph got those government-related, appointed, and elected jobs right after the Civil War. However, records did not say that he was Joseph's father. So, as Dr. Henry Gates would say, I turned to the DNA. There is a Graves organization in the country. They have a DNA registry, so I had my DNA run through them to see if there was a close match to a James Graves from Pearlington, Mississippi.

Well, I got a hit.

There was a white descendant of James Graves who had genetic markers close to mine. That was the hit I needed. The judge was in fact my great-grandfather. Joseph must have been born when James was in his late teens. We haven't been able to find any record of Joseph having brothers or sisters. We also haven't found any record of his mother.

According to E.B. Maxson's book, Joseph Graves was "the first colored man to hold a political office on Pearl River." He was first appointed Harbormaster at Ship Island during Reconstruction. He was the first colored person elected Justice of the Peace and the first appointed Postmaster at Pearlington serving under both Presidents Arthur Harrison and Benjamin Harrison. All of this happened in the First Supervisor's District of Hancock County, Mississippi.

My grandmother Fannie's side of the family also has a compelling history. Charles Cade, Fannie's father, was the son of a plantation owner's daughter and one of the white overseers of the property.

The parents weren't married, so her father really didn't know who his father was. I thought the father might be one of the slaves on the property. So he did what people did back in those days:

he gave the child to the Black Cade family to raise as their own. Charles was raised as if he was black, but we really don't know who his father was. He married a lady named Emma who was the daughter of an Italian man and a slave woman. The two of them had 15 children. I have learned that at some point during slavery, large numbers of Italians were imported into Louisiana and several southern states to do farm work along with the African slaves. The Italians lived and worked next to the African slave population, so there were naturally relationships between the two groups. Emma's family name was Fregelio, so it follows that Emma Fregelio Cade passed on that maiden name to her daughter Fannie.

Fannie named her and Joseph's second son Fregelio. Fregelio was my father, and he was born on Christmas Day, 1906. He was listed in the 1910 U.S. Census as Fregelio Joseph Graves, age 4. My dad didn't like the name Fregelio so at an early age, he and his mother flip-flopped his first and middle names. He became Joseph F. instead of Fregelio J. By 1920, when my father was only 14, Fannie told the census taker that his name was Joseph F. Graves.

The line of the Graves family is:

1.   Fregelio Joseph Graves (December 25, 1906–January 13, 1984)
2.   Joseph Graves (1838 –1908): First Black Graves in this line.
3.   John Graves (????–????): Pearlington, MS. White

My dad married his first wife, Helen Stokes, in the late 1920s. They had two children that did not live long past birth. Her third child, Kenneth, was born on April 25th, 1931. Helen died shortly afterward.

My father married my mother in 1935. He had been raised in the African Methodist Episcopal Church (AME), but my mother, being Catholic, would not marry a man who wasn't also Catholic. So one day, after they had dated for nearly a year, my father came to see her

Fannie Cade Graves McCree as a teenager.

and said that he would like her to take him to see a priest. That was his proposal. My mother knew that if my father wanted to become Catholic, he was willing to do whatever it took to win her over.

My dad converted to Catholicism and several months later they were married at Holy Ghost Church, a beautiful church that still stands on Louisiana Avenue in uptown New Orleans. It was a big wedding. My mother's younger brother Honore, or Butsy, as he was called, and my dad's best friend Herbert Oubre were in it, along with my uncle's wife Eldredge. Alma (Nunnie) Gardina served as my mother's maid of honor. The ring bearer was one of my mother's nephews, Belmont Haydel, Jr., and the flower girl

Pictured from left to right are Roy, Joseph, Fannie, and Fregelio Joseph Graves. This photo was taken in mid-1908; Joseph died that December.

was Jean Haydel, the oldest daughter of my mother's first cousin, Dr. Clarence C. Haydel.

Two years after my parents were married, my mother still hadn't gotten pregnant. But instead of going to the doctor for help, she turned to the church. She made a *novena* to the Blessed Mother at Our Lady of Guadalupe Church in New Orleans. She spent nine days praying for a child. In her prayers, my mother promised that if she were to have a child, she would dress him or her in white for two years as a thanks for that blessing. Well, one year later, on August 26th, my mother's birthday, she gave birth to me. She did as she promised and dressed me in white for two years.

My dad's mother, Emma, lost her husband Joseph in 1908. She remarried a man named Louis McCree and had two more children, Ganzalo and Mazarene McCree.

My Uncle Gonzi was another family member who adopted me early on. He and his wife, Abby, didn't have children, so they treated me like their child. Uncle Gonzi would pick me up on

A picture from the wedding of Joseph Graves and Mabel Haydel. Back row: Hubert Oubre, Eldridge Vappie Haydel, Joseph Graves, Mabel Haydel Graves, Honore Haydel, Nonny Gardinia. Front row: Jean Haydel and Belmont F. Haydel.

a Friday and keep me until Sunday night when it was time for me to go to bed. He worked most of his life for the New Orleans Telephone Company. In his time off, he fished and *shined* for raccoons, possums, and anything else that might be in the woods. For those of you who've never heard of shining for raccoons, you go into the woods at night with a little light affixed to the front of your cap and you shine your light into the woods until you see some eyes looking back at you.

"Don't take your light off whatever you shined," Uncle Gonzi would say to me.

The animal keeps looking at the light while you get your shotgun up and shoot it between the eyes. Shining takes some skill because if you move your head and the light moves off the animal's eyes, it'll run away. After you shoot the creature, you send your dog to get it. In most cases, we'd shoot a raccoon (that we called a coon) or an opossum. Either way, it was something

Curtis, dressed in white, with his mother, Mabel.

that my mother wouldn't put in one of her pots because they were, in her words, "not clean animals."

My Aunt Abby, however, would cook them up and they would taste so good. Uncle Gonzi used his brother-in-law's dogs for us to hunt rabbit and deer as well as retrieve ducks and coons, and Aunt Abby would cook the hell out of whatever he brought home. That lady could cook a snake and you would ask for seconds.

Hunting and fishing were awfully exciting activities for a young boy. I remember when I was around twelve years old, Uncle Gonzi called my dad and said that the shrimp were running on Lake Pontchartrain. It must have been a weekend or during the summer because my dad said I was available.

When I went to catch shrimp, my mother would dress me in something warm and put my knee boots on. Uncle Gonzi would pick me up and we'd go out to Pontchartrain with several ice chests filled to the brim with ice and a few big washtubs. I'd be my uncle's bait and light man all night long. We used clams as bait and I'd keep cracking clams with a hammer while he'd keep casting his net in a perfect umbrella where I dropped the clams just in front of the bottom step of the sea wall. With one weight in his mouth and the net over one of his arms, my uncle dropped the net in the right spot each time. I also made sure to keep the Coleman lamp burning. We needed to see what we were doing all night, and without that Coleman lamp we were in total darkness.

There was one other thing about these shrimping outings: we'd drink a little wine throughout the night. It was just some sweet wine and we only took little sips at a time to keep the chill off, but it was good. But my uncle said I could *not* tell my parents about the wine. He said if I told he wouldn't take me shrimping again.

Well, I haven't told a soul until now. Uncle Gonzi has been dead for many years now. For that matter, so have my parents. Now I can tell the truth.

Sure, the little sips of wine were good, but the best thing was hanging out with Uncle Gonzi. He taught me how to smoke and how to drink. I would dry my hands off and light up a Camel cigarette for him and put it in his mouth. He would take a couple long drags on it, and then I'd take it from his mouth, lay it carefully on the second step of the seawall, and wait for him to ask for it again.

I must admit that I took a drag or two myself from time to time. But it was for medicinal purposes, after all. It'd keep the chill off us and keep the shrimp coming.

We went down to the lake a few times, and on most of these shrimp outings, we'd catch at least a washtub full. But on one outing, in Uncle Gonzi's words, "we cleaned up." We caught 1,800 pounds of shrimp in just one night. We filled up all our washtubs and everything else we had with shrimp.

I know your question is, "What do you do with 1,800 pounds of shrimp in 1950?" Not everyone had a freezer at the time. Well, it took my uncle several days to give them away to anybody who would take them. But catching all that shrimp in that one night gave me and Uncle Gonzi bragging rights for a long time. The first thing we did was show them off to as many people as we could. If only there were cell phones back then to record the accomplishment. We'd still be posting pictures from that night today.

Even though I have plenty of memories with my uncle, there were many things I remember about my dad that were unique. One of these things was the fact that he always had a *"hookup."* At the time, wealthy white men would lease property to hunt duck, and in many cases these men would have a Black guy who would train and manage the hunting dogs, build the duck blinds, and take the hunting parties out to kill ducks on the weekends. From time to time my dad would get a call from one of his friends, letting him know that the hunting party they were scheduled to take out that weekend had fallen through or the boss decided not to hunt that weekend. We would go in that party's place to hunt duck on their lease. My dad would load me up in the car and we would go to some out-of-the-way place to meet one of his friends. I always knew these were going to be good hunts because it was really meant to be a rich white folk's hunt. We were not rich or white, we were just the folks with the "hookup" who knew the man who made things happen.

We'd start hunting right after daybreak. My dad's friend would be hard at work with his duck call. Now that guy knew how to call those ducks. If I were a duck I would have been there before daybreak myself.

After those hunts, we always brought home our limit and some extras. Now, I think it's worth an explanation about the "extras." After we hunted a while, we would hear a helicopter in the distance. "Here comes de man in the hell-of-a-copter," my dad's friend would say.

It was the game warden coming to check if we had more game ducks than our limit.

My dad's friend would quickly count the game ducks that we had in the blind. If we were over the limit, he'd have a decoy or two at his feet. He would tie the extra ducks to the bottom of the string close to the weight that kept the decoy in place. He would then throw it over near the other decoys and the ducks would stay down. The game warden would land and launch his pirogue to check us out. It was tied to the floats to allow the craft to land in the water. When he'd get over to us, he would ask how we were doing.

"Done any good?" he would ask.

"Not yet, boss," my dad's friend would reply. He always called the game warden "boss."

The game warden would shine his light on the floor of the duck blind and say, "Let me see what you got." Dad's friend would hold up the game and non-game ducks and show them off to the warden.

"Y'all got duck licenses?" he'd ask. We'd take them out and point them in his direction.

"OK boys, y'all have a good hunt," he'd say as he cranked up his little outboard motor, waved, and moved on back to his aircraft. We'd watch the game warden tie his boat to the float and fly away.

I'd look at my dad as the sound of the *hell-of-a-copter* grew faint in the distance. His nose would twitch as a slight smile came over his face.

He'd look at his friend and say in a firm voice, "You know your people."

His friend would respond with just one word: "Yep."

We'd go on to knock down a few more ducks before we called it a day.

My dad knew how to have a good time and duck hunting was just one of many fun outings with him. He was also a hard worker and a good businessman. When I was about ten years old, my dad and my mother's brother Honore (or Butsy, as almost everyone called him) opened an Esso service station called Butsy and Buddy's Service Station in New Orleans. Their service station was the first Esso service station owned by Blacks in the state of Louisiana.

Getting to the place where they even talked about opening a station is worth telling. Butsy was working as a grease man at a Pan-Am station own by a white man named Simmons. This was in the days when all cars needed to be greased and have their oil changed every thousand miles. Butsy was good at his job and he had a following of people who came to the station because of him.

One day, when he was working on a car on the rack next to the station office, a man walked in and asked Mr. Simmons if he had someone who could grease his car. Simmons responded quickly, "I'll put my nigger on it as soon as he gets done with the car he's working on now. I have the best grease man in the city."

Butsy overheard the conversation and came home that evening and shared the story with my dad. Butsy and his family were renting the apartment downstairs from us. At the time, my dad was teaching diesel machine mechanics at a veteran's school owned by one of my mother's relatives. Prior to teaching at the veteran's school, my dad had opened an auto mechanics shop with a friend. The shop was called H&G's Auto Shop, but the partnership went bad and they closed the shop.

After hearing Butsy's story, my dad said, "Butsy, why don't we open our own service station?"

They thought about it a bit and decided to do just that. They found a location near our house and inquired about the rent. It was reasonable, so the only thing left to do was find a gas company that would sell them the gas. They decided to try Esso because it was one of the biggest in the city and it didn't have a Black-owned outlet. My dad contacted them and started the process. Esso was interested, but they needed to check my dad and Butsy out and get some references.

My dad knew a federal judge who he thought might make a great reference. Years before, my dad had captained a large fishing boat for one of the Canal Street merchants, the Krauss family. Mr. Krauss used to take many prominent friends fishing, so during the time my father worked on the boat, he met many political and business leaders of the city, including this judge.

My dad called the judge and asked if he would write a letter of recommendation for him. The judge agreed, so one Saturday my dad told me that he wanted me to go with him to meet this judge and pick up a letter. We drove up to this large house on St. Charles Avenue and parked outside the fenced-in yard. We went up the stairs and my dad rang the bell. A gray-haired white man answered the door. When he saw my dad, his face lit up. It was obvious that they knew each other well. Daddy introduced me and they started talking about the good times they had on the many fishing trips they had taken. They talked about the size of the fish and about the others who used to fish with them. I was standing on one leg and then the other waiting for all this to be over. After what seemed like half an hour later, the judge said, "Let me go and get your letter."

"I am very glad that I could help you with this," the judge said with a big, warm smile.

My dad took the letter, shook his hand, and thanked him for

The grand opening of the original Butsy and Buddy's Service Station. Pictured are Joseph and Mabel Graves and Honore "Butsy" Haydel and his wife.

his help. I shook his hand, too. We turned to leave and the judge stood in his door and waited until we had closed the gate of the fence, waving as he went back inside.

After we got in the car, my dad turned to me.

"Did you see anything about that visit that was strange?" He asked, looking at me.

"No," I replied.

"You could see that we were good friends. But he never asked us in, he never said that we could sit down on one of the many chairs on the front porch," he said.

I could see that this took something out of him to have to explain this all to me.

"In his mind, we're not his equal and he would *never* ask us to sit or come in the house," he continued. "It doesn't matter how good our friendship was. He is white and we are not. Therefore, we are not his equal. But I needed him, son. That's why I went to get his letter of recommendation."

He was quiet for a moment. I could see that he was hurt about what had just happened. After what seemed like a minute or so, he felt like he could talk again.

As he started the car, he said, "But I know that he doesn't

think of me as his friend. If he did, he would have asked us in. This is a lesson. You get what you can out of some white people, but don't think for one minute that they think you're their friend."

With that letter (and some others), Butsy and Buddy's Esso Service Station opened in the uptown part of the city. My dad's veteran school job paid well, so he'd spend his weekdays working there and his evenings and weekends at the service station. After the veteran's school closed, they opened a second station downtown. Their stations did very well for as many years as Butsy Haydel and Buddy Graves wanted to operate them. After 40 years of successful operation, they decided to retire and closed both businesses.

THREE
CIVIL RIGHTS AT THE HOUSTON LUNCH COUNTERS

I f you were Black, or a negro as we were called in 1960, and
lived in Houston, you were listening to either KCOH, the
daytime radio station, or KYOK, the 24-hour station. They
were blaring out "Save The Last Dance For Me" by the Drifters or
"The Twist" by Chubby Checker. This was before every car had
AC, so the windows were down, and you wouldn't miss a beat as
cars went by you on the street. White radio stations never played
Black music, or what they called "race music."

John Kennedy was not yet president of the United States.
Some students in Greensboro, North Carolina staged a sit-in at
a lunch counter. At the same time, the "Freedom Riders" were
testing the United States Supreme Court decision to allow blacks
and whites to sit together on buses.

It was the second semester of my sophomore year at TSU and
by this time, I was well known on campus. I had an active social
life and many friends. I lived in an apartment building about four
blocks from campus with two friends, Otis King and Charles
Stephens. Otis was in law school and Charles, who went by Steve,
was studying to be a medical technician. Otis would later become

the Dean of the Texas Southern Law School and Steve would become a successful medical technologist.

One day in the fall of that year, I learned of a meeting in Room 214 of Texas Southern's administration building. The word around campus was that there was going to be a discussion about the desegregation of lunch counters in Houston. I decided to attend and before I knew what I signed up for, I was involved in the civil rights sit-in movement.

The meeting was led by Eldrewey Stearns. He was a TSU law student from Galveston, Texas who was stopped for a traffic violation several weeks earlier and was arrested because he had a picture of a white girl in his wallet. He went before the Houston City Council and talked about the beating he received at the hands of the Houston police after his arrest.

The following Friday, March 4, 1960, we gathered at the flagpole outside of that administration building. Twelve of us walked six blocks to the nearest Weingarten on Alameda Street, a "whites only" chain grocery store. We gathered at the lunch counter inside, left of the grocery store entrance. We planned it like a military operation. We arrived moments before the press, who we called before we started walking. We reasoned those cameras and reporters would stop the police and others from violent actions against us.

Only a few members of the press showed up, so we just went in and sat down at the lunch counter. Two of the three white people who were eating paid their bills and left quickly. The counter was immediately closed. The store management tried to talk us off the stools, but we wouldn't move. In retaliation, they closed the entire store. Once the store was closed to all shoppers, we were also forced to leave.

So, following Greensboro, which took place at a Woolworths lunch counter on February 1, 1960, we made our stand against segregation. It turned out that our brief protest in Weingarten was the first "sit-in" in the United States west of the Mississippi River. That evening we went back to an upstairs room in the Grove Grill, a night club across the street from campus, and planned our next move.

Within a short time, I became Stearns' first lieutenant. Along with Rev. Earl Allen, Holly Hogrobrooks and several others, we formed a student group called the Progressive Youth Association (PYA). Our goal was to desegregate Houston. We felt like we made a stand, and nobody could stop us. We asked the Black citizens of Houston not to shop at Weingarten stores until they would serve us at the lunch counter, just like other patrons. By the next Saturday that store was empty. As Holly Hogrobrooks said in *The Strange Demise Of Jim Crow*, a documentary about the integration of Houston, "You could have shot a scatter gun down each aisle and not hit a soul."

She was right. The Black newspapers and local TV covered the story of us asking the Black community not to shop and it was done.

But we weren't finished. The next day, we decided to expand our efforts to Madding's. At the time, Madding's was one of the largest drugstore chains in Houston. As a result of the press coverage we received the day before, many students on campus were behind us. It was at this point where I had my "crisis", as Stearns called it. It was time for me to make a decision, a commitment to a cause that I really believed in, to the point that I would be willing to give my life.

I will agree, "willing to give my life" sounds a little dramatic, but at that time, in that place, it was a realistic thought. The cause was really that important to me and most of the people around me. We saw Dr. Martin Luther King and others stand up in the face of overwhelming odds. I sat at dining room tables with people who talked about risking everything to make it better for those who would follow us. Now it was my time to make the sacrifice.

When Saturday morning arrived, more than two hundred students wanted to participate in the sit-in. We checked the store out and knew how many stools were at the lunch counter, so we decided to send students in waves so that everyone who wanted to be involved could be. The plan was to have each wave of students to stay for an hour or so before moving in the next wave. I was in the first wave. We went into the drugstore, again without any press present. Entering the store, the lunch counter was to the right. It ran the length of the store and had about twenty stools. A mirror was mounted on the wall from one end to the other. There were about eight to ten people having breakfast. I took a seat near the middle. As more students came in, the white patrons paid up and left quickly.

In less than five minutes, we took every seat. One of the counter workers took off in a little trot looking for the store manager. He arrived in short order and told us that we had to leave and we would not be served. Our response was simple: we would not leave until we were served. He stepped back, not knowing what to do next. I assumed that he was trying to get some direction from the corporate office.

It was about that time that I noticed several young white guys in leather jackets come through the door and position themselves behind us. As I remember it, there was less than four or five feet between us and them. As I investigated the mirror to my left, I could see a Black reporter with a big Speed Graphic camera held up to his face. He was the lone press person in sight. As the one and only camera in the room, he was ready to get the picture of us getting beaten up or worse that would run in TV reports and newspapers all over the nation.

People say that these are the times that your life flashes before your eyes. Well, I thought that this might be that moment for me. I had been thinking about the possibility that I would have to confront violence of some sort and I already decided that I was not going to hit back.

A number of us spent some time talking to Rev. Bill Lawson, the minister who ran the Baptist Student Union on campus. He educated us about Dr. King, Gandhi, and non-violence. His words rang in my ear and I repeated them to myself. "It is important that you not fight back. It is important that you not fight back."

I was ready to take a punch or even a knife in the back, whatever was to come my way. The tension was high and the crisis was there, right in front of me (although technically it was behind me in the mirror).

I prepared myself and accepted that I might die, yet I was secure in the knowledge that the cvil rights cause was worth it. I was so focused on what was to come that I was surprised when, out of the corner of my eye, I saw a lone police officer walk through the door. He was wearing a white hat, which led me to believe that he was not just another cop, but a captain or some other higher-ranking officer.

No words were spoken. He slowly walked between us and the leather-jacketed white guys. It was so quiet that I could hear his footsteps behind me. It could have taken just one or two minutes for him to slowly walk to the last stool at the counter. But for me, it felt like two hours. He walked to the back end of the store, turned around, and walked back towards the door. By the time he made the second round trip, the motorcycle boys started to leave. First one, then another, and another. The officer defused the atmosphere with his mere presence. I'm sure there must have been other officers present, but I saw only this one with a white hat. No words were exchanged, but his deliberate, slow walk stopped something that could have turned ugly.

That morning, my life changed. The movement became more important to me than my life. I felt free. I was determined

Rev. William Lawson and Curtis

to do whatever it took and would not stop until Houston's thick walls of segregation had fallen. As I reflect on that time, I think that this is what Dr. King was telling us the night before he died. "I may not get there with you, but I have been to the mountain top and seen the other side."

Looking back, I can say that I knew why I was there and why I needed to be a part of the movement at that time. It often takes us a while to discover ourselves, but that day I felt a purpose and a place. I found myself. This was a cause for my community that I could believe in and give myself to.

A few days later, on March 7th, a 27-year-old Black man named Felton Turner was forced into a car at gunpoint by white supremacists in Houston. He was taken to a secluded area, had "KKK" carved into his abdomen, and was left dangling from a tree. He survived and recounted how the white men said to him that they had been paid to hurt him because "those Texas Southern students were getting too much publicity."

The attack had the opposite effect on us and the Black community. Before Felton Turner was attacked, I don't think that most of the community was with us. As Rev. Lawson said in a *Houston Post* article, "We had seen far too many cruelties, far too many lynches, far too much violence. It was too much, and it galvanized us."

Within a few days, we decided to expand our protest to the Henke & Pillot supermarket a few blocks down from the Weingarten on Alameda Street. After the Felton Turner incident, we felt sure that pressure was mounting and we needed to keep it up. After we notified the press, I led the group to the store with the local NBC news crew and other TV camera crews filming.

The lunch counter was closed in anticipation of our arrival. I made a split-second decision and jumped the barricade. I motioned to the other students to follow and take every stool. That moment was captured and made the national news.

After an hour, we gathered the students and went back to the campus. We called it off for the day because we got the press coverage we needed.

That night as I studied in my apartment, the phone rang. It was my mother, and she wasn't happy. My parents had seen me on *The Huntley-Brinkley Report* on NBC. "Your dad wants to talk to you, and he's angry," she said.

I didn't tell either of my parents about my sit-in activities. I didn't want them to stop me. My dad got on the phone. "Son."

I could tell from that one word that I was in for it. This was the same stern voice that I heard from time to time growing up. He was a man of few words, but when he spoke, you listened.

"We did not send you to Houston to do this," he said. "We sent you there to get an education, not get killed."

I felt all his weight on my back. I was silent at first, thinking of a response. I wanted to say something to explain myself.

All I could come up with was the truth. "But Daddy, you raised me to do this."

The silence made me feel like he was trying to fashion a comeback. A few seconds passed, but it felt more like several minutes. When he finally spoke, his voice carried the same authority as before.

"I understand."

Those two words touched my heart, and they reverberated in my head. I knew right in that moment that he wanted me to continue fighting for the cause. All those lessons I learned at his hand came together in those two words. I think he recognized the cause was bigger than his son and it was worth whatever sacrifice had to be made.

That moment became a turning point in our relationship. I was no longer his little son, the young boy who he needed to protect. I was a man choosing to stand up for what he believed in. From that moment forward, he was my biggest supporter. I might not have appreciated it then, but I realized that all the time I spent sitting around the table with the Thurgood Marshalls of the world molded me into a person who could stand up for what's right.

I called him to tell him what I was doing most of the time from then on. The bottom line was that he didn't want any surprises. In many cases, I asked him not to tell my mom. I thought she might worry and try to stop me. It worked; he kept my words to himself.

There was pressure building in the city to bring this protest to an end. The mayor of Houston at the time was Lewis Cutrer. He had campaigned on a segregationist platform with billboards around the city reading, "Will the Negro Rule Our City?"

He formed a 41-member biracial committee that included the president of Texas Southern University, Dr. Samuel Nabrit. Cutrer pressured Dr. Nabrit to stop us and save the city from national embarrassment. But Dr. Nabrit wasn't the sort of person to be pushed around by the mayor or anyone else. An accomplished marine biologist in demand both in the United States and around the world, his job as president of the university was secure. He also knew a little something about the struggle for equal rights. His brother was Dr. James Nabrit, then president of Howard University and one of the NAACP attorneys who worked against the Texas White Primary cases in 1935. These were legal cases made against the practice at that time that did not allow Black citizens to vote in primaries.

Dr. Nabrit was the kind of guy who we needed to be sitting as our university president at that time. He knew that something needed to be conveyed to the students to help the process.

President Nabrit called an *all-university assembly*, a really big thing at the school. In fact, I don't remember all the students and faculty ever being called together at one time before or after that. The word around campus was that we might be thrown out of school if we continued our protest. We began to think this might be it for us. None of us knew just where Dr. Nabrit stood on all of that. Not knowing what to expect, we crowded into the auditorium for a command performance. To say the least, tensions were high.

We had many thoughts and fears. Should we walk out if things didn't go our way? Should we disband the effort and go back to classes with our heads down? Do nothing until we decide our next move? As we sat, the curtains were opened—the stage was empty but for a single podium in the center. Walking slowly, Dr. Nabrit, who at that time was a balding, slightly overweight man in his mid-fifties, walked in alone from the left. He had no papers in his hand. I also noticed that he did not have a smile on his face. I don't remember everything he said, but I do remember his opening words:

"Mrs. Nabrit and I are very comfortable. I don't need this

job. Primarily, you are citizens of the United States of America."
He paused to let that sink in. "Secondarily, you are students at this
University. So, you have to do what you need to do."

Both the students and faculty stood up, applauding. We had
done it. We knew in just those few words that he was one of us
and was not going to side with the whites that controlled the city.

He closed with something like, "They can have my job before
I allow anyone to come on this campus to stop you from doing
what you need to do."

We considered this carte blanche to continue our fight. The
school administration was not going to stand in our way. I didn't
find out for more than thirty years that Dr. Nabrit was talking
to Mack H. Hannah, Chairman of the TSU Board of Directors. In
turn, Hannah was talking to Lyndon Johnson, formerly a senior
senator from Texas and then vice president of the United States.
Johnson was pressuring Price Daniel, the Texas governor, to make
sure the state police would keep a lid on a potential explosion of
anger. We could not know at the time, but the fix was in. It was
all about money. The white leaders were going to do whatever it
took to keep Texas from looking bad in the eyes of the public and
risking the big money that was slated for the city of Houston.

Not too long after that, protests broke out on the campus
of Southern University in Baton Rouge, Louisiana. At the time,
Southern had the largest enrollment of any Black university in the
nation. It was less than two hundred miles east of Houston but
thousands of miles away in the way things were handled by its
administration.

Southern's president was Dr. Felton G. Clark. His father, Dr.
Joseph S. Clark, was president before him. After my first cousin,
Honore Haydel, and several other students took to the streets of
Baton Rouge, Dr. Clark took the opposite approach of Dr. Nabrit.
Like Dr. Nabrit, Dr. Clark called an all-university assembly.
Emphasizing that his parents were buried on the campus, he told

the students, "You need to stop this or they [the governing white folks in the state] are going to shut down this university."

I was told by Honore and several others that Dr. Clark had tears in his eyes. Many students were arrested and some were expelled from the university. A few students were even charged with treason against the United States of America.

Honore told me that Dr. Clark's attitude towards the protests caused the students to turn on him. They gathered around his house on campus and did not leave for several days. Signs were made calling him an "Uncle Tom." I guess with all his PhDs and everything, they could have elevated their name-calling to "Uncle Thomas." I can even remember my dad telling me that Felton came from a long line of Toms. His dad perfected the art of "Tomming" many years before.

I remembered Dr. Clark from when I was involved with Bayou Boys State. At the end of the ten-day program, Dr. Higgins always invited some state senator or state representative to speak to the students. At the time, there were no Black members in either House. Dr. Clark would meet the white representative at the tracks that were located on the road entering the campus. He had a chauffeur-driven car, but on those days *he* would be the chauffeur. He would run around and open the door for the rep. It was sickening to see him "Tom" like that.

It was months before things settled down at Southern University.

Meanwhile, back in Houston, the biracial committee was meeting behind closed doors and we started feeling like we were about to be compromised. No adults were talking to us and we began to feel like something or somebody was going to stop us from our quest towards desegregation. I suggested to Stearns that we needed some adult supervision. We needed some help from someone like Dr. Martin Luther King. We agreed that I should call

Andrew Young, who was my YMCA camp counselor way back when I was in elementary school.

The Dryads Street YMCA was the hub of activity for many Blacks in New Orleans when I was a child. My dad took me to see Jackie Robinson there. My cousins, Honore and Elphege Haydel, and I would go each summer to the YMCA camp in Waveland, Mississippi. I think I was about seven years old when I first met Andy Young, who was my first YMCA camp junior counselor. His younger brother, Walter, was my junior counselor when I went back the second year. Eventually, when we were old enough, we became junior counselors.

I called Andy and told him the story and he suggested that we talk to Dr. King. He gave me a phone number and a time to call.

We went to Stearns's apartment to make the call because he had a two-bedroom apartment with a phone extension in each bedroom and we could both be on the line. With much excitement, we waited in his apartment for the time to talk to Martin Luther King himself.

With his national reputation, we thought that he was just the person to keep us moving in the right direction. We wrote down our points. Firstly, we needed him to revive the enthusiasm among the students. Secondly, we needed him to put his weight and national reputation behind our movement. Thirdly, we needed adult leadership and whatever else he could bring to the table.

He answered the phone himself on the second ring. We introduced ourselves and he confirmed that he talked to Andy about me. Stearns and I must have talked for nearly thirty minutes. We made our points as best we could. We gave him the background and our best shot. King didn't say a word during the whole time we were talking. When we were done, we expected something big to happen. After all, he *was* Martin Luther King. We thought he might catch a plane the next morning and come to our rescue. We thought he might send some of his trusted lieutenants.

He paused after our pretty much one-way conversation and said in a low but positive voice, "I'll tell God about it."

We thanked him, hung up the phones, looked at one another, and said, "What the hell was that?"

He will tell God about it? We felt a little like we were the butt of a private joke. We considered that maybe this was his standard answer, or maybe as a reverend he really did have a direct phone number to "The Man."

Both of us decided that we wasted a long-distance call. Back in the day, long distance calls cost money and as students, we really didn't have that much money to burn. It was not a good night or, for that matter, a good week for us. We played our one card, as we thought, and got shot down with, "I will tell God about it."

However, without our knowledge, a group of Houston's Black leaders were meeting and working. Members of the Houston Black civic, religious, and business communities were gathering with the mostly white business community types to stop the kind of things that happened in many other cities. We feared police aggression and as it turns out, these business and community leaders also feared police aggression. What we did not know was that the Mack Hannah, chair of the Texas Southern Board of Directors, Vice President Lyndon Johnson, Governor Price Daniel, state police, and city police were working on a solution behind the scenes. They didn't want the desegregation process in Houston to turn into something ugly. To this day, I don't know exactly all the people who were behind it, but I do know that Quentin Mease of the Wheeler Street YMCA, Chairman Mack Hannah, Justin Robinson, a Black realtor in the city, a few doctors like John Coleman, and several ministers were talking to the right people.

All these folks had some strong motivators to create a peaceful transition in Houston. First, it just happens that at the same time, there was an effort to get a major league baseball team in the city. Not only was that cooking, but the city was about to be the NASA's Space Center of the free world. If you're old enough, you remember the words, "This is Houston mission control." Houston needed to attract the best and brightest scientists in the world. Added to all of that, Houston was vying to be the oil and gas capital of the country. Money has always been and will always be the biggest driving force for many people to do the right thing. As Reverend Lawson put it in an article in *Texas Monthly*, "Houston couldn't possibly have a Bull Connor or have the type of things that happened in Birmingham, Alabama."

So, slowly over the next couple of years, the city started desegregating lunch counters, hotels, and movie theaters. Surprise, surprise, it was all done without fanfare.

But the way it was done was interesting. We, the PYO (Progressive Youth Organization), thought we were really making things happen. We devised a plan that would disrupt an astronaut's homecoming parade. Our big plan was that, with the national and international press that would be covering the parade, we would get all the press we needed for our cause. By this time, our organization was meeting at the Wheeler Street YMCA. The director of the Y was Quinton Mease. He heard that we were planning this protest at the parade and alerted John T. Jones, the publisher of the *Houston Chronicle,* and Bob Dundas, then vice president of Foley's, the city's largest department store.

The pressure was on. What they decided was that they would desegregate restaurants, department stores, hotels, the transit authority, and everything else in one day. Now, this part is hard to believe, but they convinced the major media outlets to agree not to cover the story. It was all done without a word being said in the press.

Just minutes before we were going to do our thing, Mr. Mease contacted Stearns to say that the deal was done. We were ready.

Our signs were done. I was sitting on a stool in the Y coffee shop when Eldrewey came in and told us that we won. I could not and did not want to believe it. It was too surreal. How could the deal be done without our knowledge? But the money spoke. The city couldn't deal with a bad name at the time. The behind the scenes work of many people of good faith won the day.

A few days later, I decided to go into the segregated, all-white Men's Grill at Foley's department store on Main Street all by myself. It was a popular spot for businessmen to have lunch in the middle of the day. I thought I would shut it down when I walked up alone to have lunch. It was a second floor walk-up that had its door on a side street beside the building. I didn't have much money in my pocket because I didn't expect to be served.

When I sat at the bar, a Black waiter from the other side of the bar approached and asked, "Can I help you?"

The menu was written on the mirror in front of me. I thought to myself that I'd better order something since I came this far. I calculated the money I had in my hand to see what I could afford. I had enough with me for a cup of soup. I said, "Tomato soup, please."

"Yes sir. I will have it out in a minute," he said as he turned and walked into the kitchen.

I was shocked. They must have been waiting for me. The Black staff didn't look shocked at all, nor did the white men sitting by the grill. I was the only one.

One by one, the lunch counter and every other place was desegregated. For more than a week, nothing was in the press. After the media black-out, it was all done. As Rev. Bill Lawson said, "No mobs could convene over events that weren't publicized."

"White" and "Colored" signs were taken down from buses and water fountains. Black customers were allowed to use the fitting rooms in department stores. The forces in the city who would've tried to stop it were out-maneuvered. Money is often more powerful than anything. We were about to disrupt the flow of money in the city and wiser heads said that it was better to bring down the barrier then stop the flow of the almighty dollar.

That is a lesson. It's good to know that many wars can be won with cash used as an incentive. The dollar can trump any old southern ideology.

Even with that done, we realized that not all barriers were down. Train and bus stations still needed to be desegregated. One evening after school, a group of us went down to the Union Station coffee shop to push what we thought was one of the last vestiges of segregation off the cliff. By this time, we had white students from the University of Houston and Rice University who were willing to join us. Only about three or four carloads of students, both Black and white, showed up at the train station. We were stopped as we attempted to enter the coffee shop. Just like before, we told the press we were coming. This time, however, they were expecting us. Very soon after we arrived and tried to enter, a police officer said to us, "You must leave or be arrested."

One of us spoke for the group and said that we were not leaving. The officer pointed to me and six others, including two white students, handcuffed us, and took us directly out to a waiting paddy wagon. We thought it was wonderful being arrested for the cause. We sang different songs on the way to jail. Once we got there, we were fingerprinted, photographed, and booked in quick order.

Then our group was separated. The white students were placed into the white part of the county jail and we were placed into the colored part. Five of us were jailed together in the same cell block. At the Harris County Jail, every cell block had eight cells on one side and a dining area on the other. Each cell had eight bunk beds each. That meant every cell was designed for eight people, meaning every cell block held 64 people. That night there were more then one hundred men in that cell block. We were each given a mattress when we entered and told to sleep on the tables in the dining area. The tabletops were filled so we slept on the floor, but we knew that we weren't going to be there for long. I thought that we'd be bailed out in a few hours, so the night on the floor didn't seem too bad.

As it turned out, we made bail in less than three hours. All of us wore proud smiles as we left the jail. We hugged and patted each other on the back, then made our way to pick up our cars at the train station and then home. We got ourselves arrested; it was what we wanted from the beginning. We thought that arrests were what the movement needed to gain attention.

We didn't even think about a court date, which arrived a few months later. We were all charged with unlawful assembly at the Union Station Coffee Shop. We had a law firm representing us. Court began on a Monday morning at nine o'clock. The five of us showed up on time and looked around for our attorney, George Washington, Jr., the man who got the five of us ready for our day in court. The white students from Rice University already had their cases severed. We didn't see them in court that day. It was just us. The time for our case to be called came and went. There was only one problem: George Washington, Junior was nowhere to be found. We had no idea where he was.

The judge asked for the five of us to stand by name. He asked, "Where is your attorney?"

In confusion, we all answered and explained that we didn't know where he was. Without our lawyer present, the judge made his decision and convicted all five of us with unlawful assembly. He set our fines at $500.00 each or thirty days in the Harris County Jail. With little warning and the shock and surprise still clear on our faces, we were handcuffed and taken away. We thought it was a mistake that would be fixed in an hour or two.

Again, we were each given a mattress and shoved into a cell block. The cell block in the colored wing hadn't changed. The only difference that time was the amount of people being jailed. There were more people in the cell block, at least 120 people.

As soon as we arrived, the most intimidating inmate in the cell block greeted us. He wasn't a big man, but when you looked at his ruddy face you could see in his eyes that he wasn't someone to mess with. He had the top bunk in the back of Cell No. 8. He had the window, and we could immediately see that he was in charge. When I arrived, he pointed to the top bunk diagonally across from him.

A man was already lying in the bunk the inmate pointed at, but my new friend yelled, "Move! This boy needs to have that bunk. They got arrested for us and now we need to take care of them."

He went to four more cells and said the same thing. I knew right away that there was nothing to fear in that jail. We were among friends and people who understood what we were fighting for.

I slept that first night fully believing that we'd be bailed out at any time. I was deeply saddened to awaken in that jail cell. It felt like we were forgotten. Our meal trays were pushed through a hole in the door. Someone on the inside had to catch them. I sat on the edge of my bunk and thought all was for naught. Did anyone know we were in here? My inmate friend looked at me and must've sensed pain. He said something to me that morning that I never forgot.

Sitting on his bunk across from me, he looked at me like a father talking to his son. With all the meaning he could muster, he said, "Do the time, don't let the time do you."

I looked up at him and said, "I didn't think that I'd ever spend a night in jail. But now that I have, I don't feel like it was what I really wanted to do."

Again, he counseled me with all the meaning that a person who was awaiting a murder case against him could. Looking straight into my eyes, he said, "You can do this. You will look back upon this and see that it was all worth your time in here."

I picked my head up after a few minutes and went to look for the other four guys that were jailed with me. I thought they also needed to hear my protector's words. When I found them, it was clear they had the same dejected, saddening thoughts I did, so I told them what my cell mate had said and made my way back to my cell.

When I made it back, I had a smile on my face. My friend reached under his mattress and pulled out a paperback book. I don't remember what book it was, but it was a gift from a man who wanted me to feel better. He handed it to me and said, "Read. It will pass the time."

I spent four more nights in that cell. Eventually, I moved into a routine. On the sixth morning, a call came over the PA system. The voice called us by name and told us to report to the front of the cell block. We did as we were told and were taken to court. I took a few showers in the open shower area behind the dining tables but I didn't get to shave and looked like hell.

As we were led into court, I spotted our attorney, George Washington, Jr. He had a big smile on his face and hugged each of us. He said, "It's all over. We needed to raise the money to pay your fines and needed you in jail to bring that to the attention of the community."

That might have been worth it all to raise the money. It might have been worth it to get the attention of the community. However, I wished someone told us that was why we remained jailed.

I felt better about myself and the process as I shaved later that day. I wanted to forget about it all but I struggled. The whole ordeal brought real mental anguish.

Several years later, all our convictions were reversed. I look back at that time as another turning point in my life. I learned more about people in those five days than at any time in my life.

No matter what your station in life, no matter what bad hand you were dealt, no matter how society looks at you, you always have something to offer someone else. When you start to see that, only one question remains. Do you have the courage to reach out to someone in need and help in whatever way you can? I never would've thought an admitted murderer could give me so much when I really needed it. But he did, and I'm a better man for it.

I graduated in June of 1963 and walked away from Texas Southern University with more than a bachelor's degree in Business Administration. I walked away with skills that you cannot find in any classroom in the nation. As time has passed, I now see that those skills were just as important in my life as the skills I learned in classrooms. I better understand that who you are and what you become is a composite of all those experiences we have through time. Some are formal and some not so formal; some are good and some are not. However, all of them make us what we are. We are truly the composites of our experiences.

Even more, we are composites of the experiences of our ancestors. None of us simply show up where we are. Someone paved the way for us to get there. Someone paid dues for the space we are in. It is our responsibility to make sure the dues others paid do not go to waste. But the truth is that all of them accumulate into something much greater in the end. You never know where the gifts are going to come from. You must always be in a place where you can receive them and allow them work to make you a better person.

FOUR

THE RIGHT TO VOTE

In the state of Louisiana and across the southern states, there wasn't an organized Republican Party to speak of. Our state was represented, both in the halls of Congress in Washington, D.C. and in Baton Rouge by very conservative Democrats. When you went to the polls to vote for congressional or state officials, you were voting for the lesser of two evils. The only vote that someone like me could cast and feel good about in New Orleans was a vote for president.

That being said, the time came for me to have "The Talk" with my father. It was August 23, 1959, a few days before my 21st birthday when my dad called an "executive meeting" at the dining room table. "Executive" meant that it was just me and him. He said it was something serious, and indeed it was. As we sat down at the table, I could see that he was wearing his most solemn face.

"Son, you'll be twenty-one in a few days, and we need to talk about you registering to vote," he began. "I think you know some of what I have to say, but there is more that we need to talk about to get you ready for that day."

"The first thing is that you have to look like you're a

professional to get around the hurdles they might have for you," he continued. "You need to get to the voter registration office before noon. I think about ten in the morning would be best. You need to have on your best suit, a clean, white shirt, and a tie. Your shoes need to be shined."

I was a little amused. "Daddy, I'm just going to register to vote."

He cut me off. "Son, this is why we're having this talk. In this state, the system is set up to keep you from voting. Voting is the most important thing a citizen can do in this country. They will throw something at you if you don't look right or sound like the kind of person who *they* think should be a voter"

"You need to look like you have your stuff together or they are going to give you a hard time," Daddy continued. "You just don't know how many people there are who show up in that office and they tell them that they're not qualified. So, you need to look, sound, and act qualified, and things will go better."

I really thought he was overstating the case. However, the state of Louisiana had a literacy test that you needed to pass to vote, and your qualifications was within the discretion of the registration clerk. That was why I needed "The Talk."

"The clerk will ask you questions," Daddy explained. "You should always answer with 'Yes, Sir or Ma'am' or 'No, Sir or Ma'am.' You want to be as respectful as you can. They are looking for a reason not to register you. You don't want to give them one."

I nodded. "I think I understand."

"There are several more things," he said. "The person is going to ask you to read something from the Constitution. Take your time to read it and answer any question the person may ask. Always look at the person and answer with a smile."

He paused. "Not a grin, but a respectful smile."

"And remember that you are a Democrat," he continued. "If you were to say differently, you won't be able to vote for anything that really counts in this state. There are no Republicans running for anything in the state. The only vote you could cast is in the general election. There will not be any Republicans or Independents running, so you wouldn't cast a vote that counts."

On August 27, 1959, I did as I was told and put on my best suit. I put on a matching tie and shined my shoes. I parked about a block away from the building right next to city hall. It was where the registration office was located at the time. As I walked into the office around 10 a.m., there was no one there but me. The white lady sitting behind a desk some ten feet past the counter looked up and said, "Yes?"

I could see from her stern face that she was not going to make things easy for me.

In my most polite tone of voice, I said, "Ma'am, I would like to register to vote today."

She appeared to be in her late 50s and had dyed black hair pushed up to the front that made her look taller than she was. Dressed in all black and without a smile, she stood and asked, "Are you a Democrat?"

I responded with a smile, "Yes, Ma'am."

She reached under the counter, got out a clipboard, and shoved a single page under the clip. "Fill this out," she said, pushing the clipboard in my direction but not close enough for me to reach it. It was as if she wanted to do her job but not really be of any help.

I stepped over and picked it up. "You have to fill it out in my presence," she said.

"Yes, Ma'am," I responded with another smile.

I filled it out and handed it over with still another smile. I made sure to check the block marked "Democrat." My dad's words were bouncing around in my head.

She reached under the counter and picked up a book. She turned a few pages and said, "Read that paragraph."

I recognized it immediately and started carefully reading out loud, "'We the People of the United States, in Order to form a more perfect Union, establish justice, insure domestic Tranquility, provide for the common defense, promote the general Welfare, and secure the Blessings of Liberty to ourselves and our Posterity, do ordain and establish this Constitution for the United States of America.'"

I looked her in the eye. "Okay?"

She was expressionless. "Now tell me what you read."

I smiled respectfully. "This is the Preamble to the Constitution of the United States of America. It was written by our forefathers to establish the rules and regulations of our government."

I was prepared to tell her all about Benjamin Franklin and James Madison or the Bill of Rights, but before I could get my next sentence out, she reached under the counter again, pulled out a big black stamp, and pressed it down with a bang.

It read "PASSED." If my dad was next to me at that moment, I would've kissed him. His prep work paid off. I looked the part, smiled when I could, and felt like I was on top of my game.

Without saying a word, she turned and went to a file cabinet on the other side of her desk and picked up a book. She confirmed my address on the page I filled out earlier before fingering through the book and stopping at one particular page. "Your voting precinct is 3-1."

Proudly, I turned and walked out the door and had a devious thought. If this clerk only knew that I already voted—twice. In both 1952 and 1956, I took my grandmother to the polls to vote. She had trouble with her sight, so I went into the booth with her and pulled the lever on her behalf to vote for Adlai Stevenson for president.

The next time would be my own vote. Oh, did that feel good. The lessons I learned over the years at the dining room table and from that last" executive meeting" with my dad paid off. Ever since that day when I first registered to vote, if the polls were open, I voted. No matter where I have lived and no matter how big or small the race on the ballot, I follow my dad's advice. Voting is the most important thing that a citizen can do in these United States. Every vote counts.

We see now that efforts are still being made to suppress or discourage voting in some places, a clear sign that voting is now even more important then ever. In a democracy such as ours, if you don't vote you aren't really a citizen. You're not exercising the primary right that makes you a full citizen of the country.

Soon after the Civil War and the passing of the Thirteenth Amendment to the Constitution, the power structure across the south found ways to jail as many Black people as they could. If they were convicted of a felony, they were denied the right to vote. It's just in recent years that after someone serves their time, they're given their voting rights back.

The second obstacle to voting was economic. People were told in many states across the south that if they registered to vote or voted, they should not come back to work. That'll keep you home in most places.

The third method of voter suppression was intimidation. Highway patrolmen or other police officers were stationed at polling places. In many places in Texas it was the Texas Rangers. They would frighten minority voters and deter many from staying and casting their vote.

In contrast to our system, in many places around the world, voting is done on the weekends. There isn't a need to take off from work and stand in long lines just to exercise your most basic right as a citizen. Many states are moving to a mail-in vote. I can see a day when everyone could vote online. It'd be cheap, verifiable, and easy.

FIVE

NOW TO THE WORLD OF WORK

I was poised to start a new life after a short vacation to New Orleans and Detroit with James V. Haydel, Jr., or Lil JV as we called him. We'd spend a week with my mother's first cousin, Pauline Haydel Milton. JV and Michael Haydel, my two second cousins, spent their freshman year at TSU with me while I was in my senior year. Lil JV and I bonded that year we spent together with Michael. The close relationship we developed has lasted my entire life.

My dad, who was always keen to find a deal, got me a 1955 Opel convertible in nearly mint condition. It was bought in Germany by a guy who was in the military. He brought it home after his service only to die that same year. His wife kept the car for several years, tucked away in a small garage. She told my dad about it in 1961. He bought it for next to nothing, then had it reupholstered, painted, and installed a new black vinyl top. Oh yes, it was unique. So JV and I drove my Opel to Detroit.

I heard so much about Detroit and a night club called the Flame Show Bar. It had some of the best acts in Black American entertainment appearing nearly every weekend. My mother would come back from visiting Aunt Pauline and tell me stories about seeing Billie Holiday, George Shearing, or some other well-known entertainer at the Famous Flame. I wanted to have that experience for myself.

After a few days of hanging out with Aunt Pauline and her husband, our Uncle Dotty, JV and I went to the Flame one night to catch Dinah Washington. The Famous Flame was all it was cracked up to be. JV and I had good seats less than thirty feet from the stage and Dinah Washington. We enjoyed every minute. I can still see myself listening to Dinah singing as the crowd in the Flame Show Bar talked and enjoyed their drinks. The murmurs and mutterings of the crowd grew too loud for a lady of her talents. Without notice, she stopped singing and looked at the audience as if to say, "You are not giving this lady the respect she deserves." With a wave of her hand, the band stopped playing. The room instantly lost volume and grew quieter by the second. She slowly walked over to the barstool next to her and sat. The seconds accumulated into minutes and the bar got so silent that you could hear a rat piss on cotton.

She moved the microphone to her face and said in a low voice, "Detroit knows me, and I know Detroit. I will walk off if you don't want to hear me."

She turned to the band and with a nod of her head said, "Oh, What a Difference a Day Makes." The band started playing and she finished her set without a person saying a word. You couldn't even hear a glass clink during the rest of her set.

She was *good*. I still sing "What a Difference a Day Makes" to myself and think fondly about those good times. Dinah was on top of her game at that time and that was her million-selling hit.

Aunt Pauline was married to a very prominent Inkster, a Michigan physician we called Uncle Doddy. They had a large house on Michigan Avenue and his medical clinic was in the building next door. I remember so many things about that house. One thing I always marveled at was a regular nightclub jukebox sitting in the basement. Someone came to the house every week to change the records, something I've never seen anywhere else. I was sure they were living higher on the hog than anyone I knew back in New Orleans.

Aunt Pauline had a den in the back of her house. The large den had a color television set that sat right under a big picture window. Not many people, black or white, had a color TV at that time.

It was in Pauline's den where I watched President Kennedy's speech about civil rights on June 11, 1963. During the heyday of the civil rights movement, two African Americans were enrolled into the University of Alabama, but not without protest and defiance from local government officials. To quell the civil unrest and calls for segregation, President Kennedy deployed the National Guard to Tuscaloosa. He delivered the address to the nation to call for the end of Jim Crow-era segregation.

Several things stood out to me about the Report to the American People on Civil Rights. The first was the fact that President Kennedy sent National Guard troops to accompany the first Black students admitted to both Mississippi and Alabama Universities. That must've bothered him. He said, "It ought to be possible... for American students of any color to attend any public institution they select without having to be backed up by troops... It ought to be possible for American consumers of any color to receive equal service in places of public accommodation, such as hotels and restaurants and theaters and retail stores, without being forced to resort to demonstrations in the streets, and it ought to be possible for American citizens of any color to register to vote in a free election without interference or fear of reprisal."

How did he know? That is just what I was fighting for during my years at Texas Southern—the right to go to a school of your choosing, eat in a place of your choosing, sit in a theater of your choosing, stay in any hotel of your choosing, and shop in a store of your choosing. He even mentioned the right to register to vote in a free election without the fear of reprisal.

Kennedy went on to say, "If an American, because his skin is dark, cannot eat lunch in a restaurant open to the public, if he cannot vote for the public officials who represent him, if, in short, he cannot enjoy the full and free life which all of us want, then who among us would be content to have the color of his skin changed and stand in his place?"

To me, those words were stronger than the Holy Ghost. I never heard a president of the United States say anything like that.

His words needed to be made into the law of the land. Unfortunately, he didn't see that happen in his lifetime. But it did happen, even if we're still fighting to keep those rights alive today.

After a few more days living high on that hog, JV and I drove back to New Orleans and I was ready to move on to the next stage of my life. That week bonding with Aunt Pauline and Uncle Doddy has always stayed with me. Uncle Doddy was from the Washington, D.C. area and loved a particular candy that you could only buy there. It was only sold at one store in northwest Washington. Every time I took a trip to Detroit, he'd call and say, "Pick me up some Velatis candy."

Uncle Doddy was a diabetic and didn't need the candy, but he loved the caramel treats. "Don't tell your Aunt Pauline," he would whisper before he hung up the phone.

I sneaked the near-pound of candy to him when I arrived.

He lost both legs to diabetes but still practiced medicine until his death. All the time, he was eating those candies he loved so much. I figured a man ought to be able to enjoy the things he likes, even if he knows they're not good for him.

SIX

STANDARD SAVINGS AND LOAN: MORE THAN A JOB

After my trip to Detroit, I went back to Houston to take a job as assistant comptroller at Standard Savings and Loan Association, an old-fashioned savings and loan bank. The Association's only office was near Texas Southern and just down the street from the store where I had my first sit-in experience. It was what we called The Heart of Third Ward and the middle class Black community. There was a night club across the street and a drug store around the block. Houston's upper class Black community was less than eight blocks away, made up of lovely homes owned by TSU professors, doctors, and other members of the professional Black community.

I had interned at the Association in my senior year and Mr. Mack H. Hannah, the Association's president, had offered me the job. Mr. Hannah was also the chair of Texas Southern University's Board of Directors. That was good in more ways than I could have imagined. A big man, Hannah must have weighed nearly 350 pounds, but his weight wasn't the biggest thing about him. That would be his heart. He took me in and let me learn about the business and how decisions were made.

At the time, the Association had about three million dollars in assets. Small, perhaps, when you compare it with other financial institutions at the time, but Hannah made the most of it. He provided loans to Black churches and people who might not qualify for loans at other banks. Many Black churches had congregations large enough to afford a larger church but the downtown banks would not give them a loan to build one because they didn't think it was a good use of their money. Mr. Hannah, on the other hand, thought that this was a great investment because the congregation would support the bank and Black people support their ministers and churches. Because of him and his foresight, the churches flourished and the members used our Association for all their banking needs.

I wasn't on the job six months when my dad called to tell me that I had received notice back home that it was time to fulfill my military obligation. It was not a draft notice, but a notice that my student deferment needed to be renewed. With my dad's connections, he found out that if I said that I was no longer enrolled in college, I would be drafted in short order. That meant that I needed to enlist in the reserves or some branch of the military quickly. I decided on the Army Reserve. I was able to get a leave of absence from my job to do the six months of military service. Within days of my dad's call, I took a trip to New Orleans and enlisted in the Army Reserves.

It was the second week in October of 1963 when I reported to Fort Polk, Louisiana for my basic training. It was an interesting process. I was assigned to a platoon of about sixty guys. The platoon was housed in a two-story building facing a parade field. The first days were more stressful than any time I can remember.

Standing outside of the building in our civilian clothes on

our first day, we were facing a Black guy right out of central casting. He looked like Louis Gossett, Jr. from *An Officer and a Gentleman* on steroids. That movie didn't come out until 1983 and my basic training was in 1963. When I saw that film, the first thing that came to mind was my platoon sergeant.

This man did not have a low or calming tone in his DNA. Every word came out as loud as he could project it. His instructions were for us to run into the building, find a bed and footlocker, and stand at attention in front of it. He would give us further instructions when he came in. If we were not standing at attention at a bunk bed, he wanted ten push-ups on the spot.

Needless to say, we found a top or lower bunk bed and footlocker, stood at attention, and waited for his instructions. One or two men weren't standing just the way he wanted us to and he pointed them out and demanded his ten push-ups. As I think back on it now, everyone was doing as they were told but he needed to make an example of someone on each floor just to get our attention.

The platoon sergeant stood in the middle of the room and shouted at the top of his voice, "This is your home for the next eight weeks. If it is not as clean as it is now, if your bed is not made up just as it is now, if your locker is not in order, your ass belongs to me."

Now I obviously did not want my ass to belong to Louis Gossett, Jr., so I needed to do as I was told when I was told it.

Within two days I realized that only two other men in my platoon had finished college. They were Phillip (Phil) Fry from Beaumont, Texas and Eugene (Gene) Godley from Dallas, Texas. We bonded quickly because the rest of the sixty or so men were from small towns in Texas, Arkansas and Louisiana and really spoke a different language. Some of these towns were so small that the only way you would have been able to understand them was to be from that town or a town near them. The one town that stands out in my mind is Marked Tree, Arkansas. This guy from the big city of Marked Tree was named Donald Ford. We called him Donny. The reason he stands out in my mind is that on the second night we were in the barracks, he came up to me and told me that he had never spoken to a Black boy in his life, so he wanted to talk to me. Most of those kids had little education and had never been exposed to diversity of any sort.

It was a new experience for all of us. I had never seen that kind of provincialism in my life. After all, I was a city boy, raised in the big city of New Orleans and educated in Houston. I guess you could say that I was as strange to them as they were to me.

Our sergeant's name was Chang. He was a very fit Black man of about six feet who took no prisoners. When he entered the barracks, we were to come to attention and stand wherever we were until he gave the word. About five days into our training, he made me acting sergeant. The same exulted title was given to Gene Godley. We were moved from the large bay of the barracks to a room on the left side of the front of the building facing the parade field. Now *that* was a good gig because we got to sleep in a private room and call the cadence for the platoon when we were drilling.

Basic training is no joke. We worked hard every day. Sgt. Chang saw to it that we were made into fighting machines that could take orders and carry them out. After eight weeks of his training, we really *were* fighting machines.

We were allowed our first weekend of liberty after our fourth week of training. Gene and I caught a bus to the nearby little town of Leesville, Louisiana to relax and get a beer. After about a fifteen-minute ride, the post bus dropped us off at a bus stop on one end of a street that looked like the one John Wayne walked down in the movie *High Noon*. It was a dirt road with bars on both sides and if I remember right, a store or two. A few cars were parked in the street, and you could hear country music coming out of the open doors of the bars. Now, this was before country music was "cool." This was more like the old time country of Hank Williams or Roy Acuff.

We meandered over to the first bar we saw and entered. Within a very few minutes we learned our first lesson of where we were and what we were.

The Army might have been integrated, but Leesville was not. The bartender promptly told us that they did not serve colored people. Well, the truth was that we were not colored "people." We were one colored person and one white person.

As we looked around, it was obvious that this was not our bar. The few soldiers that were present would not have had our backs if things were going wrong. The locals looked like they came from the same casting agency as Sgt. Chang. Their rednecks were so thick that you could see it on the front of their faces. To put it another way, they looked like Klu Klux Klansmen at their day jobs. Since we were made as colored people, we needed another venue.

Standing in the dirt road, we made a quick decision. We would enter another establishment in town, I would pretend to speak Spanish to Gene, and he would order beers for both of us. Of course, I was counting on the fact that nobody in the place actually spoke Spanish. We went across the street and tried out the scheme. It worked and we were able to down our first cold ones of the evening. That was the first beer we'd had in four weeks.

Beyond the drinks tasting good, the bar was pretty boring. The music was the same brand of country that was blaring across the street. As I looked around, I noticed that nearly everyone who wasn't in Army uniform was dressed in khaki shirts and pants or jeans. We had a little more time to look around and we noticed that the patrons were all men. To say the least, the place wasn't friendly so we left as soon as we finished our beers.

When we stepped out on the street, I heard a train. I turned to Gene and said, "Let's walk in that direction."

He agreed and off we went.

Since no colored people were drinking or even *standing* in this part of town, I surmised that the Black community would be on the proverbial "other side of the train tracks." And, surprise, surprise, it was just where I thought.

"The wrong side of the track" was in every city that had a train running through it. It was side where the smoke and soot would blow when the steam engines came barreling through. That is not the side that you want to live on. So that's the side where Black communities were located.

We crossed the tracks and right in front of us were three or four night clubs, but back then, they might have been called colored juke joints. We went into one and it was *hopping*. The music was good, the patrons were both men *and* women, and people were dancing and having a good time. We downed a few more beers, laughed a lot, and enjoyed the music and the happy faces. The only song I can remember is one by The Impressions:"It's All Right." The jukebox was a nickel a play so for a quarter, you could pass a good bit of time.

From that point forward, it was clear that to have a good time we had to go to the other side of the tracks. Gene was accepted into the group and the joint was always jumping. We were free to be ourselves.

On November 22, 1963, everything changed for us in that barracks and across the rest of the nation. For that matter, the entire *world* changed.

We left before daybreak on a forced march with all our gear on our backs. It was the kind of training that you needed if troops needed to move to another location and did not have transportation. We did not return to the barracks until nearly 2 p.m. The only stops in all that time was to relieve ourselves or to eat our Army ready-to-eat meals. With all that gear on our backs, it just might be the hardest walk I have ever taken. We came back to the barracks and literally fell over. Most of us didn't want to dirty our beds so we just fell right on the floor. That all changed about 45 minutes after we got back. Someone burst through the door and yelled, "Kennedy has been killed!"

What happened next took my breath away. The barracks broke out in cheers, yells, and applause. The sergeant wasn't there and the only people who weren't cheering were me, the few other Black people, Gene, and Phil.

I was stunned. I ran out the door that led to the parade field and stood as tears rolled down my face. I saw the post chapel on the other side of the field and ran to it. The door was unlocked, so I went in and sat. I must have sat there for more than an hour. As I cried, I thought to myself, *"Who could have done something like this?"* Then there was the cheering and clapping. I didn't *ever* think that I was doing my basic training with men who nearly all thought it was a good thing that the president was dead.

This was *my* president. The same man who had given that speech not too many months before about civil rights as I sat in my Aunt Pauline's den. The same man who had given so many in the nation and the world hope.

I've never gotten over that hour I spent alone in the post chapel. I returned to the barracks still with tears in my eyes. I closed the door as the men were still high-fiving. Gene and I just looked at each other for a long time.

As I showered in an open bathroom, washing the dirt of the forced march from my body, I could still see happiness on the faces of the men around me. The water flowing down my face hid the tears that didn't seem to stop. Later that evening, Gene, Phil and I moved ourselves to an empty part of the dining hall to eat without saying nearly anything to each other.

The next day we were all unexpectedly given a three or four day pass. Phil had friends in Beaumont, Texas, who were willing to put us up for a few days, so we took advantage of the offer and caught a bus. I called my parents once we got in that night and they weren't doing well after the previous day's tragedy either. The nation, both black and white, was in shock. That was the first time that the assassination of a president was seen on TV. We went from Camelot, the cheers of the crowds with our First family riding in an open car with the Governor of Texas and his wife, to full stop. A nation of people wringing their hands saying, "How did this happen?"

Well, not *everyone* in the nation. We had just left many who were cheering because the Catholic northeastern liberal that had taken over our government had perished. Not everyone was lamenting the loss of Camelot.

It was now the 24th of November and the three of us were sitting in the living room of our borrowed house with our eyes glued to the 14-inch black-and-white TV. We saw Jack Ruby kill 24-year-old Lee Harvey Oswald in real time. He was the person who they said shot President Kennedy. Now, how did a Dallas night club owner get close enough to Oswald in the custody of the Dallas police to kill him with a single shot?

That question and many others will never be answered. There were many questions about the events in and around November 24, 1963 that will never be known. If my memory serves me right, we didn't speak for more than a half hour. We could not believe what we had just witnessed. The air was sucked out of the room and we sat looking at the chaos unfolding on the small TV screen. There was so much pushing and shoving on the tiny screen. We didn't realize it at the time, but our nation had just turned an important page of our history book. We were now entering the post-President John F. Kennedy history of the United States. Camelot was over. The scenes of the beautiful First Lady

Jackie and their storybook-looking kids running through the White House was done.

We reported back to Fort Polk on time to finish the rest of our basic training, but the rest of the training was pretty much a blur. The only memory that I still have is the night I went through the infiltration course. I think most people would always remember bullets and tracer bullets flying only a foot over their head. It rained that night so I went through in the mud. I do remember the sergeant saying, "You need to keep your head from touching the barbed wire. If you should stand up, you die. You will *die*."

The remaining days went by quickly. We, and by "we" I mean the nation and the world, were left with memories and images; the young president's widow and children, the funeral procession through Washington, the burial in Arlington Cemetery. It was all a little more than a person could take packed into such a short time. It might be because these images have been played over and over that I still remember so much. Whatever the reason, John Jr.'s. salute, Jackie with the black veil over her face, and the horse with the boot turned backwards is still with me and nearly everyone who lived through that time.

After being sworn in on Air Force Once on the Dallas tarmac, the new president, Lyndon B. Johnson, took office and life was different for the next few years. The voting rights bill passed, many of the civil rights laws passed, and Johnson, the "accidental president," as he was called in playwright Larry King's book, pushed through many things that he would not have touched if it were not for the blood that was let on that awful day in Dallas.

My basic training ended around the first week of December 1963. I was shipped to Fort Ord, near Monterey, California. It was a great place for me at that time. Honore Haydel, my first cousin who I'd been raised with, had gone into the Army nearly a year before I did. He was stationed at Fort Ord and was serving as a

Military Police Officer (MP). My father also had several friends who were non-commissioned officers there, and it was a short drive to Oakland where my cousin/sister Margaret was living with her family.

My orders said that I would catch a train to California, but before I shipped out I had a few days of leave to spend with my family in New Orleans. I had just enough time to think that I wanted to send a telegram to Honore saying, "Will arrive Ft. Ord at 7:00pm on Dec. 5th. Have the party ready."

My orders gave me a sleeper, so I went to California in style. I ate well in the dining car and slept in a private a room. If I remember right, I had to change trains in Los Angeles, but I still arrived at the front gate of Fort Ord at the scheduled time.

"Private Curtis Graves reporting for duty," I said to the MP at the gate.

The MP looked at a roster on his desk and pointed to another MP.

"Arrest this man!" he shouted.

I was arrested and handcuffed. He threw me and my duffel bag in the back of a Military Police car and with the red lights flashing and siren blaring, I was taken straight to the party that I had asked for. I just didn't ever think that it would happen with me handcuffed in the back of a Military Police car.

A crowd was standing outside of an officer's post home laughing at me as the MP took the cuffs off me and let me run into Honore's arms. "Welcome, welcome," they all shouted. "We thought that would get your attention," someone said.

There was music, food, drinks, and a good time. Honore sure did greet me with a flair. One that I have remembered and talked about ever since.

Most of the officers attending my welcome party were from Louisiana and were very good friends with Honore from his Southern days. Honore played football at Southern and knew nearly everyone who went through ROTC training because he was in the program himself for two years before changing his mind.

I learned that Fort Ord was one of the best places for a Black officer to be stationed in the nation. It was a beautiful, mellow place. It was strategically located right on the Pacific Ocean within sight of the beautiful little city of Monterey, and to top that, an officer of color was not an oddity. During my time there I ran into many of my own friends from New Orleans or friends that I had met at Bayou Boys State who were from other places in Louisiana. Oh, it was like old home week.

I was sent to Fort Ord to be trained as a company clerk. I had learned typing in college and the Army knew that. Because of my business degree, within two weeks I was teaching the typing class and did so for the rest of my training without any problems.

Other things worked out in my favor, too. One of my dad's friends ran the Non-Commissioned Officer (NCO) club at the Presidio of Monterey. My and Honore's connection to him gave us free drinks and all the rights and privileges of the club. We were not NCOs but he treated us better than if we were. The same man also ran the pistol range, so we could go shoot anytime we wanted. There were many good things on the post, and I took advantage of all of them.

After three weeks of training and teaching, I took a flight back to Houston to pick up my new black VW. I had just bought it after I took the job at Standard Savings. It was new, but I got it for a good price because it was made to be driven in Europe, not on the streets of the United States. Many of the safety features that the US required were not built into it. But what did I know? I was shopping for the best price and I bought it at a lot, not a dealership.

Because I was only given a three-day pass, I needed to get back to Fort Ord as soon as I could. I convinced one of my new friends to make the trip with me to Houston. Our plan was to drive all the way back without stopping. Well, we made it back from Houston in 33 hours, but it was *not* easy! We took turns driving while the other tried to sleep. We really tired ourselves out, but we made it.

Now I had my car and the means to get around without any problems. I drove to Oakland and other places nearly every weekend. Margaret saw more of me than she wanted to. Her girls were about four and six years old and we all spent many good times together. I even went to a Black and White Ball with Margaret and her husband, Joseph Zimmerman. He and I had both pledged Kappa Alpha Psi fraternity in college. The Black and White Ball was one of the events that our fraternity put on in most cities. Margaret arranged for me to meet some girls for me to take out and for several months they made my visits to Oakland memorable.

I was discharged in April and decided to drive across the country to Chicago to visit a girl I had known from my days at Xavier University. I got all the way there only to find that she wasn't home. She had gone to visit her mother. I decided to make the most of my time in the area, so I spent a few days with my cousin, Fallon Williams, and his wife, Mary. Then I headed south to visit another friend living in Nashville, Joseph Labat. He was in medical school then. I spent a few days with him and we had a great time.

After my cross-country drive, I still had two weeks before I had to be back on the job in Houston so I headed to New Orleans to see family and friends. My dad asked if I wanted anything special to take back to Houston with me when I left. I didn't have to think about it very long. "A dozen soft-shell crabs," I requested.

Sure enough, when it was time for me to head back to Houston, I had a dozen soft-shell crabs packed on ice. By the time I got back to Houston, I didn't quite know what to do with them. I went to the owner of a club called The Black Cat and asked him if he could cook them for me. He agreed, and I invited some friends over that night to polish off the dozen.

Not too many days after I arrived back on the job, I received a call from Mr. Hannah asking if I would drive him over to a party at President Johnson's ranch. It was about a three- or four-hour drive. He had also asked a big lawyer from Dallas, also an invitee, to ride with us. His name was W. J. Durham, a prominent civil rights and family attorney who had been practicing law in Dallas for many years. The drive over to Johnson's ranch with these two old warriors who had been in all the trenches was an educational experience. Their "war" stories were wonderful.

Mr. Hannah had submitted my name so I had my own invitation to the party. We proudly showed them off at the front gate and parked the car in a VIP parking area.

Now there I was at the LBJ Ranch; I was transported into another world. Supreme Court Chief Justice Earl Warren was there along with other Supreme Court Justices, cabinet members, Governor of Texas John Connally, and many members of the Senate and House of Representatives. Governor Connally was still wearing a sling from the injuries he suffered sitting in the front seat of the limousine when President Kennedy was assassinated in Dallas.

Amongst themselves, this display of ease by the high-powered elite of America was almost unimaginable to me. It was truly a revelation for this young man who was raised in the shadows of a New Orleans Catholic Church, made even more shocking by the liberal use of "MFs," "SOBs," and other words that I assumed would not come out of the mouths of high-ranking individuals.

It was some kind of a day. In time, the president spoke to the several hundred people gathered in his ranch house front yard and formally introduced the governor and several other high-ranking attendees.

I didn't talk to many people besides Mr. Hannah and Mr. Durham. After all, I didn't know a soul besides the two men I drove in with. I was like a fish out of water, but I played my part. I didn't look like I didn't belong. I must admit that there weren't more than ten Black people among the several hundred guests. I didn't really see any Black people serving at the party, either. I learned many years later that President Johnson had been using this same barbeque caterer for many years. It was a company from the Texas hill country that had grown famous doing these "Out Back" parties for the Johnsons and by the time Lyndon was president, the restaurant had worked enough of them to have it down to a science. Most of the servers were Latinos and most of the pitmasters were white. They made it seem like an easy job. But I must say that I saw the biggest barbeque pit I had ever laid eyes on at that party. It was a set of trailers on wheels tied together as if they were one. It must have been 100 feet long! On one side the pitmasters were turning all kinds of meat and on the other side the guests were getting whatever they wanted that was cooked.

That day is one that I will never forget. There was more raw power in one place than I have ever seen. Since Johnson was at one time the majority leader of the Senate, he had more friends who were senators and as many friends who were members of the House as you could imagine. On top of that, the partisan divide was not as deep at that time. Republicans would show up in numbers at an event such as this one because the president had invited them; it wasn't as big a deal to fraternize across party lines. But the truth is, I didn't recognize many people in attendance because I was not aware of the national leaders as we all are now. Even now, I remember the party not for the people I met, but for the grand scale of the whole event.

The trip back was just as colorful as the trip to LBJ's ranch.

The stories were nonstop and I was all ears. They both talked about the times when they first started in business and law, the women that cross their paths, the law cases that were interesting and business deals that were closed. They never stopped talking. From time to time, Mr. Hannah would say, "Curt, you need to pull over at the next service station so we old men can pee."

So I would find the biggest station to pull over at because they would not be likely to tell us that we couldn't use the restroom.

I slipped back into my job at Standard Savings knowing that I was in the active reserve for another six years. Within two years, Mr. Hannah decided to open a branch of the Association in The Fifth Ward section of the city. This was an all-Black section that was really underserved by any financial institutions. It also had a large neighborhood of Catholics who had migrated over the last twenty years from Louisiana. Houston was looked at like a boomtown for many who had come in from Lafayette and other western Louisiana cities. This was a Creole population very much like the one where I was raised in New Orleans. Since I looked and sounded like the neighborhood, Mr. Hannah appointed me without any competition to be branch manager. I had the opportunity to build out the bank and open the doors of the first Black bank in The Fifth Ward section of Houston, Texas.

It turned out to be a great place for me. I became the hub of lots of activity on Lyons Avenue, the main street of Fifth Ward. A law office and an optometrist shared the first floor of the building with the Savings Association. The lawyer was Asberry Butler and the optometrist was Dr. Theodore Youngblood. Asberry opened an account at the Association and Youngblood and I became close friends. The owners of the building occupied the top floor. It was The True Level Lodge Hall. I didn't know it then and would not have ever thought of it, but that friendship with Dr. Youngblood opened the door for me to recruit the second Black Page in the history of the Texas House of Representatives. I also did not know it then but the True Level Lodge Hall would be my place for many fundraising activities and the membership of the Lodge helped me in my political career.

One day I was sitting in my office when Asberry came in to tell me about his desire to run for a seat on the Houston school board. Mr. Hannah wanted me to jump in headfirst into the community, so it was an easy step for me to help him. A known segregationist named Joe Kelly Butler had been on the school board for many years. All the Houston Independent School District (HISD) meetings were broadcast on the Educational TV channel, and Joe Kelly Butler was one of the most popular people in town. The mayor didn't even have a platform to be on TV as much as the school board did.

Asberry and I thought that the way to win this campaign was to never be seen in white Houston. It was a citywide race and with the last name Butler, a down-low campaign on one side of town and a non-media campaign on the Black side of town might just pick up enough white vote to win the day. We ran as low to the ground as we could. When the Houston daily papers asked for a picture, we did not send one. Asberry's picture was never seen in the white media. On the other hand, we visited every church in Black Houston that we could find. No matter how small the church, we were there on Sunday to talk to the preacher and meet his flock.

We wanted white Houston to think they were voting for Joe Kelly Butler and not Asberry Butler. The election was at-large, meaning that the entire city would have to vote on all the members who were up for election. This system had been in place since 1876 and it was proven to dilute the minority vote and keep most minority candidates from ever being elected. Only one person had broken the code. She was Hattie Mae White, a Black former teacher who got elected even under this bad system.

Well, our campaign plan worked. We successfully convinced enough white people across the city that they were voting for Joe Kelly Butler, not Asberry Butler. He was elected and joined Hattie Mae White on the school board.

The other factor that worked for us was that after the *Smith V. Allwright* decision, more Black Texans had registered to vote than in any other southern state. (Coincidentally, the Smith in *Smith V. Allwright* was Dr. Lonnie Smith, a Black dentist who lived and had his dental practice in the Fifth Ward.) Asberry went on to become an outspoken member of the board and worked hard to bring to the everyone's attention the problems that plagued the children of Houston be they Black, white or brown.

SEVEN

WHY I RAN FOR OFFICE

Not too long after Asberry Butler's election, I went to a meeting of the Holy Name Society at Our Mother of Mercy Catholic church where I was a member. A year or so before, I joined the Society because it helped poor people in the parish. The speaker at this meeting was Henry Grover, a member of the state Senate, a fellow Catholic from across town, and a member of the Society at his respective church. He was known by the name Hank. The senator was invited to speak to our group because he was running for office in our county. The main message of his speech revolved around the merits of voting for all the candidates county-wide. Our Mother of Mercy was an all-Black church in an all-Black neighborhood.

We listened to him trying to convince us of his view. After all, he was invited by our pastor to be a guest at our church, so we all tried to remain polite. However, I was not persuaded. After a while, I could not sit silently. I stood and asked a question.

"Senator, did you not know countywide elections would stop

and make it nearly impossible for a Black or brown candidate to ever get elected to the legislature from Houston?"

The congregation grew quiet and still. I just asked a white elected official a question that was, without a doubt, going to cause some discomfort. They were not completely ready for that.

"All the people of the county should have the right to vote for all the candidates in Houston," he answered.

I stuck to my position. "That approach is unfair."

The room remained quiet during this exchange and heads bounced around tracking the conversation like they were following a tennis match. They looked forward, then back at my response.

Finally, he ended the argument. "If you think you have a better way of doing things, why don't you run?"

Without saying anything, I sat down, deep in thought.

In the following weeks, I got a call from a good friend who was a lawyer. He said that he was going to drive to Austin in a few days for a legislative committee meeting. The meeting would discuss the redistricting of Harris County, where Houston was located. The member who sponsored the bill was State Rep. Robert Eckhardt of Humble, Texas. Humble was in Harris County and his bill created eighteen single-member districts for the county.

Because of the number of people attending, the committee hearing was held on the floor of the State House of Representatives. The attendees were invited to sit in whatever seat they wanted on the floor. The members of the committee gathered around a press table in the center of the room. The seats were quickly filling with other attendees, but for some reason, I paused to take a moment and decide which seat I wanted. There, amongst the moving crowd, I saw the perfect seat for me. I sat in seat number 69 because it had great view of the entire hall, from the floor to the entrance in the back. I looked around and up at the ceiling of the room and listened to the proceedings. By the next day I made a decision: I was going to declare my candidacy for state representative. Senator Hank Grover had challenged me, and I was ready to answer.

What I didn't know was that just a year earlier, a case called *Kilgarlin v. Martin* was decided in federal court. It forced the state to redraw the state House of Representatives electoral map in accordance with a Supreme Court decision. The districts only represented population size, not land area like a county. In the end, the eighteen single-member districts didn't pass. Eckhardt was forced to compromise his bill. What he ended up with were three legislative districts that were synonymous with the congressional districts. So, there were six members that would run at-large in the congressional district.

The congressional district on the northeastern side of Harris County included Humble, Bay Town, the mostly Black Fifth Ward section of the city, and a large part of the Hispanic community. If a coalition ticket could be put together, that coalition might stand a good chance of winning. I thought to myself that the ticket needed a Black, a Latino, and four whites to appeal to the large labor/working class people who lived there.

I turned to Hattie Mae White for advice. She was a long-time member of the Houston Independent School District. At the time, she and Asberry were the only two Black elected officials in the county. She advised me that it was imperative to get the backing of the Black Ministerial Alliance. After that, I needed to work on the Black coalition that had an active "Get Out the Vote" machine in place. The group was known as the Harris County Council of Organizations (HCCO). They were necessary because they could garner more support from several other labor organizations.

Hattie Mae's advice was golden. I first went to the Ministerial Alliance. I showed up at a church where they held their monthly meeting and asked to speak. The group was a collection of mostly older Baptist pastors who had large congregations. After a few minutes of talking, I was able to explain to them why I was the man to support. In the past, they always called candidates before them to decide whether they would support their campaign or not. I jumped the gun, but before they had their candidate forum, I had their endorsement.

I then went to the HCCO to align myself with them. They knew and liked a woman named Barbara Jordan. Barbara was a local lawyer in the Fifth Ward and her father was a well-known Baptist minister. The labor community asked her to run twice before to get out the Black vote, but they knew she couldn't win in an at-large race. I never met Barbara and didn't know if she'd be of any help to me. What I *did* know was that I needed someone to give me some inside help.

My inside person was Mrs. White. She recommended that I meet Christia Adair and arranged a meeting. Adair was a woman in her late fifties or early sixties with a really forceful personality. With a little effort, I was able to win her over. We talked and she shared thoughts about me being a Catholic in politics. I remember her saying, "If you're asked if you've been saved, or born again, always say 'yes.'"

I didn't know of or hear sentiments like that before. In general, Catholics didn't talk about being saved, or, for that matter, being born again. But that was something that I needed to know if I was questioned by a Black audience. It meant that I accepted Jesus as my savior. Now *that* was a concept that I hadn't been exposed to. Mrs. Adair had a lot of insider perspective. She shared information that I needed to know about core constituencies that I needed support of to win.

If my memory serves me right, I called Mrs. White that very afternoon to ask her what it meant to be "born again." She broke it all down for me. After our conversation ended, I felt ready to talk the talk and walk the walk.

It was Mrs. Adair who took me to HCCO for their support. With her in my corner, I was a shoo-in.

Barbara Jordan was a known personality, a familiar face after running for office. The labor and liberal coalitions in Harris County put her on the ballot. She thought that she paid her dues and felt, rightfully so, like this was her time to get elected. There was a new state senatorial district that was drawn in a way that made her the best and most logical person to get elected.

I, on the other hand, was not a known quantity. I had to earn my supporters, one person at a time. I had my work cut out for me. I needed to work the field as hard as I could. With the backing of the HCCO, my next challenge was to get Big Labor behind me. The white part of the district consisted of factory workers and other workers from unionized jobs.

But before I did that or anything else, I had to qualify for the race by paying my filing fee of $500. I gathered some friends, raised a buck or two from each, and off I went to officially file as a candidate for the Texas State House of Representatives. I enlisted several friends to stand behind me when I filed so the picture that ran in *The Forward Times* and *The Informer*, two Black newspapers, would show readers that I wasn't simply acting on a whim and that I had support.

Once I was official, I felt it was time to put myself in front of larger groups like the labor unions. There was a meeting called at the American Federation of Labor (AFL) union hall on the Gulf Freeway. I showed up with a host of other candidates. Every one of them was a stranger to me. We were each allowed to say a few words about our candidacy. After a day or so, we were informed of their decision.

They announced endorsements of Joseph Allen of Baytown, Glenn Vickery of Houston, Rex Braun of Houston, Lauro Cruz of Houston, Lindon Williams of Houston, and Curtis Graves of Houston. I made the cut.

I quickly bonded with the other five endorsed candidates. After a meeting or two at the union hall, we decided that our approach would be to campaign together as much as we could. Taking turns speaking, we would allow the candidate to lead in the community where he was strongest. I suggested speaking last whenever there was a mostly white audience because I wanted to portray an image of a person who was not going to rock the boat.

Being a Black candidate during those times meant I needed to be acutely aware of how my race affected my campaign for candidacy. I called myself "The Mop Man" at a meeting in Humble one night. I wanted to mop up after those guys to make sure that everything goes right. The approach worked well in the white sections of the district. The nickname didn't stick but it served its purpose—I didn't come off as someone who would push a Black agenda.

At that same Humble meeting were Bob and Nadine Eckhardt, the same State Rep. Bob Eckhardt that I'd seen in action in that Austin hearing a few months earlier. He was there not only for his community but also because he was running for the U.S. congressional seat in the same district. That night, he and Nadine invited us all to their house. As a result, I picked up two new lifetime friends.

Bob went on to be elected to the U.S. Congress. We remained close until his death in November 2001 and her passing in December 2018. Friendships like that don't come along every day. We spent many great times together around a fire in their backyard telling stories and getting to know each other. The life lessons I learned are priceless and remain with me to this day.

It was around that same fire that I heard stories about the beginnings of liberal labor-oriented politics of Texas. I wish I was wise enough to have taped some of those conversations. I learned the importance of Senator Ralph Yarborough and the liberal movement in the state.

Even though I already started, I soon realized that I didn't know much about organizing or running a real campaign. I started getting invitations to speak or make appearances at many events in the Black community, largely because of the articles that ran in the two Black newspapers.

One of the appearances I was invited to speak at was a national meeting for well-known Black realtors. Their keynote speaker for their banquet was Dr. Vivian Henderson, president of Clark College in Atlanta. I was introduced to those present at the meeting as a candidate for the State House. At the end of the program, I went up to Dr. Henderson and introduced myself as a candidate for the Texas House of Representatives. I told him that I needed some help starting my campaign and asked if he knew Georgia State Representative Julian Bond. By this time, Julian Bond had gained a reputation of fighting for Black causes in the Georgia State House. I learned about him after reading articles about him in *Jet* and *Ebony* magazines.

His response wasn't what I expected. He did know Bond and shared how great he was, but Dr. Henderson was sure that he wouldn't be the ideal person to help me get my campaign off the ground. Instead, he suggested that I speak to Ben Brown. Brown was also a member of the Georgia House and had excellent organizational skills that could be of great use to me. With that, Henderson gave me his card and said, "Call me Monday when I'm in my office. I'll make the introduction for you with Ben."

Within the civil rights movement, there was a network for successful Black Americans that I was unaware of but needed.

I did just as Dr. Henderson said and he arranged an introduction to Rep. Brown. I called Brown with my plea for assistance and he readily agreed, saying he would give me a week.

All along, I was little concerned — could I even afford one week of a high-priced political consultant?

"What will this cost me?" I asked with some dread.

"A plane ticket and hotel bill," he answered.

Even on a budget, I could afford that. Within the week he came to Houston and spent a week with me, attending my speeches and helping me organize volunteers. I rented a small house on Lyons Avenue and set up a campaign headquarters. Brown set up some files for me so I could get more people to help raise the money I needed and eventually, with his help, I had a real campaign in place. He made suggestions for my stump speech and put me on my feet. I finally felt like I knew what I was doing for the first time. A few years later, I was happily able to return the favor for all his help.

I believed that my role in desegregating Houston when I was a student needed to be told. However, it only needed to be told in the Black community. The notion of desegregation and integration might've caused some problems in places like Baytown or Humble, but two precincts over from Humble was an all-Black community called Barrett Station. As it turns out, a precinct judge at one of the large precincts was a Creole from Lafayette, Louisiana. I hadn't met him before but being a Creole from New Orleans meant we understood each other. He was the political leader in his community and whatever he decided was the way the community voted. Whenever I was asked to speak in Barrett, I was there. I always brought my friends and they got the same respect and voter turnout because they were with me. Well, as it turns out, I got every vote cast in Barrett Station every time I ran.

Despite my success in Barrett Station, extensive voter targeting still needed to be done. With the experience I gained with Asberry Butler's campaign for the Houston school board, I learned how to say a lot in some Black communities and nearly nothing in some white communities. It was imperative for my campaign success to learn how to present myself and speak according to the setting, and I learned.

Running for Congress in the newly realigned 7th Congressional District, adjacent to mine, was George H. W. Bush. He was the chairman of the Harris County Republican Party and ran an unsuccessful campaign for U.S. Senate in 1964. A major factor in Bush's campaign struggles stemmed from a Black community in his district, Acres Homes, that gave him very little support. Our paths crossed somewhere on the campaign trail and I got to know George and his wife Barbara quite well.

Of course, since Bush was a Republican and I was a Democrat, we had our differences. But as I got to know him, I realized that of all the people running in that district, he seemed to be the best.

One time when I was speaking in Acres Homes, I spoke about Bush to an all-Black audience. My mention of Bush did not go unnoticed by him; we became friends and would talk regularly. I even endorsed him when he tried running for the U.S. Senate in 1970. That endorsement was used against me later on, but I never regretted doing what I thought was right at the time. Bush lost to Lloyd Bentsen, who, in my opinion, never did anything to help the poor and minority people of Texas.

Since the candidate gatherings crossed district lines in many cases, Barbara and George Bush and I were often in meetings and forums with Bob and Nadine Eckhardt and the other candidates endorsed by the AFL-CIO.

After several weeks, we started to get to know each other well. Bob, Lauro Cruz, and I came up with a plan to campaign together nearly every Sunday. I was the only Catholic in the group so we would start off early at different Catholic churches around town, Black and white. We were not allowed to speak in the church, but we could stand outside and greet people as they came out of Mass.

Sometimes the priests joined us and introduced us to some of their people. Other times, we were on our own.

Lauro was the lead person in the Hispanic churches and I was the lead at the Black churches. After hitting the Catholic churches, we'd have a quick breakfast at a Mexican restaurant, then by 11 a.m. we'd hit the Black Protestant churches and end the tour by getting lunch at another restaurant.

Congressional candidate George H. W. Bush and Curtis, 1966.

One Sunday morning, we were short a candidate because Lauro had another engagement. Bob brought along both Nadine and their two-year-old toddler, Sarah. Sarah is now the State Senator for Travis County, Texas, but back then she was just a beautiful little blonde blue-eyed girl who was just beginning to walk. It must have been close to 3 p.m. that Sunday when we pulled up at this Humble, Texas Veterans of Foreign Wars (VFW) Hall where there was a planned political gathering.

Bob and I borrowed a black Buick with a phone. We called it the Batmobile. A car phone was a completely revolutionary thing at the time, extremely rare and far beyond the means of all but a few. We knew a city councilman who had one. It was useful because we could let people waiting for us at events know that we were on the way. Many of the Protestant ministers would let me speak as soon as we arrived if we gave them enough notice.

Bob placed a call to someone who couldn't talk right at that moment. The person returned the call just as we drove up to the VFW Hall. We were a little late, so Nadine and I decided to go in and let Bob finish his call.

The gravel parking lot was filled with pickup trucks with rifle racks in the back window. Not only did they have rifle racks in the window, but most of them had a rifle hanging one way and a shotgun hanging the other way. To say the least, it was redneck country.

Nadine wore heels and a cute hat cocked down on one side. She was having some difficulty carrying Sarah and navigating the parking lot in heels. In order to speed things up, when we got out of the car, I took little Sarah to help her. Carrying Sarah, I followed Nadine as we entered the hall.

As I followed Nadine in, I immediately noticed how the room grew quiet. By the time we reached the middle of the room, all eyes seemed to be on Nadine, the baby, and me. Barbara and George Bush were on the other side of the room, but from out of nowhere

Barbara Bush made a beeline straight towards me. She spoke in a stage whisper, "Curtis, you give Nadine back her baby."

I was a little befuddled. "What?"

Her whisper was gone. "Give Nadine her baby *now!*"

All at once, it hit me. It appeared that Nadine and I were a couple and "Pie," as we called Sarah at the time, was our baby. I handed Sarah off to her mother and looked for Bob, who just walked into the hall. I went over to him. "Go over to Nadine and kiss her and take Pie away from her," I said under my breath.

He looked at me, puzzled. "Why?"

"Just do it," I replied. "We'll talk later."

He went over to Nadine and kissed her. As he took the baby, you could feel the tension leave the room.

Now we needed a plan for how to address the meeting and huddled with George and Barbara. Our collective decision was that George would speak first. At the end of his remarks, he'd recognize Barbara. She would wave, and then Bob would speak. At the end of his remarks, Bob would introduce Nadine and Sarah. Nadine would grab Sarah's hand and wave it. At the end, Bob would just make mention of me, standing somewhere in the back of the room, as a friend who is running for a State House seat. Standing nowhere near Nadine, I would quickly wave.

That was about all the attention I needed. More attention among those folks might've been fatal. It wasn't a community that I needed any real visibility in and I felt quite unwelcome. It wasn't uncommon to hear word of Ku Klux Klan meetings being held in the area. Truth be told, the group looked like Klansmen out of their white robes. The pickup trucks in the parking lot should have been my indicator, but I missed the signals. The situation demanded that someone else needed to talk for me. Bob was the guy for the job, and he did it well. If I remember right, we received the primary elections returns by precinct a few days after the election. I carried that precinct with a double-digit percent lead. Bob had a twelve percent lead, while I led by ten percent.

On another occasion, it really *did* feel like we were at a Klan rally. We were given an opportunity to speak at the Fraternal Order of Police's union hall for their candidate endorsement meeting and we encountered open hostility. I could almost imagine a stack of crosses ready for burning in the back room along with their white robes.

I was sitting in the front row of the union hall with Bob and Nadine. The meeting opened with a film called *The Watts Riots*. It was produced by a group called the White Citizens' Council. Yes, *that* White Citizens' Council, the white supremacist and segregationist group known for its racist rhetoric and ideology.

Nadine, Bob and Sarah Eckhardt with Curtis

This film was one of the most derogatory statements towards Blacks that I'd ever seen. I wanted to get the hell out as quickly as I could and even whispered to Bob that I was going to bolt. Bob grabbed my leg. Nadine made me sit between them and grabbed the other leg.

"You just sit," Bob said firmly.

Nadine was gentler. She whispered in my other ear, "Just close your eyes and sit."

It was all I could do. Every time I heard the word "nigger" I flinched. Since the word was heard every minute or so, I guess I must have looked like I was dodging bullets or having a seizure.

When the film was done, I said to Bob, "If I speak, I'm sure I'll call them a sack of MFs and then run for the door. I really cannot do this."

He understood. When the time came for Bob to speak, he said more about me than he said about himself, making sure the audience knew that he was only speaking for me in the interest of time.

Bob's instincts were right. Both the Police Union and the Fraternal Order of Police endorsed me before the night was over.

While I was in the legislature, the union leadership came to Austin and asked me to sponsor a bill for them during the session. It was a bill to change some aspect of their pension system for Houston. As a result of my support, the legislation passed, and they gave me a gift in appreciation at the end of the session. Would you believe they presented me with a five-shot .38 caliber Smith & Wesson Police Special? Those police boys sure knew how to take care of their legislators.

I enjoyed running for office. It was a lot more fun than I expected it'd be. We would get the word from the AFL-CIO or some other supporter about an upcoming candidate forum and we would promptly descend on it. After a night of perhaps several of these forums, Lauro and I would hit the streets to put up our signs. I bought a staple hammer to make it easy to hang signs in seconds. We would find a post or tree or some other place where we could hang our signs, jump out of the car, and put up as many signs as we could, as quickly as we could.

One night, we were hard at work putting up our signs. Near midnight, we crossed a fence to put up our signs on a post that held up a regular-sized billboard. We knew that this was private property but we figured it would stay up on that private property until the person who changed the billboard came to make changes.

We only put up a few signs that read "GRAVES for State House" and "CRUZ House of Representatives" just below the large billboard that we could never afford when a Harris County police officer rolled up. The stoic officer got out of the car and asked, "What are you guys doing?"

We knew we were caught but we thought fast. "Taking these signs down, officer."

We calmly introduced ourselves and explained. "Some of our supporters put these signs up and we knew that they shouldn't be here on private property."

He thought about it for a moment. "OK," he said as he got back into his Harris County police car.

We waited until he pulled away and had a laugh. We put up two more signs on the other post before finally leaving. There were lots of places we hit under the cover of darkness where signs should not have been placed, but that was politics, after all. We were hungry and needed to get our names out in any way we could. The two of us once pulled up to a rally somewhere in the district and placed our bumper sticker on as many cars as we could before being caught. We stopped and went into the rally like nothing happened.

About a week out from the primary election day, I received a call from Don Horn of the AFL-CIO. Don was one of the union's top people and the person who we had the most contact with. He wanted me to attend a meeting at the union hall the next day. As I walked in, I noticed that Barbara Jordan was already there. Jordan was running for a state senate seat within the boundaries of our congressional/legislative district. It turned out that the meeting was only for the two of us. Don had set aside some money to use for us on Election Day. One purpose, I learned, was to hire poll workers to stand outside of each of the predominantly Black precincts and give information on the candidates and instructions on how to cast your ballet.

After everything was explained to the two of us, I admitted that I didn't have nearly enough people to man all the precincts in the Black community, so I thought it would be best if Barbara was given the money. She agreed and we struck a deal. The poll workers would hand out information supporting the entire slate of endorsed candidates of the AFL-CIO. This included the congressional candidate, the state senatorial candidate (her), and the six State House candidates, including me.

Two days later, I received a call at my campaign office. It was Mrs. Adair, the woman who was instrumental to my endorsement by the Harris County Counsel of Organizations. I could tell from her voice that she was distressed.

"I attended a meeting at Barbara's headquarters last night and she informed the poll workers that they should instruct voters to go in and pull one lever. 'Only pull the lever for me,'" Mrs. Adair relayed.

I had no doubt that Mrs. Adair was reporting accurately. Jordan was giving these instructions to poll workers who were going to be standing outside polling places where I was also on the ballot. That's called "single-shotting" the ballot. The voters would be instructed to only vote for Jordan and leave.

I thanked Mrs. Adair and hung up. I decided to call Jordan immediately and set this straight. I was sure there was just some misunderstanding.

I reach Jordan at her campaign office. As soon as I got her on the phone, I told her that I knew she was instructing her poll workers, which were at this point really *our* poll workers, to tell voters to only vote for her.

"Barbara, that is not fair. We were given that money by the AFL-CIO to support the entire ticket. That means that everyone endorsed by the AFL- CIO would be pushed by the poll workers," I insisted.

Her response was shocking. In her best and deepest Barbara Jordan voice, she said, "That is not *my* agenda."

Each word felt like a shot from a double barrel shotgun and left me stunned.

I didn't know what else to say. I politely, but coldly, thanked her for her time and hung up.

Without taking my hand off the receiver, I dialed Don Horn and explained what just happened. I'm sure he could tell that I was pissed.

"This money was not given to us just to support *one* of us. It was given to us to support the full ticket," I said with all the force I could muster.

Don calmed me down and told me not to worry.

"I will take care of it," he assured me.

Whatever he did must have worked. I received another call from Mrs. Adair. Barbara Jordan called another meeting to change the poll workers' instructions.

Don must have gotten Jordan to change her mind. I went to many of the polling places on Election Day and sure enough, voters were being instructed to vote for the candidates on the endorsed ticket.

If not for that exchange with Jordan, I would have assumed that we were going to have a cordial, professional relationship. But she made it clear that that was not meant to be. It also became clear that it was going to be my job to keep our exchange "out of the public" and keep whatever wars we had out of the newspapers.

That night, the ticket for Vickery, Cruz, Williams, Allen, Braun, and Graves was elected to the Texas House of Representatives. Barbara Jordan was elected to the State Senate and Bob Eckhardt and George H. W. Bush were elected to the U.S. House of Representatives. Well, the truth is that we were all nominated from our parties for these positions. Since we had no Republican opposition and George Bush no Democratic opposition, we were essentially elected.

This was really a big thing, not only in Texas, but also in Louisiana, Mississippi, Alabama, and Florida. Texas joined the ranks of only Georgia to elect the first Black people to serve in either of the state legislative houses.

After too many drinks, I showed up at Bob Eckhardt's headquarters for a celebration with a permanent grin on my face. We all won handily. History was made that night of the primary. None of us had an opponent in the general election.

I don't know if the others did, but that night, I received a call from President Lyndon Johnson. I really don't remember what he said and what I said back to him. I had a little too much to drink and honestly, in the glow of victory, he wasn't that important to me that night. It was the people in the room who made it all happen and it was our supporters who were getting my attention that night. I was driven home by one before I made a fool of myself.

The next day was filled with calls from across the country. I posed for pictures and *Time* magazine ran a story headlined "Texas: A Quiet Change," noting that I had captured 50.3 percent of the total vote, including 25% to 40% in "non-Negro precincts."

It wasn't really quiet, but it certainly was a change. Before me, the last Black man who served in the Texas House of Representatives was Robert L. Smith from Colorado County, 68 years before the night I was elected. He served from 1894 to 1899.

I learned that he was a passionate speaker against the rampant lynchings that were happening all over the South. At the time of his service in the State House, the word *nigger* was in common usage, although even in 1966, it was often interchangeable with "negro" and "colored boy."

Then, the Civil War was over, but the pain of slavery was still a very recent memory. Just as impórtantly, former slave owners were still alive. Reconstruction was in place, but it was taken away quickly. The short-lived gains in the South were to end quickly. We were beginning a new period of segregation that, if you think about it, was the same slavery under new management. A Black person could not eat, sleep, or sit where a white person ate, slept, or sat. However, you had some relative freedom. You could walk *somewhat* free without your walking papers. But that really was an illusion. The real thing that was not open to the average Black person was the ability to earn a living commensurate with their skills and abilities. Even with the election of a Black president, that fact unfortunately is still with us.

It was at that same time that the Civil War monuments went up all over the South. The South lost the war, but if they didn't tell anyone in the South, they could *act* like they won. Monuments and statues were put up on Stone Mountain in Georgia, on Robert E. Lee Circle in New Orleans, and on Confederate Avenue in Richmond, Virginia. Statues of Jefferson Davis, president of the Confederacy, were in so many cities and towns that it would be hard to name them all. General Stonewall Jackson was another favorite to memorialize. All over the South, monuments went up like someone was building them for free. Stone masons and monument builders must have had a field day carving and fashioning these artifacts of the losing side.

Someone must've sent a message to almost every major southern city that if we put up these things to memorialize a lie, then no one will realize that we really lost. The internet wasn't invented yet, but word got around the South just like it was written in Facebook: we could change our coats and continue slavery under a new name. The sheriffs would arrest as many Black people as they could and rent them out to former slave owners so the crops of the South could still be grown and harvested under a new and revised system.

The criminal justice system has, in both small and large ways, turned its back on people who are not white males. We can still predict, with a high degree of certainty, that a Black male has the system stacked against him. We can say, and back up with statistics, that a Black male is more likely to die before he is thirty than his white counterpart. Those same statistics show that Black males are disproportionately sleeping in more jail cells across the nation than their white counterparts. They might have committed the same crime, but they get convicted at a higher rate and serve longer sentences than their white counterparts.

During the Covid pandemic, we saw Black people dying at a higher rate than their white counterparts. The disproportionate distribution of medical services and the history of not having a doctor to go to when you feel ill, added to obesity and high blood pressure, has given the virus a field day in poor Black and brown communities.

Despite the odds, I moved from Louisiana to Texas and won a coveted seat in government. Several tried for many years since Robert Smith in 1899 but none made it across the racial obstacle. Winning the election was a feeling that I have never forgotten. All those days sitting at my father's knee. All those stories I heard from both my parents and grandparents. All those years sitting at the dinner table half understanding what the adult conversation was all about came to a head and gave me what I needed to move into this next phase of my life.

The next day I remember thinking about the very first time I stood before an audience and spoke. It was a YMCA father/

son dinner. The planned speakers all spoke and the master of ceremonies asked if there were any boys who wanted to say something about what the Y experience has meant to them. My dad said, "Get up and tell them what being involved in the YMCA means to you."

I have no memory about what I said. However, I do remember what he told my mom when we got home. He said, "Curtis got up and made a speech at the dinner."

"About what?" my mother asked.

"About what the YMCA has meant to him," he responded.

She looked at me with a big smile and asked, "What did you say?"

"I don't remember," I said.

My dad jumped back in. "He talked about the things he's learned at the Y and why it was important for him to be able to meet so many boys and make good friends," he said. "I was shocked. He spoke like he planned his words."

My mother gave me a big hug and I went off to bed. That memory of recognition for saying what I had inside me has stayed with me for my entire life.

Many years after my speech at the Y, Dr. King said that he had been to the mountain top and seen the other side. Well, that election night was my mountain top moment. I made it to a place where no Black person had been since Reconstruction. It took several days for me to come down.

That same night that we were elected in Houston, Joseph Lockridge, a Black lawyer from Dallas, was also elected. Since he was selected by the business community of Dallas, there wasn't much press in Dallas about the historic nature of his election. I didn't learn much about him running in the primary. It was also strange that I really didn't meet him until a few days after the opening day of the session the next year. The big news was that there would be three new faces in the upcoming session that didn't look like the faces that served for nearly seventy years in the Texas State House and Senate. It was historic and I knew it. While it was important for Black history, there weren't any women in the State House and only one in the Senate.

The general election would be held in November without anyone running against us. It was currently August. In the Texas valley, the farm workers were being organized into a farm workers' union. Texas did not have a minimum wage, so the AFL-CIO and other unions encouraged leaders to march to Austin to raise the minimum wage. It was something that both Lauro and I very much supported, so we decided to march with the farm workers every weekend. The march was timed to end with a big rally on the steps of the Capitol on Labor Day, the first Monday in September 1966.

There were three things of significance that still stand out in my mind about the marches. The first happened the second weekend after we joined the marchers. Each weekend we would call our AFL-CIO contact to see where we should meet the marchers. They were somewhere in south Texas, so we drove up in two cars. One car would be where we started, and one car would be where the march would end that day.

We decided that we were not going to camp out but rather find a local motel to stay at each night. When we arrived on Friday night, I overheard some of the marchers saying something in Spanish: "*grandes cucarachas.*" I had no idea what that meant, but they kept laughing and pointing our way. I waited until Lauro and I were alone to ask what they were talking about. He laughed. "They call us the Big Roaches."

At first I didn't quite get it, but it began to dawn on me why they were calling us roaches. We rolled in on a Friday night and took a lead position in the march for Saturday and Sunday, but we didn't walk all the way like most of them did. We didn't face the hot sun day in and day out. We never slept in tents on the side of the road or in a vacant field. We didn't eat the cold lunches that were provided by the union organizers. So I guess we *were* roaches. After all, what gave us the right to walk up front when we hadn't paid our dues, figuratively or literally? It was because of our relationship with the AFL-CIO that we were put up front. Roaches or not, I admit that we enjoyed our front marching status.

The second significant thing happened as the march approached San Antonio. We arrived at a hotel outside of San Antonio on a Friday night and planned to march all day Saturday. Unlike the real marchers, we were staying in a nice hotel and not sleeping on the ground. We were back in a hotel room on Saturday night preparing for the next day. We were joined by two union officials and a Catholic priest named Father Antonio Gonzalez.

Father Gonzalez said that we should not forget that tomorrow was Sunday and that we should start the day by attending a Mass. Most of the real marchers were Catholic, after all. We all agreed, and the union guys started to make arrangements for a stage to be erected very early so that they could set up a makeshift altar for Father Gonzalez to say Mass.

In the middle of these plans and various phone calls, I thought about going to Holy Communion at the Mass. I hadn't been to confession for some time and thought it might be good to do so before Mass. I leaned over to Father Gonzalez and said, "Father, I want to go to Communion tomorrow and I need to go to confession."

Without hesitation, he stood up. "Come with me."

He led me into the bathroom and put the lid of the toilet seat down. "Sit," he said with a broad gesture.

He sat on the edge of the bathtub and said, "OK, let's have it."

I looked at him. Then I realized that he was talking about holding my confession right here, in the hotel bathroom. My only thought was that this must be a first. Here I am at a hotel on the outskirts of San Antonio, Texas, sitting on a toilet seat in a bathroom about to give my confession to a priest who is sitting on the edge of the bathtub. We should have erected a plaque outside the room memorializing the fact that a confession was given sitting on the toilet seat in this bathroom on that day. Now I didn't know if this was a first for him, but it was truly one for me. Every time I went to confession, from my first time when I was just seven years old, I was in a little confessional in a quiet church. Amen and amen.

I looked straight at him and began. "Bless me Father, for I have sinned."

He heard my confession and together we walked out of the bathroom. I sat on the edge of the bed, thinking to myself about how many people in the history of the Roman Catholic Church could say that they went to confession sitting on a toilet.

The third and last significant memory comes from the last weekend of the demonstration. We were in San Marcos, Texas, marching the last stretch before we went into Austin, and Cesar Chavez, the well-known labor leader from California, joined us for the last leg. With his efforts on behalf of migrant Mexican workers in the fields of California and activism for farm workers everywhere, he certainly paid his dues. With his reputation, I don't think anyone called him "*cucarachas*." He flew in and took his rightful place in the front line of the marchers.

I met him on the Saturday morning of Labor Day Weekend of 1966. Several of the Texas Labor Union organizers arranged for a few of us to meet him and have breakfast at a small Mexican restaurant near San Marcos. He was warm enough, but a little standoffish. After breakfast, we started off on a full day of walking.

Chavez was a soft-spoken, small man with a hauntingly serious look on his face. You could tell that he was a person of resolve who was on a mission, and he would do whatever it took to complete it. In 1966, I don't think his true sacrifices had really started yet, but by then he had led strikes in California and had the battle scars to show for it.

By Sunday night, Chavez warmed to us. He smiled during our small talk and we began to see the personal side of him. We walked side by side most of the day on Sunday. At another small restaurant outside of Austin, I had my last semi-private time with him. There were six or eight of us at a table and I happened to be sitting next to him.

He was more open by then. He started telling stories about working in the fields, picking grapes in the hot California sun. He talked about being fired by the growers because he was informing the workers that they should be earning more money for such hard work. It was a good evening; lots of tequila and laughter came from the table. That was the last time we were together.

On that Monday morning, I thought to myself that it was really an honor for us to march in the hot early September Texas sun for such a noble cause. We heard that Governor Connally ordered the Capitol building closed when the marchers arrived later in the day. We marched on with the pride of knowing that we would be meeting opposition when we arrived.

The rally on the steps of the Capitol was more than we could have asked for. There were at least 10,000 people gathered to listen to speeches and thank the marchers for their sacrifices. I was honored to be introduced to the crowd.

As I think back on that moment now, I realize that as we crossed the last bridge leading to the Capitol, we crossed First Street, now called Cesar Chavez Street.

Most people who did not participate in that march would not have known that name in September 1966, but it is fitting that the street that we crossed on the way to the State Capitol is named after the man who gave so much to help the living conditions of so many.

With the marching over for now, I needed to prepare myself to be a working politician. I researched issues that needed addressing and talked to as many people as I could about their concerns. I attended a meeting in New York City called by the NAACP Legal Defense Fund. The meeting was held at the New York Hilton Hotel and well attended by civil rights lawyers and others who could help us fashion our agendas. The attendees includded the Black members of the Georgia House and Senate, Tennessee House and Senate, and others from around the country. Louisiana, Mississippi, and Alabama hadn't elected anyone of color yet.

The New York meeting gave me some good insights into how it would be possible to operate in a legislative body where there would only be a few people of color. One member of the Georgia delegation suggested I always carry a real crazy bill in my pocket.

Curtis at the rally with Joe Allen (foreground), Father Gonzalez (behind), and Cesar Chavez (right).

Whenever you were approached to co-sign something that you did not want to be involved in, you could just pull out your bill and say, "Sure. However, I would like you to be a co-sponsor of *my* bill."

That would surely send them running. Once in office, I did just that and it worked well. Most of the legislation pushed by individual members was of interest to their local constituents. It was benign stuff and I signed without thinking much about it. However, there was legislation that I did not want to put my name on in any way. They fit in all kinds of categories. Bills to raise taxes on various things, bills to keep the state from passing a minimum wage. That's when I pulled out *my* bill.

I knew it was always going to be a bridge too far for most of them, but it would get them off my back. My "back pocket bill" would have changed the function of the Texas Rangers to basically museum guards. Not only would it send my fellow lawmakers running, but it also made my point. Too often, the Rangers continued to be used in parts of Texas to intimidate minority voters and make them leave the polling places. Texas Rangers might have had a useful role to play at some point in the history of the state, but in 1967 they were being used to enforce voter suppression. Still, they had the support of most of the members of the House at that time, so I had a good wedge issue that would remove the smile on their faces so quickly that you would think they were having a heart attack. They tensed up and shrank right in front of me like bacon in a hot cast iron skillet. Seeing them slither away like albino snakes was one of my great joys.

As a lawmaker, I did have an agenda. High on my list of priorities was changing the way African Americans were depicted in the schoolbooks used to teach history in elementary and secondary schools of the state. I knew I might not be able to change it right away, but the bill would serve as education for those who thought that the books reflected the true history of Texas and the nation.

My list also included slowing down the rapid sale of guns in the state. I once said at a rally that most white male Texans think that their manhood is best depicted in the gun strapped to their hip and not what's behind their zipper. I needed to find a way to push that one in the right way. Within the last few years, I have been invited to attend some legislative functions at the Texas Capitol. Today the members walk around the metal detectors, so if a member wanted to be packing that day, they could get away with it. The public, on the other hand, cannot go in with a firearm.

Banning DDT was another thing on my agenda. DDT was killing wildlife across the state and the nation. It might have been a good pesticide, but the side effects outweighed the benefits. I knew that getting it banned was a heavy lift, but I also knew that someone had to educate the public about the harmful effects of the wide use of DDT in agriculture. It killed more endangered wildlife than harmful bugs.

At the committee hearing, one member of the House brought a bag half full of DDT to use as a prop against my bill. He was an older farmer who represented a farming district in northwest Texas. During his remarks, he ran his hand down into the white powder and went through it like it was flour for baking. "This is harmless to humans, animals, and anything but bugs," he said. "Why, I could eat some of it now and it would not harm me!"

As I think back on it now, I should have asked him to prove it.

Today, DDT is banned as an agricultural pesticide. Politically, I think I might have been a little ahead of my time.

Raising the minimum wage was also high on my list. I had just marched from the Texas valley to effect that change, after all. The federal minimum wage in 1967 was $1.60 an hour. Tell me, how could you harvest crops for less then $13.00 a day? Texas last had a minimum wage in 1919, so I knew that we would first need to educate the state's citizens. For the most part, it was an issue that wasn't talked about. I hoped that the introduction of the bills and the hearings that I would demand would inform people about needed changes.

But before I could start working through my agenda, I had to get to Austin for the session and find a place to live. I also needed to find an office in the State Capitol and hire local staff. Friends and supporters were going to be present for my swearing in and my family from New Orleans was planning to attend. After all, I was the first Black person to be elected to anything in my family since Reconstruction. That was so long ago that no living person would have any memory of it. Even the history books had little mention of it. To say the least, I was full of pride. I knew that everything I did or said would be closely watched and, in many cases, criticized. Therefore, I needed to watch my every step.

On top of all of that, as one of the first two Black members in the Texas House of Representatives since Reconstruction, my swearing in would be a real historic moment in the history of modern-day Texas.

I made a customary trip to the Capitol to pick out my seat on the floor of the House. I was surprised and thrilled to find that Seat No. 69, the seat that I occupied a year before when I first contemplated entering politics, was available. I knew I needed it.

Next, I had to pick an office. Because there weren't enough offices in the Capitol to go around, some freshmen members would have to share an office space. Lauro and I decided to share an office and live together. It would save money and the logistics were almost perfect since Lauro didn't have a car to take to Austin that first session. It was a great decision. We got along well, so it was a real good fit.

As the day grew near, my mother informed me that she and my dad were going to be there along with my brother, my aunts, and their husbands. A veritable caravan of cars was coming from New Orleans. I needed to get rooms in a hotel for them and take care of all the other logistics of their visit. Where could they all eat? How would we move them around in Austin with limited parking? It had to be right. My parents were so proud, and I wanted their trip to Austin to be something that they would remember for the rest of their lives. With the large group of first cousins my mom had, I'm surprised that they didn't have to get a bus to get all her folks there. But work and the expenses of making such a trip laminated the attendants.

EIGHT

MY TRIP TO THE EXECUTIVE MANSION

Shortly after my primary victory, I received an exciting invitation to attend a meeting in Washington, D.C. called "The White House Conference to Preserve These Rights." The meeting was slated for the first and second of June 1966.

President Johnson proposed the conference the previous June when he gave the commencement address at Howard University. It was meant to give action to the important civil rights legislation of 1964 and 1965. Later, in planning, it was expanded to include the issues of poverty and education.

Ben Heineman, the chairman of the conference, followed up with a letter in mid-May with details about hotel reservations, meals, and registration. The conference staff arranged everything. Over 1,000 participants were expected for the June conference at the Sheraton Park Hotel in Northwest Washington.

While I was making plans, I got a call from presidential advisor Louis Martin. He had the highest position of any Black man in the Johnson-era White House. A former newspaper war correspondent, he became a trusted confidant of President Johnson. I knew who he was through the Black media, but I had never met him.

Martin called me because he wanted to know if I was attending the conference. "The president would like to meet you."

"I would very much like to meet him, too," I replied, as if I thought it was a possibility.

"Come up a day early and I will make all the arrangements for you to get into the White House," Martin responded.

He gave me his private White House number and left it at that.

When I arrived in Washington, I called to confirm that I was in town and could be at the White House any time he wanted. We set 11 a.m. as the time to be at the front gate. I assured Martin I would be punctual.

I arrived at the Pennsylvania Avenue gate at the appointed time, still not exactly sure what I was doing there. A uniformed Secret Service guard manning the gate had my name. I was given a badge and instructed to go through the door they pointed to on the west side of the White House. Walking in, I was immediately greeted by a woman who asked that I sit and wait for someone to get me.

Within a minute or two, Louis Martin introduced himself to me. He was a tall man about my complexion, mid-fifties with black rimmed glasses. He seemed genuinely glad that I was able to visit the White House and make it to the conference. I learned many years later that he had been first recruited by Sargent Shriver to work in Kennedy's 1960 presidential campaign. Martin was instrumental in persuading Kennedy to call Coretta Scott King to express dismay over the jailing of her husband, MLK. Many believed that phone call helped Kennedy win a larger portion of the Black vote.

We stood and talked in the waiting room just inside of the

entrance to the West Wing of the White House. He excused himself, saying he had some calls to make and would see me the next day.

I started a conversation with the receptionist in the room, an attractive white woman in her late twenties or early thirties. She spoke on a phone with a long cord so wound up that she could barely get it up to her ear. "Let me fix that phone cord for you," I offered.

She had a pitiful look on her face. "Would you?"

I went over and unplugged the cord and let it start spinning in my hand as I held out the receiver and pulled it down. "I never knew that the cord was that easy to detach from the phone," she said.

"Well, this is a learning moment for us all," I responded with a smile. "I don't know what's more surprising: that someone at the White House would be having so much trouble with a phone cord, or that no one would come to your rescue."

We laughed as I sat for what seemed like a month waiting for someone to come for me. I made more small talk with her about the clock hanging above her desk. She explained that it was an old wooden face clock that was in the White House for years.

A man finally came for me at 1 p.m. He said the president was ready. I was taken to another room outside of the Oval Office and instructed to wait again. There was a lot of coming and going as I sat in the adjacent room in the company of another secretary working at her desk. At 1:30 the secretary said, "Go right in, the president will see you now."

I opened the door and President Lyndon Johnson got up from his desk with a sprint and greeted me before had gotten two feet past the door. He grabbed my hand with his right hand and secured my elbow with his left, a real two-hand politician's shake. It could've been a normal practice from his part of Texas, but I'd never seen a handshake like that before.

President Johnson was a tall man about my height, six foot four inches. Flashing a big smile, he warmly directed me to sit. I didn't say anything about visiting his ranch years before, but I did mention Mack Hannah. He shared that he was glad I was elected from Harris County.

Reaching over to the intercom on his desk and pressing a button, he said "Get Jake for me." Within seconds a tall, thin, silver-headed guy walked through the door. "Jake, this is Curtis Graves. Give him your card," Johnson directed. "This is Jake Jacobson, my special assistant," he said to me. "If you need anything out of the White House, just call him."

Jacobson passed his card to me and I thanked him, glancing at it. Officially, the card said that he was Legislative Assistant to the President. After a signaling nod from President Johnson, he left the room.

Johnson and I chatted for about fifteen minutes, mostly about Texas. When he stood, I knew it was time for me to leave. I thanked him for inviting me to the White House and made my way to the front gate. One guy handed me off to another and I was pointed to the gate for my exit. A Secret Service agent collected my badge and before I knew it, I was out on Pennsylvania Avenue looking at the traffic.

It was pretty heavy stuff for a young, twenty-something political novice. I'd just met with the president of the United States privately in the Oval Office. The only thing left to do was call my mother.

In those days, long distance calls were expensive, especially when calling from a hotel room. The usual solution was to call collect. I reached my mom as soon as I got in my room at the Sheridan Park. "Can you guess where I am and what I've done?" I teased.

"Where are you and what have you done?"

With as much glee as I could muster, I said, "I have been to the White House, and I met the President in his office."

"Who was with you?"

"It was just me," I boasted.

"Just *you*? Why did he want to see you?" she asked.

I still wasn't completely sure myself. "I guess it's because I'm one of the first Blacks elected from Texas to state office."

"Now that is really something," she said.

I gave her every little detail and she sounded as happy as I was. I closed with, "Tell Daddy as soon as he comes home."

I used that card from Jake Jacobsen twice. That summer, a father of one of the solders in Vietnam called to say that he and his wife hadn't heard from their son in more than two months. I got their son's name and service number and asked Jacobsen to help. Within two days, their son called from Vietnam to say that he was all right.

The second time was more serious. I got a call from a mother who said that her son died at an Air Force base in Alaska. She and her husband received a visit from two Air Force officers who reported that their son committed suicide on base, jumping from a window to his death.

I asked them to come over to tell me the entire story. They'd spoken to their son that same day and he gave no indications of depression or any other problem. They convinced me it was worth checking out.

Jake promised to investigate it. It was months later, but we finally found out the truth. Two white airmen had gotten into an argument with the victim and threw him out of a window. I was told that they would be tried and convicted.

There was an informal reception that evening. Still on a natural high from my meeting with President Johnson, I went down to the hotel lobby to see if I recognized anyone coming in for the conference. I didn't, but I introduced myself to several people and went out to eat with a few of them that night.

By the time it began, the conference swelled to a few more conferees. There was a cross section of people from across the land. Government officials, which at that point included me, made up about a third. Religious figures, business and labor leaders, the Black media, and academics were all well represented. I was told that even Bill Russell, the legendary basketball player and, by 1966, the player-coach of the Boston Celtics, attended. He was hard to miss but I never got close to him.

Every Negro civil rights organization was there, except for one. The Student Nonviolent Coordinating Committee (SNCC) vocally rejected the conference, calling it "absolutely unnecessary" and a "useless endeavor." They favored "direct action" and "Negro self-reliance" instead of government intervention. They weren't alone, but every other organization participated.

Ironically, it wasn't an increased militancy that alone accounted for the rift in the civil rights world. It was the growing mistrust of the Johnson Administration over the Vietnam War. LBJ wanted a consensus of the next moves in civil rights and the involvement in Vietnam made the leaders suspicious. By this time, even Dr. King expressed misgivings about the war, although he was steadfast in his commitment of non-violent means to achieve his civil rights goals. I never got close to Dr. King at the conference, either.

The conference was opened the next day by A. Philip Randolph, the honorary chairman, and Vice President Hubert Humphrey giving the morning address. He was wonderful. I was impressed by how warm he was and how well he was received by the attendees.

"We are here to go to work," he said. "And there is much work to be done. But our task at this conference—as it will be America's urgent domestic task for many years to come—is not to recount the progress of the past, but to fulfill the promise of the future."

"Now, this will be a hard, sometimes unglamorous, frequently frustrating responsibility," he continued. "We can rejoice that the time has arrived when millions of Negro Americans can step out of the shadows and walk forthrightly into the bright sunshine of human rights. But a man too long walled off from society cannot easily adjust his senses and his capacities to the light—yes, and the heat—of equality. This generation of Americans has the task and, I may add, the priceless opportunity, of walking side by side with the Negro American as he strides into that bright sunshine and stands erect, equipped, trained for his opportunity."

There was a break after Humphrey's remarks and many of us went up to shake his hand. He stood for what seemed like a long time to shake nearly every hand that reached out to him.

Twelve working groups were established to discuss and debate recommendations to deal with housing, education, and economic welfare as well as the administration of justice. We met not only at conference headquarters at the Sheraton Park Hotel off Connecticut Avenue, but also at the nearby Shoreham Hotel. Each working session was about three hours, twice each day.

The first evening, Wednesday, there was a dinner. Thurgood Marshall, then the solicitor general, was to deliver the address. We waited. Shortly before 10 p.m., we learned why when President Johnson arrived. He hadn't been listed on the program.

Johnson didn't say much that could be taken as earth-shattering or jarring. He mainly defended the progress his administration achieved and laid the groundwork for the next widely anticipated civil rights act. He concluded his remarks with a surprise.

"I have a very unusual pleasure and pride to introduce to you a great soldier. I might say that the president of the United

States does not often have the opportunity to introduce another speaker."

And with that, after recounting some of his accomplishments, first as a judge and then as solicitor general, he brought Marshall to the podium.

It was almost exactly one year later that President Johnson nominated Marshall to the Supreme Court, where he would serve for 24 years.

Marshall used his remarks to give a brief history of Negros in America. He called attention to correspondence in 1782 between Thomas Jefferson and Benjamin Banneker, the Black astronomer, surveyor, and mathematician who helped survey the original plans for Washington, D.C. Banneker told Jefferson, "I hope you cannot but acknowledge, that it is the indispensable duty of those, who maintain for themselves the rights of human nature, and who possess the obligations of Christianity, to extend their power and influence to the relief of every part of the human race..."

One part of Marshall's narrative that might not be as widely known is this:

"If slavery persisted in the southern states, it was the northern states that did much to deny free Negroes their rights in the dark days before the Civil War. In 1830, a mob drove eight Negroes out of Portsmouth, Ohio. For three days, in 1829, bands of whites in Cincinnati took the law in their own hands and ran out of the city those Negroes who did not have the bonds required by law. In New York state, there were riots in Utica, Palmyra, and New York City in 1834 and 1839. In 1834, a mob of whites marched down into the Negro section of Philadelphia and committed numerous acts of violence. American antislavery organizations and Negro conventions were unable to generate sufficient public opinion to put down the wholesale denial of the rights of the darker peoples of the United States."

Marshall placed the first modern battles for equal rights from

1948 with the early struggles to remove restrictive covenants and other forms of government discrimination in the nation's capital.

"Now, at last, the movement toward equality was under way. Two years later—again at the urging of the solicitor general, who took issue with the I.C.C.—the Supreme Court outlawed segregation in railroad dining cars."

He continued, "By 1953, the Court declared illegal discrimination by places of public accommodation in the nation's capital—the Department of Justice having once more intervened on the side of Negro rights against the local authorities, as it would do henceforth with increasing frequency."

The next day, Louis Martin showed up at the hotel to make an announcement. Some of us were invited to the White House on Friday for a "meet and greet" with President Johnson.

The next morning, I was standing outside of the hotel waiting for the buses. When they arrived, we were invited to board, and I just happened to get on the first bus. I really don't know how many buses were in the convoy, but they were all filled. I sat next to Leroy Johnson, a senator from Georgia.

Louis Martin stood in the front well of the bus as two police motorcycles with lights and sirens led the way through the streets of Washington, D.C. directly to a side gate of the White House.

Louis Martin signaled to the bus driver to open the door and he hung his head out and waved to the Secret Service guard at the gate. He yelled out, "They're all with me!"

The guards on duty waved all the buses in.

I leaned over to Senator Johnson and pointed to Martin. "That man has real juice." Johnson agreed and we both smiled.

As we got off the buses, we were ushered into the Rose Garden, where there were chairs for us in front of a podium with the Presidential Seal attached. As soon as we were seated, President Johnson came out to speak to us.

About two minutes into his remarks, he turned his attention

to one of his beagles chasing a squirrel up a tree. He left the podium as if we weren't there and started clapping and yelling to stop the dog. I remember thinking to myself: the president of the United States of America is chasing his dog who was chasing a squirrel up a tree on the White House grounds?

I imagined I'd seen it all. Lyndon Johnson truly wasn't your average president. He was from West Texas and no matter what, West Texas was in his bones. I don't think he could help himself.

The conference concluded with a speech from Roy Wilkins, executive director of the NAACP. "The need is for urgency because our nation's neglect of the past is about to rendezvous with a worldwide technological expansion," Wilkins said.

Stressing our common goals, he wanted to bypass any disagreements of how to attain them. He stressed that we should all work together to achieve the passage of the Civil Rights Act of 1966. The Act was filibustered in the Senate and never passed.

NINE

MY FIRST SESSION

I was sat at home in Houston just after noon during the first week of January 1967 when my phone rang. I was not sworn in as a member of the Texas House yet, but duty was calling. It was Bob Eckhardt, newly minted member of U.S House of Representatives, and he needed some advice. He had given me so much good advice and guidance about the world of law and politics by then that I found it a little ironic that *he* was reaching out to *me* for my advice.

"Curtis, I just don't know what to do," he said somewhat apologetically. "I was just sworn in and now my very first vote is going to be about Adam Clayton Powell, and it's in about 25 minutes. What should I do?"

I was so involved with my own entry into the state legislature that I hadn't really followed Powell's latest struggles with the leadership in Congress. "What's this vote on?"

Bob sounded harried, which I guess was understandable since he now had less than twenty-four minutes to decide.

"The new session of the House of Representatives is voting to not seat him because of some infractions of the House rules," he explained.

The story about Congressman Adam Clayton Powell was all over both Black and white media for months. He took a girl-friend to Paris at the government's expense and done many other things that upset the white members, so they wanted to unseat him. This would take away his chairmanship of Committee on Education and Labor. Powell's answer to his fellow congress-mens' anger was, in every case, that he wasn't doing anything that other chairmen haven't done for years.

"Can they really do that?" I asked.

"I think they can." Bob paused. "No, not really, at least in my opinion."

"Well, let me give you a quick tutorial," I began. "Adam Clayton is a national hero in Black America. He has been a trail-blazer in Congress. President Kennedy once said that he was one of the most effective legislators in Congress. He has taken so much abuse just to get a committee chairmanship and he cer-tainly speaks his mind. He's right that most of the accusations against him have also been done by the white chairmen of vari-ous committees for years. But now it's a criminal offense because a Black man is doing the same thing."

Bob was silent, but I could feel the wheels turning in his head through the phone.

"Bob, you *cannot* vote to expel him. Because of what he's done for all of us, most Black people will not forgive that vote."

I knew that his vote would not make news in Washington, D.C., but it would come back to haunt him in the Fifth Ward that both he and I represented.

Finally, he answered in his familiar warm Texas drawl. "I'm sure that the Constitution is on my side. But I think the majority of the House will vote to not seat him."

"Well, do you want to stand with the United States Constitution, or the majority? That is the real question,"

I paused. "Well Buddy, I think that takes the monkey off your back," I added, emphasizing the last four words.

"I hear you," Bob said.

"Call me and let me know how it goes down," I said.

"Before the day is done," he assured me.

The detail of the vote is provided by Gary Keith in his book *Eckhardt:*

"The committee recommended to 'exclude' Powell (there is no constitutional language on exclusion). In his maiden congressional speech, Eckhardt argued that the House had no constitutional authority to refuse to seat Powell. The Constitution, he said, only allows *voters* to determine whether members are qualified. He urged the House instead to approve Mo Udall's motion to seat Powell, then strip him of his committee chairmanship as a punishment for his violation of House rules and ethics. But by majority vote the House 'excluded' Powell from its membership: Eckhardt voted nay in what he called his most difficult vote. With the House action, Powell's seat was declared vacant and a special election called to fill it. Powell won the election, but was excluded again. Eckhardt wrote a *Texas Law Review* article arguing that the House violated the Constitution. The Constitution alone, he wrote, spelled out the qualifications for members. He cited constitutional convention debates to sustain his position that Congress could not judge the qualifications of its members, as the House had done in its resolution. .... Powell sued the House and successfully won reelection in 1968 (he was seated, then fined for his unethical behavior). But in 1969, the Supreme Court overturned the House's action, vindicating Eckhardt's constitutional arguments. Indeed, Chief Justice Earl Warren quoted Eckhardt's law review article."

With the clear vision of hindsight, I can say that this kicked Bob Eckhardt up several notches in my estimation. He stood up and did the right thing in the face of making himself an outsider on the first day of his freshman term in the U.S. House of Representatives. Not many would have done this. He swam upstream with his party and the leadership of the House.

When Eckhardt called me back that night, he was a happy warrior. "I made my first speech on the floor of the house in favor of seating Adam Clayton Powell," he reported.

"Well, how did it go?"

"Several members came up to me to compliment me on my argument. I really think that many wanted to be on my side but thought that it might not work for them in their districts."

He went on to say something to the effect that it was hard for him to be voting against such a large bipartisan group, but he felt good about what he did.

"Bob, only time will tell if you came down on the right side of the constitutional argument, but I know you came down on the right side of the political argument for your district," I said.

I really don't remember if he agreed or disagreed with my analysis. However, history has shown that he came down on the right side of both the Constitution and the political issue. I am only taking a little credit for providing him some support to do the right thing for his district and the country.

• • •

According to the constitution of the state of Texas, the state legislature is sworn in at noon on the second Tuesday of January of the odd numbered years. The time was getting close, and I needed to get my ducks in a row.

A few days before opening day of the Texas legislature on January 10, 1967, I finally found myself a secretary. The connection was Dr. Theodore Youngblood, a friend of mine who was raised in Austin, Texas. His mother was a principal of one of the local schools and his father was the head waiter at the Driskill Hotel.

It was his father, Youngblood, Sr., who once told me that his wife took him to work every morning and dropped him off two blocks from the hotel. He wanted (and needed) to hide his success. "If they knew that I had a new Cadillac, I would have lost my job."

He walked the last two blocks to work to hide his personal status symbol. He worked covertly for all those years, hiding his prominence in Austin's Black community from his bosses.

The Youngbloods had a friend whose daughter was a college graduate and needed a job. Her name was Jo Cash. She came from an outstanding family in Austin and was ready to take on the responsibility of getting things running in my office as well as watching my back.

The latter was just as important as, or maybe even *more* important than the former. I never forgot what an old man told me one day in Houston after I was elected. He said, "Son, watch out for those who pat you on the back, because with the other hand they will unzip their fly and piss in your boots."

I laughed it off at first, but I soon realized that it really was sound advice. I can't even remember the names of the numerous people who greeted me in the first few weeks and would have stuck a knife in my back if I were not watching them with both eyes.

Many members of the House came up to tell me how glad they were to meet me. I quickly realized that their words were just that. Words! Just something you say to the first Black person you have ever spoken to in your life. I could see that many were in that category.

Some members wouldn't get close to me on the floor of the

House. They might say something to me in the members' lounge or in the restroom, but never where others (meaning *the public*) could see. I can even remember some walking away from a group when I approached them on the House floor.

The incoming legislators as well as veteran members received an invitation to attend a breakfast at 8 a.m. the morning of the swearing-in. We were told that we could bring a guest. Since my parents arrived in town the night before, I asked my dad if he wanted to go to the breakfast with me the next day. He said he'd be glad to go with me. I told him that he would have to wear a coat and tie, but he was ready to wear a coat and tie to everything he attended regardless of the dress code. After all, his son was going to be the first Black man sworn into the Texas Legislature since Reconstruction.

Bright and early the next morning, I picked him up at the hotel and we drove the few blocks to the Capitol. We arrived at the Capitol at about 7:30. Because it was so early, there weren't many cars parked behind the building. I pulled up to my very own parking spot. I think the parking spot number was 101. The governor's spot in the front of the building was Number 1 and I was Number 101. My assigned spot was right behind the beautiful granite Texas State Capitol building built by the hands of men who were just freed from slavery.

As I pulled in, my dad asked, "Will they let you park this close to the Capitol?"

"Yep, this is my spot," I proudly responded. For emphasis, I added, "I'm the only person who can park here."

I could see on my dad's face that he was impressed.

We were going to walk through the building because it would take much longer to walk around it. It was quite cold that morning with an even dusting of snow in the air. We walked up the steps and through the Capitol Building's back door. Right inside the door was a capitol guard. He was a tall white man in his fifties who didn't look like he smiled easily. He nodded to me with a half-smile. He seemed to know who I was even though I'd never met him. We walked through the rotunda of the building and into an entranceway. On the right-hand side of that entranceway today holds a plaque that memorializes Black people that were members of the Texas House during Reconstruction. The main portion of the plaque is a simple black and white picture, but below it is another plaque that has my name on it along with Joseph Lockridge and Barbara Jordan. We were memorialized as being the first Blacks to be elected in post-Reconstruction times.

As we approached the front door to make our exit, another white guard flashed a full smile as we passed him. When I walked to the door, I recalled being introduced to the crowd on Labor Day just five months before in that same spot. We walked down the front steps and through the grounds that surround the building. Those grounds would be filled with well-wishers in a few hours. Those grounds also still have a monument to the Confederate Soldiers erected in 1903. It was a part of an effort to "romanticize the motivations that drew Texas into the Civil War."

My dad was looking back at the building. What was going through his mind? He fought the good fight for so many years. He groomed me to stand up for what I believed in. He took a back seat so many times to push me and others up front. I was fully aware that I was standing on his shoulders that morning. I remembered that talk about registering to vote. I remembered his understanding of my involvement with the sit-ins in Houston and other civil rights efforts at Texas Southern University. He had prepared me for just this moment in time and I very much wanted him to be a part of it. I wanted him to be proud of me. I wanted him to know all the work he did for me and all the sacrifices he made paid off, big time. His son was about to take a step that hadn't been taken by a Black man since Reconstruction. It was a big deal and I knew he was just as aware of it as I was.

I was trying to be nonchalant and maybe even a little cavalier about parking in my designated spot, walking through the Capitol, and having the white guards nod their heads and smile at me. I nodded back with the confidence of a person who was going to run the Capitol that day. I knew that Boss John Connally was the Governor of Texas, but I felt like I was going to make a mark in that building and on the state that would be remembered for a long time to come.

Yep, there was pep in my step. I really felt like I had arrived, and I was going to let everyone know about my appointment with destiny.

We crossed 11th Street, which runs right in front of the Capitol grounds, to walk down Congress Avenue for another few blocks to the Driskill Hotel. My dad and I walked the few blocks in silence. It was cold, the snow continued to fall, and we were walking with a mission in mind.

We stepped into the lobby of the old hotel. The doorman, a tall Black man, nodded at me. I smiled and nodded back. We caught the elevator and got off on the second floor. Set up outside one of the larger function rooms was a table for members of the Legislature and their guests to sign in and pick up their name tags. I identified my dad, got him a badge, and clipped it to his lapel. By the time I turned to get my badge and have one of the ladies clip it on me, Dad disappeared.

I entered the room and couldn't find him. In the meantime, there was a lot of glad-handing going on. Nearly everyone I passed shook my hand and greeted me with a hearty "Welcome." Of course, being the only noticeable Black man in the room that was not carrying a tray, I stood out like a sore thumb. My dad, who was lighter-skinned than me, sort of blended in.

I finally spotted my dad's bald head in the very back of the room. As I approached, trying to make my way to him, members were telling me, "I just met your dad."

I couldn't believe it. He was working the crowd like a good politician. When I grew near, I could hear him saying, "I'm Joseph Graves. I'm Curtis's father."

I could tell from the grin on his face that he was a proud man that morning.

I was also filled with pride. For the first time in my life, my father was defining himself by saying that he was my father. All my life, it was the other way around. I thought back to when I was growing up in his shadow. He had a lifetime membership in the NAACP and was a trailblazer in his own right. He did everything he could to advance the cause of civil rights. Many times, he said to me, "Just tell them who your dad is. They'll help you with what you need."

But now the roles were reversed. I was becoming a man of some importance in his eyes. It was only the presence of so many people that I'd never seen before that stopped me from crying right there.

I really don't remember much else that happened that morning beside being introduced to the attendees and introducing my dad to the public after we had our breakfast. But the walk back to the Capitol in the blowing snow sticks in my mind. It was an uphill hike back and I think I cried most of the way. My dad was a quiet person by nature, but the quiet on that walk was nearly more than I could take. Looking back, I can see that with each step back towards the Capitol Building, I could feel him making the last little cuts on the umbilical cord that connected us and that he was wordlessly guiding me as my dad one last time. Now I was out there on my own, a man in my own right.

Walking along, I could see some pep in his step and a bright smile on his face. Driving away from my very own parking spot, I could feel the change in our relationship. He set my little boat free. He did his job and decided that I was now able to chart my own course. It might not be what he would have chosen, but it was mine alone, although both our names would remain attached. As I look back with the luxury of time I see many more names, those of my ancestors whose shoulders I was standing on that morning.

The blowing snow and the cold on my face froze the tears as they streamed from my eyes. I never had a conversation with him about that morning, but now that he's gone, I wish I would have. He needed to hear from me directly that the dues he paid for me to enter manhood made me the person that I was. He needed to hear from me that I appreciated him working hard to get ahead and push societal boundaries so that I wouldn't have to walk that same path. He was a man who knew what it took to move us from where we were to where we ought to be.

Life is funny that way. In too many cases, you only think of thanking people for what they did to bring you to another level when, in too many cases, it is too late for them to hear it.

We collected the rest of the family and headed back to the Capitol for the swearing-in at noon. I showed off my new shared office to my family while a steady stream of supporters from Houston and folks from other parts of the state dropped by to express congratulations.

Jo Cash, my new secretary, was at her best. She was the perfect hostess that I needed on that first day to organize and make everyone feel welcome. My guests blended in with Lauro's family and guests and we were all on cloud nine.

I stepped on the House floor at the right time with my mother, my father, and my big brother Kenneth behind me. I walked up to Desk #69 and took my seat in the large brown leather chair that was my seat for the next three terms. As I stood nearby, an assistant sergeant-at-arms came up to assist me. I never saw him before, but he knew who I was.

"Representative Graves," he said quietly. "How many chairs do you need for your family?"

"Three would be great," I answered, trying to convey authority.

Family on the First Day. Pictured from left standing, brother Kenneth Graves, , Mother Mabel Haydel Graves, father Joseph Graves, Sadie Haydel Woods, Olga Haydel Argierd, Clarence Woods and Ann White, a cousin-in-law.

My desk mate, James Lovell, was a House member from East Texas. Our desks were separate but they touched each other, with the right side of my desk touching the left side of his. It felt almost like the desk I shared with Charles Neville in the second grade, although that desk had one top for the two of us while Lovell and I each had a separate space and key for us to lock up our personal items. We also had a phone that was a direct line to our office and a key to our own personal voting machine. We could turn it on and vote "yes" or "no" ("aye" or "nay"), or "present," if we so chose.

I could tell by Lovell's tentative handshake when we met that he did not know that he would be sitting next to the first Black man to take the oath of office in 68 years.

My parents and brother were seated behind and beside me. My mother was euphoric. She wore her Sunday best with a bright and stylish hat that matched her dress perfectly. She looked at me and said, "Curtis, this is one of the proudest moments of my life."

I knew she was proud. I guess all those lies she told me about

Curtis' Mother, Dad and brother Kenneth at his desk on the House floor.

Jim Crow and segregation to make me feel like I could do anything in life paid off. I did feel that morning like nothing could stop me. From the first day I could understand right from wrong, my folks instilled that feeling in me. I'm pretty sure I teared up as I looked at her.

The time came for us to take the oath of office. When I stood to take the oath, I made sure to stand close to Lovell. I never met him before that day and was not sure how he would react. I wanted to show everybody that I was being sworn in with all the rest of the white boys.

And make no mistake, that day it was *all* white boys. For some reason that I can't remember, Joseph Lockridge, the other newly elected Black representative in the House, was not sworn in on opening day. He took the oath of office several days later.

So the cameras were on me, more cameras than I'd ever seen in one place.

Lovell did not move. He could be seen in photographs taken of me.

Two days later, as we sat side by side on the House floor, Lovell whispered to me, "I'm glad you moved over next to me on the day we were sworn in."

"Why?" I asked, surprised.

"Turns out, that picture was seen all over the country. My name was listed along with yours. That was a good shot for me," he said.

It turns out that the picture of us was not just seen around the country, but all over the world. UPI and AP, the two big wire services, carried the story worldwide. Papers all over Europe, Asia, and Australia ran the story. People sent me clippings from everywhere.

I smiled. I thought to myself at the time that I might've made a friend out of him. Indeed, we did become friends. He never voted for any legislation I was interested in, but we remained friendly. We respected each other and our different points of view.

As I look back at that time and our relationship, I can see now that the lack of respect and understanding with those who we have political differences with might be the biggest problems in today's politics. Today there is such a strong animosity between the Democrats and Republicans that it makes it difficult to meet in the middle. Before you can reach a compromise, you need to talk to each other. That talk comes easily if there is friendship at its base.

After my family departed for New Orleans that evening, I went to my first big gathering of the Legislature and other state officials. It was a biannual event at the Capitol Country Club on the outskirts of the city. This was the tradition of welcoming in the new legislative session. Lauro and I rode to the event together. After parking my car, we entered the main room of the club at the same time. Lauro looked up and noticed that Governor John Connally spied us and was heading towards us.

I stood my ground, but when I looked around, Lauro was

gone. We talked about Governor Connally so many times at so many rallies that I think Lauro might have vomited right there if he had to shake his hand that night. He was the enemy, and sometimes it's not good to greet the enemy face-to-face on the first day. In many cases, you must get your stuff together to know what to say and how to act in that first face-off.

With a big smile on his face, the governor grabbed my hand, pulled me towards him, and said, "Curtis, I am so glad that you were elected. You are going to be a real addition to our House of Representatives."

James Lovell and Curtis Graves take the oath of office

Without letting go of his hand and pulling him in a little closer to me, I responded, "John, I really want to thank you for that. I look forward to working with you."

Still holding on to his hand, our faces were about a foot apart. I could literally see the color drain from his face. He paled as he pulled his hand and the rest of his body away from me. The big smile faded away, too. He looked as serious as a heart attack. I'd seen that look on people's faces before, but never that close. I remembered the words of that old man and thought Connally might've pissed in my boots if the conversation would have gone on past that point.

Looking back on it now, I'm sure that no Black person ever called him by his first name in his life, especially in those days when things were more formal. However, I figured if he felt free to call me, a stranger, by my first name, then I was at liberty to call him by his.

He turned around so fast that I could feel the wind from his body as he passed by. We did not speak again for some time. He never looked for me at any other gathering of state officials in the entire time I served in the House. We *did* have several encounters in the six years I served, but most of them were not pleasant.

The last time I laid eyes on the former governor was on one of those people movers at Dulles Airport years after I was out of politics. He was in the front as I entered the back. He recently went through a trial accusing him of corruption. He was found not guilty but he left with a tarnished reputation. As I stepped on the people mover, I shouted after him, loud enough for everyone to hear, "John Connally!"

I could see that same paleness come over his face. He did not want to be recognized. I went up to him, shook his hand, and walked away just like he did to me many years before.

During the time that he was governor, rumors were always swirling around him concerning corruption of one kind or the other. I remember another encounter with him when I was invited to a reception at the governor's mansion. I had too much to drink and knew that I shouldn't stay at the mansion's backyard party any longer. As I made my way to the door, I decided to think about how I would arrange things when I was governor. He walked in behind me and looked at me. I saw him out of the corner of my eye and, looking him straight in the eye, I said, "I was just deciding how I would rearrange things."

He did not say a word and I made my way to the door that was opened for me by one of the state police officers.

Even though I did see him from time to time, we were never on friendly terms. I certainly didn't think about him very much. I almost forgot about him entirely until the morning of June 16, 1993, when I picked up the *Times Herald* newspaper slipped under my door at the Nile Hilton Hotel in Cairo, Egypt. I was there on business as president of the Aerospace Education Organization. A little picture of Connally was featured at the top of the right-hand column. The article under the picture said that he died the day before in Houston.

During the first days of the session, I noticed that there were no Blacks among the page boys in the House. Of course, there were only page *boys,* never any girls. They were there to help run errands for the members. Their duties mostly consisted of going to offices to get documents or delivering something from one office to another. They were helpful, and it was an internship of sorts for a young person.

After asking around, I learned that there had never been a Black boy to serve as a page in the history of the state. That gave me an idea that, again, would forever change my life. I decided to find out the qualifications and try to find a young Black man to serve in that capacity.

Again with the help of Jo Cash, I found a young man named

Michael Arnold who was, again, from one of the outstanding Black families of Austin. I had him to come up and interview with me and decided that I would make a case to have him hired as the first Black House page in the history of the state.

Young Michael was an outstanding candidate, so I brought him down to meet the Secretary of the House. She was a very pleasant lady who told me that if I needed anything, I should just let her know.

Well, I needed something. She had him to fill out the necessary paperwork and within days, he got an excuse from his school and was at work in the Texas House. He was there to serve *all* the House members, not just me. However, I did keep an eye on him.

The process was that the page boys would sit on the right side of the chamber in a line. The boy in the first chair would be the next to respond if a member signed that he needed one of them. I wanted Michael to show that he could do the job as well as the other boys. I would like to report that he did, and in nearly every session of the House since that day, a Black boy, and eventually girls, served as pages.

I think it was only my second or third week in office when House Speaker Ben Barnes sent one of his people down to get me. I think it was the Cruz guy who sat in front of me. He often ran legislative errands for the Speaker. He leaned over my desk and whispered, "The Speaker would like a word with you."

Joe Lockridge was finally sworn in by this time, and I guess he must've also been invited. We stood in front of the Speaker's podium, nearly at attention. After all, this was a *command performance*, and that is what one does. We were summoned.

Barnes leaned over and grabbed my hand. Then he did the same with Joe. "I wanted to personally welcome the two of you to the House. If you have any problems with anything, please let me know. I think you will be welcomed everywhere in Austin," he said with a big welcoming smile.

Both of us knew what he was *really* talking about. I could see in his eyes that he was concerned and wanted proceedings to continue without any problems or tension. He didn't need to say anything else. With all the publicity that our elections got, most places that were "whites only" would know that they really couldn't stay segregated anymore. At the very least, they couldn't be off limits to a sitting member of the State House or Senate.

We thanked him and returned to our seats. I didn't know that short conversation was really a watershed event. Surprisingly, his words would come back to me in less than two months, and I would have to go to him to share that some doors were still closed to me.

In session with his Page, Mike Arnold

Now that Joseph Lockridge was seated and I wasn't the only dark face in the place, I had an ally. I never met Joe before and I didn't really know where he stood on any of the issues I cared about. What I *did* learn from the newspapers was that he was a graduate from the Howard University School of Law and that he was very sharp. He was a little dark-skinned guy who spoke very softly and sort of blended in without making any noise.

Looking back, I wonder if he thought that he needed to create some space between us. In any case, I could tell from his demeanor that we weren't going to be best friends. I was alright with that. I appreciated the fact that he was elected at-large in Dallas and probably could not speak out on controversial issues that would make his constituents unhappy, so we basically became waving friends. We spoke all the time but almost never of anything substantive.

I saw him in the members' lounge and on the floor. I went over to his desk from time to time because he was between my desk and the bathroom. I learned that, as a practicing attorney in Dallas for several years, he was rather well known for his aptitude in his profession. When the powers that were in Democratic circles in the city knew that they should have a Black person on their ticket, they approached him to see if he would run.

He introduced me to his wife, but we never socialized. I never drank with him after the session, nor ate lunch with him at any time. Many of us on the liberal side of both the House and the Senate hung out at a place called Scholz's Beer Garden. We all loved to "shoot shit at Scholz's." We'd hang out there, throw back a few, then get some dinner. I never saw Lockridge there. I don't remember him at many lobby parties either. There were lots of those, but he kept to himself. He was very bright, but as a person, he didn't stand out much. I guess that's the way he wanted it.

About two weeks into the session, I was in the House post

office and, sporting a big smile, the lady behind the counter said, "Good morning, Mr. Lockridge."

I looked up at her and said, "Now if you can't see the difference between Mr. Lockridge and me, you need to take a trip to Texas State Optical."

She looked at me blankly. Joe and I looked nothing alike, the biggest indicator being the difference in our skin tones. Joe's complexion was much darker than mine. Joe was also about five foot seven inches on his tall days, and I was six foot four inches. Despite our differences, it seemed like people didn't care enough to notice. The confusion between us happened many more times. In each case, I would let the people know that Joseph Lockridge and I did not look *anything* alike. The thought that all Black people look alike is as crazy as the thought that all Chinese people or all white people look alike. I made it my mission to help people who were never exposed to Black people know that we are all unique individuals.

A few days after the session opened, I received a call from my buddy Theodore Youngblood. His father wanted to speak with me. He gave me his home number and asked that I call him in the evening. I called Theodore Youngblood, Sr. that very night.

We had an interesting conversation. He said that he wanted to be my ears and he would hear things that he could relay to me.

I really didn't understand all of what he was saying. In a very quiet voice, he said that the Black employees were invisible to many powerful white people. "They don't know we are in the room," he said matter-of-factly. "Is there a number I can call you at night to let you know if I hear something that might be of importance to you?"

"Mister Youngblood, you just don't know how helpful that will be to me,"

As it turns out, I got many calls from him about conversations he overheard. Many were just things he heard about some member saying something ugly about me. In a few cases it was rhetoric like, "Who does that nigger think he is?" It was all helpful because it helped me understand the crowd. Not all rattlesnakes are detectable until you hear the rattle. They just seem like any other snake. But with Youngblood's wisdom and keen ear, I could see the rattlers from a distance.

That gave me an idea. The shoeshine man in the members' restroom was another invisible person. I spoke with him one day when there was no one else in the men's room.

"I would like to call you at night to talk to you about something. Would you give me your home number?"

He wrote it down and I called him that night. We established an arrangement that was as much help as the one I had with Mr. Youngblood. He would call with information or just some negative thing he overheard about me or other Black officials that some member said, unaware that he was listening to every word. The Shoeshine Boys, as they were collectively called, were also invisible to white folks, just like the waiters in Austin. However, my new friend's ears and eyes worked just fine and he could—and did—relay conversations had in his presence.

As it turns out, most of the calls from both my Black spies were things about me.

"Can you believe he said this or that?"

"We will *never* let him pass such a bill."

I got about a call a week with the name of a member and some negative comment they made. Since Mr. Youngblood was a senior member of the wait staff at the Driskill, he got other waiters to listen for him, too. I had a spy ring working just under their noses. It served me well during the six years I served.

I got about my agenda quickly. I learned that the Legislative Council drafted bills for the legislative members. Bob Johnson led the office and served as the House Parliamentarian. He was an employee of the state who headed this office to help both members of the House and Senate put their ideas for legislation into the proper format to be introduced as a bill. Bob was one of the nicest people who worked in the Capitol Building. He made it a point to introduce me to a person on his staff who he felt would best help me with the drafting of any legislation I was interested in introducing. He knew that the person he found for me was sympathetic and that he would spend some quality time with me. Within a month, I had several bills drafted that I was proud of. At this point, I don't remember the person's name, but I do remember that he was a lawyer and excellent researcher. For now, let's just call him "Justin."

The first bill was the one dealing with Black history being taught in our elementary, middle, and high schools. At the time, state-approved texts only had one mention of Black history—a picture of a slave behind a mule and one paragraph of description.

With "Justin's" assistance, I surveyed the country and found out that Texas and California were the two states that produced history textbook content for the nation. Whatever textbooks were approved in those two states influenced the other states.

I knew that my bill would not change the content of elementary, middle, and high schools' history textbooks for years to come, but you have to start somewhere. I looked at my bill as that first step. I wasn't sure how long it would take, but I just knew I had to get the ball rolling. I knew that I was going to push the idea as far and as fast as I could. At the time, I never thought that I might write a book that might be used in these schools, but as time passed and I thought about it more, I did write a book with Jane Hodges called *Famous Black Americans*. It was published in 1986 by Bartleby Press. That book was used during Black History Month in many schools across the country.

Before a bill can become law, it has to go through a specific process. After you introduce a bill to the House, it's assigned to a committee that deals with that subject. Then you ask the committee chair for a hearing if you want one. Many bills are introduced just to get a local headline and the member who introduced it doesn't really want it to go anywhere. Many bills are introduced for local public relations purposes and then simply dropped. The member just wants to claim some credit for taking up the subject. It's truly necessary for a sponsor of a bill to ask for a hearing if there is any hope for success.

Before my hearing on the schoolbook history bill, I gathered several history books from the elementary, junior high, and high school level. It wasn't difficult to notice what I already discovered: the only reference to slavery or Black history was one picture and one paragraph on the subject. Slavery, the original sin of the nation, needed to be discussed and looked at by children at every level. If you don't know your history, you are destined to repeat it. The history of slavery and what it has done to both white and Black America is still with us today. Hiding it from our textbooks will not make it go away. In fact, I truly believe that hiding it will only make it worse because it is never faced and understood. It is never openly talked about to begin the healing process.

Most white people in our nation will never know that their thought process is colored by inherent and deep-seated racism. Take the lady in Central Park in New York who called the police on a Black man and acted like she was being attacked after he told her to leash her dog. If you were to ask her if she was a racist, she would probably say no. But when confronted by a Black man who told her to do something she did not want to do, she fell right into the racism that is just below the surface. She might not have known that it was there, but it raised its ugly head and shook its rattler.

I scheduled a hearing. Mrs. Hattie May White agreed to testify. After all, she was one of only two Black people on the Houston School Board. I also asked Floyd Stringfellow, a teacher and principal, to appear. I tried to get a representative from the Texas Textbook Committee to testify as well, but I was unsuccessful.

Together, we hammered the point across of the scarcity of information about Black history in textbooks and that none of the books presently used in our education system included any information on minority groups' contributions to the country as well as the institution of slavery.

In my remarks, I noted sarcastically that the only reference to slavery in any of the American history textbooks was one picture of "a slave on the north end of a south bound mule." That quote made the papers all over the state.

Unfortunately, my bill didn't get out of the education committee, but I did get to say my piece. The fact that many of the state papers carried the story about my hearing was all I could really ask for on my first shot out of the box. I realized that as a freshman legislator and one of only two Black legislators in the State House, it wasn't likely that something like changing the textbooks for the public schools in the great state of Texas was going to come without a fight.

Not only was it not going to come about without a fight, but it also wasn't going to come about without the deaths of many Black people and a change in the way we as a nation look at race. I knew after the vote to table my bill in committee that I may not see it come to pass, but one day it would. I did not have the foresight in 1967 to know that the pain and death would be as great as it has been, but change will come. Sometimes it takes something as horrible as the public execution of George Floyd to show the nation that change must come.

One day in March 1967 the phone rang in my office. It was Robert Casey, Jr., an attorney I knew from the campaign trail and the son of a sitting congressman from Harris County, Robert Casey Sr. He said that his firm tasked him with lobbying for a client who was interested in a bill that was going to come up in the Legislature. He didn't know anything about lobbying and he asked me what he should do.

"Bob, get yourself some club membership cards in Austin, take me and Lauro to lunch, and we'll show you how it's done."

Credit cards weren't yet in widespread use. At that time, membership cards would do what a credit card does now.

A few days later, Robert called and said he was driving to Austin. Lauro and I met him in our office and for over an hour, we talked about his bill and the objectives of his law firm's involvement. He took my advice and got a few club memberships from his firm. "I have one membership from a club called the Austin Club," he said.

Neither of us had been to that one. "Well, let's try that one," he said.

The Austin Club was a short walk from the Capitol on Congress Avenue. It turned out that Bob's firm were members for years. We walked up to the second-floor reception area and a Black waiter seated us in the lounge outside of the dining room for drinks. More than half an hour passed while we talked before we finally noticed that not one person approached us.

Finally, a waiter appeared, but instead of taking a drink order, he leaned over and said to Bob, "Mr. Casey, can you step over to the office for a moment?"

At the same time, I noticed some of the Black kitchen help stick their heads out and take a peek at me and Lauro. We both noticed it but we didn't think that much about it.

A few minutes later, Bob returned with a look of discontent. He just spoke to the president of the club, Mr. Homer Leonard. He told Bob that we could not be served.

Words cannot describe the heat and anger that overcame us. But as frustrated as we were, we got up and made our way down the stairs to the street. As we were leaving, Representative Jake Johnson and two other members of the House were just coming in. Jake was a tall man in his early forties with an easy smile. He was known for his quick wit. Jake was a member of the Houston delegation. The delegation was divided between conservatives

Testifying in a hearing

and liberal members. He and I were both on the liberal side. "Jake, they just refused to serve us," I said in a loud voice.

"They did what?" He asked in an equally loud voice. "If they don't serve you, we won't eat there, either!"

Then he and the other members with him stormed out. We all made our way to the Driskill Hotel dining room. We had a great meal there and managed to still use Bob Casey's card from his firm.

I didn't want to let the incident drop and planned to bring it to the attention of the Speaker the next day. I had no idea what would come of it. But before I could even report it, Jake Johnson introduced a House resolution that said in part, "If one member of the House is refused service by a restaurant or club, then all members will not go." It was the first order of business that morning.

Before any vote, I was summoned to meet with Speaker Barnes. He asked me to sit next to him and whispered, "What happened at the Austin Club?"

I told him the story of yesterday's aborted meal and the embarrassment of being asked to leave the club. I made sure he knew we were with a person whose law firm had a valid membership in the club and that that had nothing to do with why we were asked to leave. The president of the club even spoke to our host. There was no mistaking the fact that my presence was the reason that we were not served.

The resolution was moved to a vote. The Speaker stood tall at his podium and asked for a division of the House. "All in agreement with the resolution, say 'aye.'"

The House responded with a loud, "Aye."

He then asked for the "nays." There were none.

He yelled out in a booming voice, "There are no nays, therefore the resolution passes without objections."

With that, a spike was driven into the hearts of the segregationist white establishment of Austin, Texas. The truth is that I really did not know what would happen. I had my doubts, but I hoped that with that wooden spike in the heart, the vampire was dead forever.

Before the day was over, I received a call from Homer Leonard, the president of the Austin Club, trying to smooth things over. It was an unfamiliar gesture. He apologized for turning me away but said that changing the discriminatory practice would take a vote of the club members since it was a private club policy. Leonard insisted he would make it his business to fix it. He thought it would take him a few days.

It turned out Mr. Leonard had another reason to get on the

right side of the House members; for his day job, he worked as a lobbyist for the beer industry in the state. Being president of the Austin Club wasn't where his bread was buttered. Publicity about his night job would hurt his real job and would tell Black people not to drink Texas beer.

He knew, just like I did, that the policy had to be changed. The Austin Club was under enormous pressure to do something to keep from losing the business of the members that would honor the resolution. The loss of prestige and the business that went along with it would be too much to bear. If the lobbyist would not be able to take a member out to eat and drink at the Austin Club, this was going to do some real damage.

As usual, money spoke louder than anything else. Within a week, the Austin Club's policy changed. I knew several members who continued to eat and drink there, but the negative publicity was a little more than the club wanted to take on.

From that moment forward, Homer Leonard and I formed an interesting relationship. He usually helped me with whatever I needed. Beer for a fundraiser booze for a political rally was just one phone call away. He also had the best joke file that I knew of, a very handy thing for a politician to have at his disposal. If you were going to make a speech before, say, some Catholic bishops,

A cartoon that ran in the Houston Chronicle depicting Curtis and Bob Casey being asked to leave. (Houston Chronicle)

Leonard had the right jokes for the occasion. In fact, I *did* use some of his jokes for a meeting of Catholic bishops in Houston, and for several other occasions. Every joke landed.

In the 1960s, Texas was a solidly Democrat state. The Texas House of Representatives had 150 members, all male. There were 149 Democrats and just one Republican. There were two Blacks and 148 whites. Today the State House looks very different. There are more Republicans than Democrats. Many of the state representatives are women and almost a third of the seats are held by African Americans. There are even one or two Black Republicans.

In my day, I made many friends on both sides of the liberal/ conservative divide. After all, at that time we only had one Republican member of the House. He just happened to be from Houston. He was a rabid Republican, but he didn't show it at the time. I can remember on some bills concerning the minimum wage, he spoke in opposition and turned as red as a ripe watermelon in July in defense of his cause. I think you could call that a "Rabid Republican."

Many of my conservative colleagues would come up to me on the floor or in the lounge and ask if I would help with some local bill. I always said yes. In some cases, when I knew the bill in question might not be something that I could agree on, I would drag out my crazy bill and ask them if they would help me on that. They'd run like roaches when you turned on the light.

On the other hand, many liberal members would come to me to ask my help on bills that I agreed with. Several times, they asked for my help but requested that I not speak. In some cases, it was better for me to give my help under the cover of darkness. I always understood and did what they asked.

I felt that I gained the respect of many members. Of course, they would not vote for anything that I sponsored, but they were friendly and did not show any open hostility towards me.

Even so, I wasn't under any illusions. Some members

wouldn't be caught talking to me on the floor where the press and gallery could see them. But the members' lounge was another story. It wasn't open to anyone but members and their wives. There, I could engage in conversation with some that otherwise wouldn't speak to me outside of the lounge or restroom.

With 150 guys, there were times that weren't all business. We played cards in the lounge on our downtime. There were even four of us who formed a barbershop quartet. We sang together on the floor several times to the cheers of the members and the gallery.

Before the close of the session, I got word that Joe Lockridge was going to defend his first bill on the House floor. In Texas at the time, it wasn't legal to sell chicken by the piece. Chicken could only be sold by the head or the pound, but not by the piece. In other words, you could not sell a chicken leg or a chicken breast. Kentucky Fried Chicken applied to open some franchises in Texas and needed to have the law changed.

It was unclear to me why the Dallas delegation decided to give this bill to Lockridge to carry, but it wasn't a controversial matter by any means. I will always think that there was something else behind the decision, but he had it and was running with it. He got his bill out of committee without any problems and it was set to be voted up or down on the House floor.

As the day and time came for the bill to be presented before the House, I noticed several members gathered near the back microphone. I could see that they were primed and ready to ridicule him. After the time that Joe and I spent together, I knew that he was not the kind of guy who could fend off several sharp-witted House members. Black people eating chicken and watermelon was the kind of thing that you would see on racist postcards and signs, and the fact that one of the two Blacks in the House was going to be carrying a bill about selling fried chicken by the piece was something that this group was looking forward to. They thought that they would have some fun at his expense.

I decided to come to Joe's aid. I thought that if I handled it, they would feel that they had their fun. Even so, I was concerned that he would be humiliated. I waved the group off by saying, "Let me do it. If you're not satisfied when I'm done, then you do what you need to do."

They parted and made the microphone available for me. I approached the back microphone and addressed the Speaker.

"Mr. Speaker, would the gentleman yield for a question?"

The Speaker responded, "Mr. Lockridge, would you yield for a question?"

The House went dead silent. Everyone could feel that something was going to happen. All eyes were on the two of us. I even took my time and rustled some papers to make it look more dramatic. I thought that a little humor would take the heat off him and let everyone laugh, and then Lockridge and the bill would be home free.

In a tentative voice, Lockridge said. "Yes, sir. I will yield for a question."

The House football team. Curtis is second from right on the back row. It was all in fun, but many of these members did not speak to him but one or two times during the session

I could see from his face that he was under some real stress, and the stress was only increasing with the fear of what I would do.

"Mr. Lockridge, would you take an amendment to your 'chicken by the piece' bill?" I asked with some authority.

"Yes," he responded in a voice that was a little hard to hear.

"Would you accept an amendment to allow watermelon to be sold by the slice and possum by the piece?"

The House members screamed and yelled. They were nearly rolling on the floor.

It was more than a minute or two before the Speaker could stop laughing and gavel the House back into order. When order was restored, Lockridge responded, his voice quivering, "I will take your amendment."

It was nearly another minute before things settled down again.

"Mr. Lockridge, I withdraw my amendment."

After order was restored again, the bill passed by a voice vote.

I knew by this time that most of the Dallas delegation was racist and would take delight in making fun of a Black man anytime they could. My objective was to soften the blow, try and take race out of it and off the table.

By the time the 60th session of the Texas House of Representatives came to an end in late May of 1967, I was known quite well in and around the state government.

I made many calls on behalf of my constituents to resolve issues they were having with the state government. There were more issues than you can think of, and because they never had an advocate in Austin, I received calls from all over the state. I did my best to address their problems. Most of the time it worked, but I didn't win every battle. In some cases, I would contact the representative from the constituent's district and ask them if they would help with the issue. In most cases where the call came from

outside my district, I would say that the constituent called me because a relative in my district asked that I help. It always worked.
Most African Americans from around the state didn't understand
that I wasn't their representative, so I played the role. However, if
an issue was, for example, talking to the parole board about a constituent in El Paso, I knew that the white El Paso member would
have more pull with the all-white parole board than I would. Like
Kenny Rogers said, "You have to know when to hold them and
know when to fold them."

According to the Texas Constitution, the State Legislature
meets for five months of every odd year, so there was no session in
1968. Many of the House members were lawyers and went home
to practice law. Many other members were involved in one business or another. There were lots of formers from west Texas, labor
organizers and a few undertakers. We did what we did in the off
year.

TEN

THE FIRST REAL TRIP

Within a few days of the session ending in late May,
I attended a Houston Independent School District
(HISD) board meeting. Mrs. Hattie Mae White was
working her magic on some subject and those who followed these
matters were going to be present. The board room was full. with
standing room only.

I sat on the steps beside Rabbi Moshe Cahana. He was the
chief rabbi of one of the large Jewish congregations in Houston.
It was June of 1967, and the Six-Day War in Israel had just ended.
The rabbi said that he was going to Israel in a week or so. I said in
jest, "Would you put me in your suitcase?"

He looked at me and said, "Would you go?"

"Of course, I would go." I responded without hesitation.

"Let me work on it," he answered just as quickly.

The next day I received a call. "Curtis!" I knew it was the rabbi
from his heavily accented voice. "I have made the arrangements,"
he announced happily.

I thought to myself that this could not be true. But he was
serious. I did not have a passport and I didn't know just what

that would take. I didn't know if I needed shots. I had so many questions and no answers. "When are you leaving?" I asked.

"In ten days," he responded.

The only question that circled around in my head after our conversation was, could I pull it off?

I had just rented some space on Lyons Avenue for an office. I had just hired a secretary and gotten the phones turned on. I had just named the office "Curtis M. Graves and Associates" knowing that there were not any associates but if I got some business, I would bring in some associates. I was hoping to do some political consulting or whatever came through the door.

The first call I made was to my mother in New Orleans to get a copy of my birth certificate. She mailed it to me the next day. With that in hand, I rushed to the federal building to get a passport. After I gave them some pictures, I found out that I wouldn't get a passport for at least three weeks.

I informed Rabbi Cahana of the timing, and he got back to me saying that it was not a problem. He would go and meet his rabbi friends as he'd planned and I would join them when I arrived the next week. Our deal was that I needed to stay a month for him to get a break on the tickets. He would pick up my hotel bills and I would buy my own food. That sounded like the kind of deal I could not refuse.

The three weeks passed quickly. Before I knew what was happening, I was on a Pan Am flight to New York and then off to Tel Aviv. As you can imagine, I was excited. As the overnight flight touched down at the Tel Aviv Airport, I could see Rabbi Cahana and several of his friends on the roof of the building. They greeted me with open arms. I was already checked into a nice Tel Aviv Hotel, so I settled in for a day.

For the first two weeks, I rolled with the rabbis. Their agenda consisted of our bus visiting nearly every part of Israel. They wanted to see all the places where fighting had occurred.

The war lasted only six days, but a lot had happened. Because it is not a large nation, I was able to see more than the average tourist would see.

The by-product of traveling with a bus load of rabbis was that I learned more about the Bible then I had ever known before. The rabbis were my teachers. They showed me where the sermon on the mountain happened. They showed me where Christ walked the water on the Sea of Galilee. They showed me the Western Wall, then known as the Wailing Wall. They showed me the Golan Heights. With them, I stayed at a *kibbutz* and went swimming in the Sea of Galilee.

It was a history lesson and a different kind of experience for me. I can still remember the evenings we spent in long conversations about the history of the Holy Land.

When the two weeks were up, they went back to the States. I stayed on because my ticket required that I stay a month. Now the big question was, what do I do with myself for the next two weeks? I didn't know a soul.

I set up camp at the Sheraton Tel Aviv Hotel right on the Mediterranean Sea. On one of my first days alone, I took a bus to Nazareth. It was my first time on my own but I was able to get to Nazareth and back with little trouble. I just went to a bus station and got a ticket and off I went. I visited the place where Jesus was raised and the Church of the Annunciation. I remember going to the well Mary would draw her water for her home and going to the house where they said that Jesus grew up in. Although I did not know Hebrew, Israel was English-friendly so I was able to make my way around and learn a lot. The trip to Nazareth was just a day trip, so I was back before dark.

The Sheraton was a great location for me. The room rate wasn't bad, and it was the place where all the celebrities from Hollywood were staying. I was having breakfast in the dining room on a Sunday morning when the waitress asked me, "You know Danny Kaye?"

She had a heavy Israeli accent and I really didn't understand what she is saying.

"No, I don't want any cake. I want two eggs, sausage, and some toast."

She said, "No, no, Danny Kaye, Danny Kaye!"

She pointed to him two tables over. If it weren't for the fact that I recognized him, I still wouldn't have known what she was saying. I was hearing "Denny cake." I thought she was trying to make me eat some Israeli cake.

I looked up and there he was. He was sitting alone, having breakfast. I stood and walked over to his table. I said, "Mr. Kaye, I am Curtis Graves from Texas, and I would like to meet you."

He looked up and said, "What are you, a Yemenite, doing here in Israel?"

"A Yemenite?" I repeated.

He laughed and said, "Please sit."

So I did. That was the beginning of a friendship that lasted more than twenty years. I told him that I was a member of the Texas House of Representatives and that I'd been abandoned by my friends who had gone back to the States. I needed to stay two more weeks because of the unique airline ticket I had.

"Do you have things you are doing or want to do?" he asked.

"Not really, I'm open. I'm feeling my way around," I said.

He smiled. "Then you are with me. 'I'm on my way to Jerusalem tomorrow morning, and you should go with us."

"Do you have room for me to tag along?" I asked.

"I will make room,"

It was just like what happened with Rabbi Cahana. He just stuffed me in his suitcase.

Danny Kaye explained that he was visiting several cities entertaining the troops and visiting hospitals where there were orphaned children. He went on to say that he wanted to visit wounded soldiers who were still hospitalized. "I would be honored to go with you," I said.

At about 8 a.m. the next morning, we were off to Jerusalem in a black SUV. We had a driver, so Danny sat in the right front seat and I sat behind him with his piano player named Sammy. During the ride to Jerusalem, Sammy and I bonded. He had been playing piano for Danny for years. Danny would chime in with information to fill out what Sammy was telling me.

Other than the bonding and learning how to roll with Danny Kaye, the ride was nearly uneventful until we arrived in Jerusalem. I say *nearly* uneventful because from time to time Danny would ask the driver to stop so he could speak to people gathered on street corners. He was raised in a house where Yiddish was spoken every day. He was looking for people who spoke Yiddish to talk to. Most people spoke Hebrew, so we stopped several times before he was able to get his Yiddish fix.

When we arrived in Jerusalem, things changed like night and day. We were driven straight to the Jerusalem City Hall. Teddy Kollek, then the mayor of Jerusalem, was waiting outside his offices for us to arrive. He was a rotund man with a quick smile. He embraced each of us heartily and after a cup of coffee in his office, we were off on a whirlwind tour of his city. Not just *the* city, but really *his* city. He pointed out the electric wires and water pipes on the streets that had to be connected in haste to provide electric service and water to those who were formerly under Jordanian control. Those parts of the city were under Israeli rule for the first time since 1947.

He took us to the highest point overlooking the city above the Mount of Olives to show us how the battle was waged. He stressed that the city had to be taken with as little loss of life and property as possible.

Therefore, in his words: "It was extremely important and

necessary to save not only the people who lived and worked in the Old City, but also the buildings that had historical significance to Christians, Jews, and Muslims."

Mayor Kollek talked about the soldiers leading the battle into the gates of the Old City. They didn't want a lower ranked person who wasn't sensitive to the uniqueness of this battle to be in charge. The fighting had been fierce, but they hadn't expected to get this close to victory. The Israeli cabinet debated how best to handle this unanticipated development. Finally, they entered and captured the Temple Mount.

His lecture and description of Jerusalem and its historical significance was burned into my head. Through the years, I have given that same lecture to friends and relatives twice. I stood in the same place where he did that morning. The first time I was with Bill Nixon, who worked for me at NASA, and the second time I was with my cousin Honore Haydel and his wife, Christa Bell. They got the lecture when we were visiting the Old City with Hilton Paris, a friend from New York.

It was obvious as we walked through the Old City that the mayor was respected by not only the Israelis, but also by many Christians and Arabs. As we walked through the narrow streets of old Jerusalem, without bodyguards or help, he spoke to nearly everyone in several languages. Everyone who saw him spoke to him and he answered in their tongue. He stopped several times to introduce us to Israelis, Christians, and Arabs who appeared to be his good friends. I never have understood how this man, who was not mayor of the Old City until the Six-Day War, knew so many people in every part of his newly expanded city.

After a long day of walking and talking, we ended the day at a little restaurant called Fink's. With less than eight tables, the doors to the place were closed to anyone who was not a part of our party. We were treated like royals. Without saying anything, the food and wine started coming until we could not eat or drink anymore. As they say in New Orleans, "we passed a good time." I really don't remember the ride back to Tel Aviv that night. However, in a few days we went from one end of the country to the other, visiting hospitals and other facilities.

I remember a talk with Danny one night at the King David Hotel. I told him that for the last two weeks, I visited places with the rabbis. We didn't spend too much time with people. Danny's agenda was not *places*, but *people*. I watched him talk to children with his fingers dancing. He really had a gift as an entertainer.

One evening in the Sheraton, Danny introduced me to a young man named Mike Burstyn. Mike was an Israeli-American about my age who was born in New York. He had a hit song out at the time named "Kuni Lemel." Hanging out with him for a week

Danny Kaye entertaining at one of the schools. Curtis was just one of the people in his entourage

or so was a good thing. He was a single man at the time and the ladies were all over him. Oh, it was good to be in his entourage! That friendship also lasted for more than 20 years.

When the time came for me to go back to Houston, I did not want to leave. I really don't remember all the Hollywood types I got to meet with Danny Kaye and Mike Burstyn. However, I *do* remember having drinks one night at the Sheraton with Eddie Fisher and Connie Stevens. There were lots more, but they did not mean much to me at the time and I don't remember them.

When I returned to Houston, I spoke at several Jewish functions about my experience. Speaking was something that I would do if I could get some fees out of it.

Several weeks after returning, I got a call from one of the officials of Frontiers International Inc. They are a national African American service organization much like Kiwanis. My dad was a member of the organization for several years in New Orleans. At the time, they raised money for sickle cell anemia, which is found mostly in African American populations. The organization was having a regional meeting in Opelousas, Louisiana, of all places. The region included several states around Louisiana. My dad might have somehow arranged for me to be asked to be their keynote speaker for the conference. (By the way, they did pay an honorarium for my services. I needed all the honorariums I could get at that time.)

I heard from the organization that they asked Dr. Felton Clark, the retired president of Southern University, to introduce me. I heard Dr. Clark speak many times and he was good. This was the same Dr. Felton Clark who was the president of Southern University during the sit-ins. He was the one who cried before the students and said that if they did not stop the demonstrations, the state was going to close the school. His oratorical skills were known in the Black community from sea to shining sea. I knew that I had to step up my game.

Well, the day came for me to go to the great city of Opelousas. The city did not have a commercial airport, so the plane had to land in Lafayette, Louisiana, some twenty or so miles north of the city. When the plane was rolling to a stop near the terminal, the pilot came on the PA system and announced, "Would Representative Graves please deplane last?"

I looked out the window of the commuter flight. What I saw was what looked like a high school band. Not only a school band, but also several police and sheriff cars, Boy Scout troops, and maybe twenty or so other people standing near the steps leading to the plane.

I waited as I was told for everyone to get off before me. Then all hell broke loose when I stepped through the door. The band started playing, people were waving, and I looked around to see if all of this was for someone else. The white mayors of both Opelousas and Lafayette were standing there with keys to their cities. Boy Scouts and some other Black kids were standing at attention.

As you can imagine, I was blown away. It turns out that I was the first Black elected official to visit these parts since Reconstruction. It was A Big Thing. I found out later that a story was run in both the Opelousas and Lafayette daily papers and people had come out to see this strange thing called "a Black sitting member of the Texas House of Representatives." As I think back on it now, I think that they made a little more of it than should have been made. After all, I was just a native of New Orleans who had moved to Houston and gotten myself elected to the Texas State House. I thought it was more of being in the right place at the right time than anything else.

They greeted me, gave me the keys, and I waved to the band and crowd gathered there, and put in the back of one of the police cars. With the light flashing and siren wailing, I was off for a twenty or so mile ride to the big city of Opelousas to do my thing. All of this, and would you believe, they were also going to pay me for speaking? The conference was being held at the Palace Hotel on the main street in the downtown section of the city. If I remember right, the Palace was the only hotel in the city. All the rest were motels.

My only stop in Opelousas before my speaking engagement was to pick up some boudin sausage on my way from New Orleans to Houston when I was in college. If you don't know what boudin is, I really can't explain it to you. But the city of Opelousas is the "Boudin Capital of the World." If it's not, then the t-shirt I bought many years ago that had those words printed on the front has been lying to me for years.

We arrived at the Palace Hotel about 3 p.m. and my police escort went away. I looked around for some familiar faces and did not find any, so I decided to take advantage of the suite they booked for me and rest for a few hours. After about an hour or so, I got up and checked out the TV. Finding nothing on, I decided to take a shower and shave before my dad and his friends from New Orleans arrived.

I was shaving when the lights in the bathroom went out. I flicked the switch and checked the lights in the bedroom. They were out, too. I was half-shaved with an electric razor and thought that I should put on my clothes and see what was going on in the rest of the hotel. In the back of my mind, I noted that I needed to buy a regular razor to finish the shave. I opened the door to my hotel room and found that the hallway was dark as well except for a dim, battery-powered light at the end of the hall. I made my way to the stairs and was able to find the lobby without any problems.

When I stepped into the lobby, I could see the people who greeted me at the airport. The officials of the organization were in a heated conversation with what looked like hotel management. They were arguing that there could not be a banquet because the microphones would not be working and the room would be hot.

The hotel employees tried to reassure them, saying that the food was cooked and the tables were set. Long white candles were lit and placed on each table. Well, hotel management convinced the officials that they could pull it off and everything would be just fine.

I looked around for my dad but he hadn't arrived yet, so I went into the candlelit hotel store and bought a razor and some shaving cream. I climbed back up the stairs to the top floor and, with the help of the light from the window, I finished shaving. I dressed, looked over my speech one more time, and went down to find my dad. By now he and his friends arrived. He informed me that the lights were out all over Opelousas. The town was in darkness.

In short order, the people gathered and the banquet started. After some apologetic remarks from the hotel management, we ate our meal. It was served hot and really wasn't bad for hotel banquet food. Then the speaking started. When it came time for my introduction, Dr. Felton G. Clark, the son of Joseph P. Clark, namesake of the Black high school in Opelousas, got up. With all the oratorical skill of Martin Luther King, Benjamin Mays, and Barack Obama rolled into one, he did an introduction like you have never heard.

He went into the many wonderful qualities of Representative Curtis Graves. He talked about accomplishments I didn't know about and I started to sweat from the lack of air conditioning. Dr. Clark went on and on for more than a half hour. *Oooh*, he was articulate. It was more than a man could take.

I felt so small when I stood up to make my little twenty-minute speech. I had to squint from time to time because I was reading by candlelight. But I did what I needed to do. I made it through without a microphone in the heat. The room was romantically illuminated by those long white candles. However, with all the body heat and the candles, it was hot, and before long the banquet was over. I think things ended a little before they might have if the room was cool.

We went out the front door to catch some fresh air. My dad was impressed with my remarks and with Dr. Clark's remarks about me. As he lit his cigar, he said, "I wondered if he was talking about my son or someone else's son." He went on, "If you think *Felton* can blow, you should have heard his dad, Joseph. Oh, he could hold a crowd in his hands and lift them off their seats. When he died, there were schools and streets named after him all over Black Louisiana."

In less than ten minutes of us stepping out to cool off, the lights came back on. As one would imagine, the conversation suddenly revolved around what cut the lights off before my speech and why they went back on as soon as I was done.

The next morning, the newspaper headlines said that a cat tripped over a switch at the power station and cut the lights off for just enough time for me to finish giving my speech. The paper didn't say "just enough time for me to finish giving my speech," but it could have. I can still see that cat with a Klan robe on trying to see just what switch would leave the city in darkness during my remarks.

As I look back on it now, I realize that it really could have been worse. After all, I did live to tell the story. In years past, there might have been a lynching party to string up this uppity nigger who rolled into town with a band of music, police lights flashing and sirens blaring. I got off easy with a candlelit room and no air conditioning. I got back to Houston through the Lafayette airport without any additional incidents.

Before the middle of 1968, I married Joanne Gordon, a woman from that same little town of Opelousas, Louisiana. Now I *really* needed to make a living from something that was more regular than sporadic speaking engagements. I went to the *Houston*

Informer, a weekly Black newspaper, to ask if there was something I could do that would give me the flexibility to do what I needed and supplement the $400.00 a month I earned as a state legislator.

Mrs. Wesley, a very kind and caring older lady, was the publisher of this weekly newspaper. She and her husband, Carter Wesley, funded the paper many years before. It had a long history of doing the right thing in the Black community. The late Carter Wesley was a lawyer and friend of Thurgood Marshall. Several of the briefs for the landmark Texas civil rights cases were written in the newspaper's office. His widow, Mrs. Wesley, kept the civil rights tradition going.

Considering their own history, my civil rights activities and other legislative advocacy did not raise any eyebrows at the paper. In fact, she was supportive of my activities. She named me assistant editor.

The paper was a small weekly, but it had a good readership in the heart of the Black community. It was fun to get into the news side of the paper. I wrote editorials and covered some news stories.

I remember showing up at a murder scene not long after Mrs. Wesley had given me my press pass. Some man had killed his lover. The body had just been discovered and the place was a bloody mess. I remember walking right into the house, showing the police my press pass, and just walking all over the crime scene to take pictures. If only the CSI people were there. They would not have let me *anywhere* in that house.

This was the murder of a Black woman and the TV news and the *Houston Post* did not think it was worth covering. I had a scoop. My pictures and story ran on the front-page center of the paper that week. Mrs. Wesley said that a murder always sells papers. That week she increased the press run and we sold out. My murder story on the front page with pictures I took with my own camera was indeed a success. As the story goes in the newspaper business, "If it bleeds, it leads."

Before the end of August, I received a call from Andrew Young. He was the chief aid to Dr. Martin Luther King at that time. They were trying to raise some money for the Southern Christian Leadership Conference (SCLC) and Dr. King's other civil rights activities. He said that he could get Harry Belafonte and several other singers, including Aretha Franklin, to come in for a fundraising concert in Houston in mid-October. I agreed to do whatever needed to be done to raise some funds in the city. Within a month, Dr. King came in for an airport press conference to announce the concert. I found him to be a warm and soft-spoken, innately charming with an easy wit. I never mentioned our conversation several years before when he said "he would tell God about it." I was a different person now that I was an elected official and not a student at TSU. I briefed him about our progress and we sat down to meet the press that gathered to make the formal announcement about the concert.

The concert date, October 17th, was about six weeks off, so I went to one of the ticket companies to print and sell the tickets. They agreed and we were off to what we thought would be a successful concert/fundraiser. I booked a venue, the Sam Houston Coliseum, that I thought could be filled and make some money.

About two weeks in, the ticket company called to tell me that one of their locations had been smoke bombed. There was a note left nearby saying, "If you continue to sell the tickets for that nigger, the next bomb will not be smoke."

Because of this threat, the company said that they would not be able to sell the tickets for us.

I had to come up with Plan B. I had the ticket company print out the tickets and give them all to me. They paid me for what they sold, I paid them for their services, and our relationship was over. Our team then set up a committee to put the tickets in churches and night clubs. Most churches aren't open except on Sundays, so sales didn't do well there. The night clubs were about another business and the sale of tickets was a secondary thing for them. In New Orleans, there was a tradition of buying concert tickets in Black night clubs and bars. However, that tradition had not been established in Houston. As you can imagine, the ticket sales did not go well there, either.

A week before the concert, we had only sold about one-third of the tickets. I suppose that a part of the problem was me. This was not my gig. I didn't have the money to hit the two Black radio stations with ads that might have pumped up the sales. Because I had never done anything like this before, I just didn't know what I needed to do to get out the people.

Before the event, several of the Black Houston police officers came to me and said that they would volunteer to protect Dr. King. The word "volunteer" told me that I needed to take them up on their offer.

When Dr. King came in on Friday morning for the Saturday night concert, things were not looking good. Dr. King and a few of his aides along with Harry Belafonte and several others came in at about the same time. After I got the group settled in the Shamrock Hotel, I told Dr. King that we needed to talk. He first called me in the bedroom of the suite and said to me, "Would you get those guys with the guns out of the room?"

Among the several Black Houston policemen who had volunteered to serve as security, two of them were in the salon of the hotel suite. I was thankful for their free service and thought they should stay close by. I didn't think that their presence with their guns would cause Dr. King any discomfort. After all, they knew how to do security and I didn't. But he just wasn't happy with them in the room, so I got two chairs from the suite and asked them to sit outside in the hallway. I told them about his comment about the guns and they understood. They both agreed and that problem was out of the way.

Harry Belafonte and Reverend William Lawson gathered in

the living room of the suite along with me and Dr. King. I explained to Dr. King the problems we were having. The bottom line was that we were going to look bad the next evening when only one-third of the auditorium would be filled. After nearly a half hour of talk, Dr. King said, "There is something that we have not done."

He stood, turned around, kneeled, and started talking out loud to God. I had never seen anything like that before. After all, I was a Catholic boy from New Orleans who never saw a priest talk to God as if he was in the room.

Belafonte and I looked at each other and shrugged our shoulders. Dr. King spoke out loud for some time. I really don't know how long it was, but it felt like a half hour or so. After he told God everything that we had talked about earlier, he stood, turned around, and sat on the sofa. There was an uncomfortable silence in the room. We had not said anything in the room for many, many minutes and it was really his time to say something.

He looked me in the eye and said, "Give away the tickets."

"*Give* away the tickets?" I repeated back to him, punching each word with as much emphasis as I could under these circumstances.

He repeated himself. "Give away the tickets! Right now. We need to be concerned about not looking bad."

After thinking about it for a moment, I responded, "We can do that."

I got on the hotel phone and called a friend that had a big garage. She called several friends, I quickly gathered the tickets up from wherever I stored them, and we were off to the races to give them away.

The next morning, we were putting tickets in cabs to be delivered to as many places as we could come up with. In the middle of this chaos, a long black car pulled up in front of the garage and a guy looking like a chauffeur got out. He walked in and asked who was in charge. One of the workers pointed to me. He walked up and introduced himself. I don't remember his actual name, but he introduced himself as the chauffeur for Mr. John de Menil. I had never heard the name before, but I later found out that he was a very wealthy man who lived in Houston whose money was made in the oil industry. The chauffeur said, "Mr. de Menil would like to buy some tickets."

At the same time, he handed me an envelope. I opened it and pulled out a check. As I looked at it, I could not believe what I was seeing. It was for $20,000.00. I turned to some of the workers and said, "Start gathering tickets!"

My thought was to give him tickets for that amount. I looked at the chauffeur and said, "It's going to take us a minute to gather that many tickets."

"No, no, *he* doesn't want the tickets," he said. "He wants you to *give away* the tickets."

He was gone before I thought about the fact that Dr. King said the same words the day before. I think I was in somewhat of a daze for a minute of two. Now, I can't really say that this was all God's work. But what I *can* say is that I witnessed this with my own eyes and ears.

Now we *really* had fun giving away the tickets. I had some money in the till and the rest was a matter of how many people we could put in those seats.

That night, the concert went on as scheduled. We managed to nearly fill the room, with around 4,000 people in attendance.

We had a problem, but it could have been much worse. Some Klan group showed up and disrupted the concert by throwing another device, described as a smoke bomb or a stick bomb into the vestibule of the arena . Some people in the back were chocking back tears, covering their mouths and faces and a few even had to leave, but the smoke did not get into the main part of the arena.

Even with that, Belafonte and the rest of the entertainers did their thing. Belafonte interrupted his performance briefly and said that it was all part of an effort to intimidate him, Dr King and others connected with the concert.

The next day in the paper Belafonte was quoted as saying: "I was told that if I came to Houston, I would fare no better than John F. Kennedy did in Dallas,"

I introduced Dr. King and he spoke as eloquently as he always did. He too acknowledged the disruption, saying "We've had problems here tonight. The forces of evil are always around."

Dr. King had by this point had become a vocal opponent of the Vietnam war and President Johnson's escalation of it. King had already lost a great deal of support over his stand.

Dr. King, Adie Marks and Curtis in a hotel suite.

At that time I did not share his views. As a public official, and a veteran, it was a step too far for me. My opinion would completely change later.

Dr. King had come to believe that President Johnson was neglecting the struggle here—the war on poverty—to instead prosecute a unjust war in a far-away land. He told the audience: "I feel that all war is evil and the war in Vietnam is the most evil of all. This war has left America morally isolated,"

He then returned to a familiar theme for him, stressing the need for racial harmony and justice. It still resonates until today: "We are going to build right here a nation where men and women, black and white, Jew and gentile, Protestant and Catholic will stand together and sing the words of that old Negro spiritual, 'Free at last, free at last, thank God almighty we are free at last.'"

As I look back at the experience now, I can say that somebody was looking after us. There were too many things that just fell into place at the right time. Dr. King had something that most of us did not have. He had a faith that was unshakable. That day in his suite at the Shamrock Hotel in Houston has been with me from then until now. It might have all been coincidence or happenstance, but I was there. What I saw and what I felt was real. I still think about it and wonder. Did he have something that we just don't understand? Was his belief something that we just don't see every day? Was it all just coincidence? I think I will never know for sure. But what I do know is that something unbelievable happened. I cannot explain it, but it left a mark on me forever.

ELEVEN

MAKING IT WORK

Since the Texas Legislature doesn't meet in regular session in the even numbered years, I knew that I needed to do something to hold everything together and serve my constituents at the same time. I would get calls from people who could not figure how to do something involving the state. I would also receive calls from Black people from all over the state who had similar problems and didn't know who to call. I had an office and someone to answer the phone and I could respond to their needs. I once told someone that I had the largest legislative district in the state that included *all* the Black folks in Texas. Can you believe that I got calls from people in El Paso asking if I could help with some state problem?

In April 1968 I was delivering speeches all over the southern states. As one of the few Black state officials in the nation, I got invitations to speak from not only Texas but also Louisiana, Georgia, and Arkansas. I lived off those speaker's fees for a while.

I received an invitation to speak to the Louisiana Teachers'

Association (The Black Teachers) in Alexandria, Louisiana. The Association had a rich history in fighting for civil rights and even refused to acknowledge or sponsor any school that refused to desegregate after *Brown v. The Board of Education* in 1957.

It just so happened that the Hemisphere Exhibition was opening in San Antonio that same weekend, coinciding with the 250th anniversary of the founding of San Antonio in 1718. A good friend of mine named Bill Thomas had a little airplane and volunteered to fly me to Alexandria on April 6.

On the afternoon of Thursday, April 4, 1968, I was writing my speech in my Fifth Ward apartment when the telephone rang. It was Rabbi Moshe Cahana. In his heavy Israeli accent, he said, "Are you looking at the TV?"

"No. Should I be?" I asked.

He said, with tears in his voice, "Dr. King has been killed! Turn on your TV. It is not real."

I got up to turn on the TV. It was on all three stations. I turned down the sound to listen to what Rabbi Cahana was saying. "Curtis, I am really calling you to tell you that I was with Dr. King last weekend at an interfaith meeting at the National Cathedral in Washington, D.C."

He continued, still crying. "I never met him, so I went up to introduce myself. I explained that I was from Houston. He said, 'Oh, you are! Do you know my friend Curtis Graves?' I told him that you and I were in Israel together just a few months ago. 'When you see him, give him my love,' he said."

"I didn't call you when I returned because I was busy."

I could barely understand Rabbi Cahana through his tears. "But when I heard this news, I knew that I had to call you right away."

We talked for a few minutes more until I said that I couldn't talk anymore. I walked over to the TV to turn the sound up and sat in disbelief. Dr. King was assassinated by a single bullet, shot on the balcony of his hotel room at the Lorraine Motel in Memphis, Tennessee. He was there to support a march the following day to fight for a fair wage for sanitation workers in the state.

Time passed without my noticing it. I cried like a toddler. I took off my glasses and wiped my eyes on my sleeve. After some time, I looked at my watch and realized that I needed to get dressed for a little meeting in my district that I promised to attend. I looked in the bathroom mirror at myself and saw that I was a mess. What I saw in the mirror was a man who did not need to go anywhere that night to meet anyone.

I really didn't want to see anyone, but duty said that I needed to be there. I dressed and drove the few minutes to the event. There were about twenty people in the room and they asked me to say a few words. I went to the podium and looked out at the sad faces gathered in front of me. Without saying a word, the tears started to flow. I said, "I am so sorry, but this is not a time that I can say anything."

If I remember right, besides those few words, I didn't say anything to anyone else. I walked out of the hall and back to my car. I sat there trying to decide just what to do. After several minutes, I drove home. I knew I needed to be in San Antonio by early afternoon the next day. Bill was going to fly me to Alexandria to make my speech and back to San Antonio to pick up my car. The speech was written for the most part, and the plans were made. Everything was in place. I needed to go on, but I didn't know if I could.

I didn't sleep much that night but I got up early the next morning to pack and leave for my two-hour drive. It was April 5th and the bluebonnets along the Texas road were in full bloom. I can't remember if I ever really looked at them before, but they were vibrantly blue that morning. It might be that the tears in my eyes made them seem bluer then ever. Whatever it was, I took them in as if I'd never seen them before. It's a memory that is with me still: the rolling roadside, both left and right, covered with blooming bluebonnets. However, my mind was not with them, but with the several times I spent with my friend Martin. I thought over the things he said to me. I remembered them almost word for word, the serious things and his joking about this and that. I remembered waving to him as he got on the plane back to Atlanta just a few months earlier. That was the last time I saw him.

Even to this day, every time I see bluebonnets, I think of him. From time to time, I even find myself crying. That morning made an indelible mark on me, and time has not and will not remove it.

The time went by so fast that before I knew it, I was pulling up into the driveway of the San Antonio hotel. I cried for a day and a half. I was invited to the opening program of the Exhibition and needed to pull myself together for the event.

It went well, without any more tears. I remembered meeting long-time diplomat and ambassador George Allen, who recounted his trip to the interior of Australia. When new ambassadors come to any country, they meet with the head of state. In Australia's case, Allen was told that he needed to meet with the prime minister. In his meeting, he was told by the prime minister that he should visit the indigenous tribes of Australia to get a real feel for the country and all its people.

He said that the date was set for his visit and when the day came, he caught a flight that morning to somewhere in the interior of the nation. He then boarded a train. After an hour or so the train stopped, they got on a little boat, and off into the Outback they went. He then came upon a tribal city. His guide spoke to the people who greeted them and they went to meet with the chief.

After much bowing, Allen came upon this man dressed in an outfit that he'd never seen before. The man was older and the years and wisdom was etched on his face. The man's face was painted, and it really looked like he was in charge of something. With that getup and paint, he had to be a king or a chief, someone of real importance.

The guide, who was one of several in Allen's visiting delegation, was his interpreter. He introduced Allen to the chief in the chief's language. After many long conversations in a different language, he heard the interpreter say the word Texas. In perfect sounding English, the chief turned to Allen and said with a big smile, "Neiman Marcus!"

Silence filled the space for a few seconds, then everyone laughed. It turns out that the only money that got to the tribe was from Neiman Marcus, a chain of luxury department stores based out of Dallas, Texas. Their representative came to see the tribal art that the tribe did. He bought several things and a significant amount of money came to the tribe so they could finally buy things that they needed from the outside would.

That was the only time I ever met Ambassador George Allen, but his story was so Texan that I've never forgotten it.

After the Exhibition's opening ceremonies were done, I went back to my hotel room to collect my things for the trip to Alexandria. At the airport, Bill was standing next to his Cessna 150 that he and I flew on a number of times. The 150 is a four-seat single engine little aircraft that many people use to learn to fly. It's also one that will get you into small airports that are not for commercial airplanes. On every trip we took, he would teach me maneuvers that would improve my skills in the airplane. I tossed my bag into the luggage compartment and buckled myself into the right seat. He cranked the engine and we went down the taxi way and onto a runway.

Off we flew to northwestern Louisiana. We took turns flying until it was dark. I didn't have any after-dark instrument training, so Bill took over. We were flying about an hour in the darkness before we reached the general aviation airport on the outskirts of Alexandria. The instruments said that we were there. We could see the aviation light signals on the tower. However, besides the light turning red and then white, there were no lights or any other indications that there was an airport below us.

Bill picked up the mic for the radio and said, "Alexandria Airport tower, this is Cessna 1780 requesting landing instructions."

There was no answer for nearly a minute.

He repeated, "Alexandria Airport, Alexandria Airport Tower, this is Cessna 1780, are you there?"

Again, there was no answer.

"Alexandria, Alexandria, my instruments say that I am over your airport, and I don't see any lights for your runways."

A somewhat timid voice finally came back to us. "The tower isn't manned after dark, but I know how to turn on the lights."

Bill responded, "What runway should we land on?"

The voice said, "I'm just cleaning up, I don't know anything about runways."

Within a few seconds, lights came on.

We lined up on a brightly lit runway and set up for a landing. Bill sat it down and took out a flashlight to see just where we should park. The one headlight on the airplane did not give us any side vision, so the flashlight had to be how we would find a place to park. After a little hunting, we found a place between two other small planes and shut the engine down.

There was the turning light on top of the tower and another lighted building in the distance that we started walking towards. Besides the runway lights and the turning light, the single light in the distance was the only light around. As we grew closer, we could see that it was a fire station. The big doors were open and one fire truck was sitting there by its lonesome.

As we walked through the big doors, I said in a loud voice, "Is anybody here?"

We stood still to see if we could hear anything, but there was no response.

I saw a phone on a desk in the corner and went over to pick it up. Just as I started to dial 411 to get an operator, a door on the back wall opened and there stood a white man in long johns with a large shotgun in his hand. The gun was pointed at us. From our perspective, the gun looked like a cannon. It might have been something like a 12-gauge shotgun, but it looked bigger.

"What are you doing?" the man asked in a real heavy southern drawl.

Bill, who was white, sensed that it was his time to speak up and speak up fast. "We just landed, and we're trying to get a cab to get into town," he said somewhat nervously.

The man was tall and thin, with one of those faces that you've seen in movies. To say the least, that face was not going to smile anytime for any reason. He lowered his gun slightly and said, "This is the fire department's phone."

Sheepishly, Bill asked, "Well, do you have a payphone?"

By this time, I was looking to see if his Klan robes were hanging on the back wall inside the open door. I must admit that I could feel something that made the hair stand up on the back of my neck. Without changing his expression or his stance with the shotgun, he shook his head from side to side. That was a hard no and both of us could feel it.

"Well, can we use this phone to make one call to get a cab?" Bill asked in a non-threatening, please-don't-shoot-us-mister voice.

"Yea," he responded reluctantly.

I picked up the phone and dialed the operator to get information. As soon as I heard a voice, I said as quickly as I could, "I'm at the airport and looking for a cab."

"What's the name of the cab company you want?" the lady responded in one of those real nasally Lily Tomlin voices.

I could just see her doing her "One ringy dingy, two ringy dingy" bit from the *Rowan & Martin's Laugh-In* variety show, popular at the time. But this was not the time for me to be thinking about Lily Tomlin. I had a man with a shotgun that looked like a cannon pointing in my direction and a lady on the phone asking me questions.

"Can you tell me what cab companies you have?" I answered.

"I cannot give you a name. You have to tell me."

Now this was one of those times that you have to be creative. A big white man with a gun pointed in my general direction stood in front of me and a woman on the phone worked me over with Lily Tomlin questions. Out of nowhere, inspiration struck. If there was a Black cab company in this town, it just might be named Harlem. Without any hesitation I said, "The Harlem Cab Company."

Sure enough, she quickly gave me the number. I wrote the number on my hand because I didn't have anything else to write on. I sure wasn't going to ask shotgun man for some paper.

I pushed the switch hook and released it. While I dialed the number, I thanked that good old spirit for the inspiration.

Now just think about it. How do you let people know that you're a Black cab company in a small Louisiana town? Well, you name it something like "Harlem."

"How do I tell the cab company where to pick us up?" I asked the fireman. "Where is this station located on the airport?"

He told me what to say and the cab was there in short order, but that fireman never did put the shotgun down. He didn't know what to make of two men, one white and the other Black, who awoke him that night. We were a set of salt and pepper intruders in his firehouse late at night. We didn't look like we could be trusted.

After the cab picked us up, we checked in to the hotel where we had reservations and the next morning, I was to be the keynote speaker at the opening session of the Louisiana Teachers' Association conference.

When I arrived at the conference venue the next morning, the host greeted me warmly. There seemed to be three or four hundred teachers in the room. The meeting was opened and within a few minutes, I was introduced to do my thing.

I began and within a few minutes, the tears started flowing. As I looked up from my notes, I could see many others crying, too. I was able to get through it, but it wasn't easy. I stopped several times to get myself together. I remember someone in the first few rows saying loud enough for everyone to hear, "It's alright."

I told the group about my call from Rabbi Cahana. I think that helped them understand what I was working through. When I was done, I stayed around for another hour and excused myself. I have no memory of the return trip to San Antonio. I picked up my car and drove back to Houston in somewhat of a fog. I do remember the bluebonnets giving me some comfort, but it wasn't much. It was almost like someone else was driving.

Dr. King's shooting and death was more than most people in the nation could deal with. There were riots in several cities. The back-to-back TV coverage made it look like Washington, D.C., Chicago, Detroit, and several other cities were burning down. The National Guard was called out, major parts of several cities were burned, and it seemed like the fabric of our nation was coming apart. At the end of the riots, it was determined that more than forty people were killed and damage incurred in over one hundred American cities. This had a profound effect on the nation's psyche. People were angry and they took it out in several places and in strange ways. I didn't go out for nearly anything until the funerals were all over.

The nation was shocked. It was all the nightly news and breaking into programs during the day. It went on every night for more than two weeks.

I remember calling Nadine Eckhardt a few days after I returned, telling her that I was really depressed. "Bob will be in on Thursday evening, and you should come over and spend the weekend with us," she said. "We're having a cookout on Saturday for several of the national news reporters. You would enjoy meeting them."

I took her up on the offer and was there when Bob arrived. We had a quiet dinner that night and talked about the reaction in the streets after King's death. The TV was still showing smoke rising from several cities. We spent Friday getting ready for the cookout the next day. Among the national reporters were representatives from AP and UPI, and I believe one was from the *New York Times.*

They arrived in early evening, and we worked around the property looking at the little creek about fifty feet from the main house. It was a Bob Eckhardt design. The ground floor was just his junk and mostly open. The living part was all on the second floor with a walkway nearly around two sides. There were four or five bedrooms and two bathrooms. A big great room with an oversized fireplace dominated one end of the house. There was enough room for the guests to stay over, but they made arrangements at a local hotel.

After several drinks seated outside around a fire that we cooked our steaks over, one of the reporters said that he heard something very interesting earlier that week. He heard that a person was let out of jail to murder King. The same guy said that he also heard that the person would be caught in a few days at a London airport. They knew where he was and it was just a matter of time. That night, listening to that story with our faces lit only by the backyard fire, has haunted me for years. I've replayed it in my mind more times than I can remember.

Things came to pass nearly just as the reporter had said in Eckhardt's backyard. James Earl Ray, the accused assassin, "escaped from jail." He was caught at the London airport trying to get through customs. Way too much of what was said around that fire that night came true for it all to have been a coincidence. James Earl Ray was a known racist but a financially determined criminal. His major crimes included the robbery of two banks, which landed him a twenty-year sentence in a Missouri prison from which he escaped. Did he escape? Or was he let out?

Evidence surrounding Ray's case determined that it was impossible that he acted alone and the only motive he would've had to do the job is money. Records showed that he went to several cities trying to decide where to do it. The bigger question of who paid Ray off remained. He had enough money after getting out of jail to move around from city to city, go to Canada, and then get a ticket to London. Someone knows, but will history ever tell us the truth?

Something about the King assassination still doesn't feel right to me even after all these years. Something went down funny and I might not live long enough to find out the real truth. It just might be like the Kennedy assassination. We might not ever know the real story. However, what we *do* know is that it's something that this nation will long remember. Martin Luther King, Jr., the lead advocate for racial change, was gunned down on a balcony in Memphis, Tennessee. He was there in support of sanitation workers, the garbage collectors, and died with a single, well-placed shot.

James Earl Ray did not have a conventional trial, but he was sentenced to life or 99 years in prison. After his conviction, he recanted his confession and argued that he was forced into the shooting and later, he claimed that he didn't have anything to do with the shooting at all. On April 23, 1998, thirty years after he took King's life, he died in a Nashville, Tennessee prison. He left behind the many uncertainties of the truth surrounding Dr. King's death.

Historians are still trying to figure out King's contributions to the nation. A colossal statue sitting on the National Mall in Washington, D.C. does not tell the story. Like Medgar Evers, Emmett Till, and so many others who gave their lives to make us a more "perfect nation," the assassination of Dr. King pushed the country to start looking at itself for what it is.

At the time, I thought that his death might have been a wake-up call to the nation. I thought that change might come quicker. In his final days, King's focus was more on the economic inequities that make it nearly impossible for a Black child to reach full potential. Now here we are, more than five decades later, still fighting many of the same battles he fought then.

King once said, "The arc of the moral universe is long, but it bends toward Justice." I didn't think that it would take this long to bend. I'm still hopeful about the bending of the arc, but I want it to happen faster.

John Lewis said in an article published in the *New York Times* on the day of his own funeral, "Ordinary people with extraordinary vision can redeem the soul of America by getting in what I call good trouble, necessary trouble. Voting and participating in the democratic process are key. The vote is the most powerful nonviolent change agent you have in a democratic society. You must use it because it is not guaranteed. You can lose it."

Martin Luther King, John Lewis, and many others have helped us galvanize the nation, both white and black, to move in the direction towards that justice we still need and are working for. It might be my grandchildren that see the true justice that King referenced, but I still have that optimism and I still say that it *will* happen.

TWELVE

THE LOSS OF A WAVING FRIEND

We lost Joe Lockridge in a plane crash between sessions. Isn't it ironic that our paths crossed that very day? I was on my way to Dallas to make a speech on May 3, 1968 and caught an early morning flight from Houston Hobby Airport. Joe just came off the incoming flight. We spoke briefly, then both went on our way. I learned later that someone was waiting to take him to make a speech at Prairie View A&M College (now University). Because it was Braniff Airlines, a company known for a quick turnaround, they were boarding the flight for Dallas nearly as soon as the incoming passengers were off the plane.

I had a meeting of some kind in Dallas and a speech to make. It all went as planned and I returned to Houston that same afternoon. Lockridge remained at Prairie View most of the day and caught a flight back to Dallas just around dark. Braniff Flight 352 encountered a severe thunderstorm and in the attempt to turn around, the Lockheed L-188 Electra turboprop plane broke apart and crashed near Dawson, sixty miles or so from Dallas Love Field. 85 people, including the crew, were killed.

It was a real loss. Lockridge's second primary election was in a few weeks and surprisingly, he received a posthumous vote of 76,696; 8,000 more than he received in his first run when he was still alive.

Honestly, I never really knew Joe Lockridge. We mostly exchanged small talk and waved at each other from a distance, but it's sad to say I never *really* got to know him.

His father was a Baptist minister and pastor for more than twenty years at Golden Gate Baptist Church in Dallas. His undergraduate degree was from Southern University in Baton Rouge and his law degree was from Howard University. While reading Vernon Jordan's book, I learned that he was actually Jordan's roommate at Howard.

By all accounts, Joe Lockridge was really a good guy. I found out many years after his death that he was on the board of directors of the Urban League and Dallas County Mental Health Commission. Because he was small in stature and soft-spoken, I think he might have been underestimated.

Within a few months of Lockridge's death, a special election was called to fill his seat. The Dallas community elected Reverend Zan Wesley Holmes, Jr., a prominent minister of Saint Luke Community United Methodist Church in Dallas. It was and still is one of the largest United Methodist churches in Dallas. Holmes graduated *cum laude* from Huston-Tillotson University in Austin and holds two degrees from Southern Methodist University. At SMU he served as an adjunct professor for 24 years. In 2001, Holmes was recognized as one of the civil rights movement's "invisible giants." Holmes was more of his own man from the get-go compared to Lockridge. With his church and Dallas's entire Black community behind him, he could stand on his own.

Joe Lockridge was selected by the Dallas conservative Democratic community. Holmes, on the other hand, came with the church and a larger Black community behind him.

Once Zan and I got to know each other, we bonded. Our friendship has lasted for more than fifty years. He recalls more stories about me than I can even remember about myself. He told me recently that he built many sermons on the experiences we shared in Austin.

In August of that year, the Democratic National Convention was held in Chicago. I was selected as an alternate delegate from Texas. That meant that if a regular delegate could not attend, I would serve in their place. It gave me a seat at the convention but not on the floor with the voting delegates, so I made arrangements to go to the convention. Always mindful of my finances, I asked my first cousin, Fallon Williams, who lived on the south side of Chicago, if I could stay with him and his wife. He happily agreed, so I was soon off to the Windy City for my first national political convention.

The convention venue was the International Amphitheatre. It was a big barn-looking building some distance from downtown Chicago and most of the happenings at places like the Conrad Hilton Hotel on Michigan Avenue.

Along with several other liberals in the state, I got involved in organizing a challenge delegation to the regular Texas appointed delegation. My argument was that Governor Connally, or really President Johnson, picked the delegates and they didn't really represent the majority of the Democrats in the state. The flavor of the selected delegates was much whiter and richer than the rank-and-file membership. We held several statewide meetings and I was selected to argue the case for more diversity in the delegation.

The real truth was that I didn't have enough people who could afford to get to Chicago in time to attend the convention.

At best, all I was really hoping for was some kind of compromise. With the backing of some big money liberals, I might've been able to get another ten or fifteen people to fill more of the delegate seats.

I flew to Chicago and was picked up by my cousin Fallon. The next day, August 24, two days before my birthday and the opening gavel of the convention, I arrived at the beautiful Conrad Hilton Hotel. The challenges were going to be heard before the credentials committee, which convened at the Hilton. Since the hearing was set for the next day, I went early to get the lay of the land. I hoped I could do some networking that would help me at my hearing.

I was able to meet with Representative Julian Bond and Representative Ben Brown, who were heading up the challenge delegation from Georgia. I met Rep. Bond at the White House conference and discussed his approach at the credentials committee. He introduced me to Fannie Lou Hamer, who was leading the Mississippi challenge delegation. Hamer was a person who had more than paid her dues. She was the perfect person to lead the Mississippi delegation. The Democrats in Mississippi never included a Black person in their delegation.

Word amongst the challengers was that both Georgia and Mississippi might be seated. I didn't know if I had a chance, but it was my job to make the case. The credentials committee was the official committee that determined who would be seated as a regular voting delegate at the convention. If any changes were going to be made to who would be seated on the convention floor, it was going to be made by that committee.

On Monday morning, I ran into Bernard Rapoport. He was a wealthy insurance executive from Waco, Texas who was known as a big contributor to liberal causes in the state. In the back of my mind, I thought he might pay for some of our Latino and Black activists to attend if I were able to win some additional seats. "Curtis, so good to see you!" he exclaimed. "I have a bunch of tickets to a 250-dollar-a-plate luncheon that is about to start in an hour. Would you like a few tickets?"

"I'm alone, Mr. Rapoport," I said.

He didn't hesitate. "Well here, just take one. But if you think you might run into someone that you would like to go with, take a second one."

Uncertain, I took the two tickets. I still didn't understand how fundraising events worked, with major donors buying entire tables and often passing out the seats. However, I wasn't a fool. I'd never eaten a $250 lunch before and figured it would have to be good.

We hugged and I thanked him. I was able to learn what hotel he was staying at so I could ask for some cash to get some additional liberals to the convention just in case I was able to get a few more delegates seated. This was before cell phones, so the only way to reach him in Chicago was at his hotel. He gave me all the necessary information and I watched him go on his way.

Not more than a few minutes later, I ran into U.S. Senator Ralph Yarborough from Texas. I first met him at the farm workers' march on Austin in 1966 and we became friends. I saw him several times on the campaign trail and he came to visit me and Lauro in our offices during the 1967 session. He greeted me with a big embrace. The Mexicans call it an *embrazo*. He acted like I was his long-lost brother who he hadn't seen in years.

"What are you doing now?" he asked.

"I was given these tickets to the Victory luncheon by Barney Rapoport."

Ralph looked at the tickets. "You can sit with me. I'm at the table with Senator McCarthy."

Ralph formally endorsed Eugene McCarthy, the two-term Senator from Minnesota. He was the only sitting senator to do so. I met McCarthy at a rally in Houston several months earlier

with Bob Eckhardt. I gradually came to share his views in opposition to the Vietnam War. It was the hottest issue in the run-up
to the political conventions and the presidential election. People
were protesting all over the country and we knew it was going
to be a major point of contention both inside and outside of the
Democratic Convention.

We relaxed for a few minutes in the lobby, greeting people
coming and going, and running into several people I knew including, unexpectedly, my cousin and Fallon's sister, Carolyn
Williams. She was working in Chicago and had business in the
hotel unrelated to the convention. I was delighted to see her since
I knew I might not be able to spend any time with her during my
stay in the city.

After a short chat, Ralph and I made our way to the luncheon. It was about what you would expect at a luncheon during

Nick Rays, Lauro Cruz, Curtis and Senator Ralph Yarborough © Curtis Graves

the Democratic National Convention in 1968. Dignitaries from all over, including many Senate and House members and, if I remember it right, Vice President Humphrey, soon to be the nominee, made a quick appearance, said a few words, and left to fry even bigger fish.

The lunch was fine, but frankly it wasn't much different from a $25/plate luncheon back home except for the Democratic luminaries in the room. Not quite thirty years old and still a relative political novice, I must admit that I felt quite special sitting at the table with several U.S. senators and a few well-known members of the U.S. House of Representatives. Yes, I was in "high cotton" and I could hardly see over it. If you were raised in the south, you know about high cotton. But this high cotton was even higher than that. It was so high that I was on my tiptoes all the time just to see to the other side of the table.

When the luncheon was over, Senator McCarthy invited us up to his suite for a drink. It was on the fourth or fifth floor. The two senators led me through the sea of hands reaching out to them and after a few stops, we were on the elevator.

The suite had a large sitting room that we rested ourselves in. We were making drinks for ourselves when we heard noise outside the window facing Michigan Avenue. Senator McCarthy looked out. He raised the window and signaled for us to come over. (This was back in the days when big hotel windows could be opened.) The three of us looked out to our left. Coming down Michigan Avenue towards us were two mules pulling a wagon down the street led by none other than Reverend Ralph David Abernathy and Reverend Jesse Jackson along with many others walking with one hand on the mules or the wagon.

It was the Poor People's March coming to demonstrate at the National Convention. The "Miracle Mile," as Michigan Avenue is called, was blocked in that direction by Black protesters following the mules and wagon for as far as the eye could see.

Across Michigan Avenue was a park facing the lakefront. National Guard troops stood with fixed bayonets and many of Mayor Richard Daley "The First" police were mixed in with the Guard. They were facing a crowd of anti-war protesters. In a distance to the right, in Grant Park, we could see smoke rising from tear gas canisters that were flying over the crowd. It was a mess, to say the least.

We hung our heads out the window of the Conrad Hilton Hotel like three children. We were shocked at what was happening below us. After several minutes of just looking, McCarthy slowly pulled his head in. I could see a tear in his eyes. I was the last to pull my head in and closed the window. The three of us sat in silence for several minutes over what we'd seen. Tears were flowing from all of us.

We all had the same question. *Just what was happening to our nation?* A mule and wagon on the streets was protesting the poverty and everything else that was happening in Black America. The protesters across the street focused on the war in Vietnam. To top all of that, tear gas flew all over Grant Park. Stunned, we three men, all government representatives, just sat with our drinks in the hotel suite, saying nothing.

Later, as I left the hotel to find a cab to the south side of the city, I got my first whiff of tear gas; the odor was heavy in the air. I walked down East Balbo Avenue, away from Grant Park, where the gas was coming from. I must have walked for a mile before I could find a cab to take me to my cousin's house on the south side.

The next day, I was scheduled to appear before the credentials committee. There were several challenges to be heard before mine. Fannie Lou Hamer, the lifelong activist from Mississippi who I'd just met the day before, was the first. Her argument was that Blacks were eliminated from the regular Mississippi delegation. This elimination didn't just happen in 1968, it had been happening as long as anyone can remember. As a matter of fact, the last time a Black person was a delegate to a National Convention from the great state of Mississippi was during Reconstruction. That delegate represented the state of Mississippi at the National Republican Convention.

Her argument was compelling. She looked like an aggrieved person and there was years and years of history to back her up. The word around the hall was that she and her challenge delegation would all be seated. As I look back at it now, I really don't see how her delegates could *not* be seated.

The next person to testify was Georgia Representative Julian Bond. He, too, said that the regular Georgia delegation didn't represent the rank-and-file Democrats of Georgia. It was also all white and he had the long history of Georgia and its segregated past on his side.

Julian was articulate and did a great job of representing the real Democrats of Georgia. The word in the hall was again that the committee might seat Julian's delegation when they went into their closed session after all challenges were heard.

I was the next in line. When Texas was recognized, I identified myself as the spokesman for the Texas challenge. I made an impassioned speech against the hand-picked delegates who received credentials. The governor added a few minorities to the delegation but they were not representative of neither the Blacks nor the Hispanics in the state. They were, in my view, essentially tokens of Governor John Connally. For the governor and the president, money was more of a criterion to be a delegate than the diversity of the Democratic majority of the state. I'm sure some were wondering about me. Who was I, a freshman member of the Texas State House, to challenge the president of the United States and the governor of the great state of Texas? The same governor that had been shot in the car with President Kennedy?

I was not opposed by the governor or even the head of the delegation. Instead they sent M. J. Anderson, a Black political

18   *From Behind the Screen*

friend of the governor from Galveston. In his remarks in opposition of me, he said that the delegation was in fact representative of the state population. "Look at me and [Texas Senator] Barbara Jordan," he said. "We are members of the delegation."

He went on for a bit talking about the process of choosing the Texas delegates. To complete the illusion, Governor Connally added in several wealthy Hispanics and Latinos to add some spice to the mix. But two grains of pepper and a sprinkling of cinnamon powder didn't season the delegation enough for anyone to really taste the difference.

When my time came, I was angry and my rebuttal reflected that. "You see that man who just spoke to you? You might think by looking at him that he is Black. But he is not. He is just sprayed that color by Governor Connally to make you think that Blacks are represented in the Texas delegation."

That statement made the national news that night on all three major networks.

However, I realized that a compromise was already reached. The challenge delegations brought by Georgia and Mississippi would be seated, but it was decided that the Texas challenge would be an embarrassment to the president if we would also be seated. I suspected this outcome before the committee even went into their closed session. Until the last moment, I was still hoping for some kind of Hail Mary Texas compromise to gain just a few more seats for our side, but the compromise did not break in my favor. The two state challenges would be seated and the third, ours, would be denied. With all the heavyweights on the other side, I'm pretty sure that if I would have added to the Hail Mary, "Full of grace, the Lord is with thee," I still wouldn't have been able to seat my challengers.

M. J. Anderson's remarks also made the national news that night. We actually became quite good friends. If I needed something from the governor, I could call Anderson late at night and it would be done. We always had to make it his idea, but if it was something that needed to be done, I didn't care *whose* idea it was.

I took my defeat as best as I could and attended the convention the next day with Senator Yarborough. It's hard to believe that the sitting U.S. senator from Texas wasn't a credentialed delegate. As alternate delegates, he and I had seats right off the convention floor. We were not able to vote, but at least we were there.

From a PR point of view, I didn't have much to complain about. From our first-row balcony seats, just three or four feet off the floor, we could see everything that was happening at the convention and could be seen by everybody as they passed. It just so happened that our seats were right behind the Texas delegation on the floor, and it turned out to be a really great location. We were situated where the press roaming the floor could interview us without anyone standing or sitting in our way. John Chancellor of NBC and several others spotted the senator and stopped by to interview the both of us on several subjects.

A few times during lulls in the convention proceedings, I roamed the floor to visit with friends and make some new contacts. Visiting Julian Bond in the Georgia delegation, he introduced me to several Black elected officials who were brand new delegates from Georgia.

We traveled by bus back and forth to the International Amphitheatre, adjacent to the Stock Yard on Halstead Street. That first night when the buses returned us to the Hilton on Michigan Avenue, it was a real mess. The protests in Grant Park grew and Mayor Daley vowed to keep the peace. Instead of calm, shots were fired, arrests were made, and the park was full of National Guard troops wearing gas masks and holding their bayoneted rifles out to keep the protesters back. It truly resembled a war zone. I stood on the corner of Michigan and Balbo Avenues and thought to myself that it was the worst thing I'd ever seen in my life. A riot generated by the Chicago P.D. and the National Guard, where shots were being fired at U. S. citizens, all because they were expressing their opposition to a war they—and I—considered unjust.

That night I nearly walked the entire way to the south side since I couldn't find a cab for several miles. I did make it, but it was in the wee hours of the morning before I put my key in my cousin Fallon's front door. Oh, it was so good to be in Fallon's house! I felt safe from all that was going on in the downtown Chicago streets. He and I sat and talked for hours about what I witnessed. I learned later that the mayor shut the city down for several hours. That accounted for the fact that I couldn't find a cab anywhere. The downtown streets were closed and traffic came to a standstill.

Well, the convention ended with Vice President Hubert Humphrey being nominated for president, but many large wounds were opened and the healing wouldn't come to the nation for years. As it turned out, Richard Nixon was elected president and took the nation on a ride in a different direction.

Two days later, I caught a flight back to Houston a changed man. I thought to myself that I became a veteran, not only of my first national political convention, but also of the battle for America. It left battle scars all over me. I really was a different person than the one that flew into Chicago only a few days earlier. I saw raw power exercised by city, state, and federal authorities. It was frightening and not something very many people see in their lifetime. Besides the civil rights protests, I'd never seen a powerful city like Chicago turn on people demonstrating in their streets. I'd never really seen the power of the federal government turned on citizens like that. The city, state and federal government turned on its own people.

The next Sunday I attended church. The priest decided to focus his sermon that day on the "rioting thugs" at the Democratic National Convention in Chicago. To say the least, the word *"thugs"* hit me hard. Catholic churches are very quiet when the priest gives his weekly sermon, but the whole time he spoke it was like someone was sticking a cattle prod up my rear end. I simply could not let it go. I needed to address it and knew right then that that moment was the perfect time. When mass was finished, I made my way to the church sacristy to wait for him.

The priest was a small, rotund white man in his late fifties. He opened the door of the walnut-paneled room followed by two Black altar boys. Still dressed in his vestments for mass, he looked surprised, but I'm sure he knew exactly who I was. Mindful that I was in the sacristy of my parish, I spoke softly. "Father, I would like to talk to you about your sermon."

He was silent, but I could read the look on his face. It said, "Well *boy*, what do you have to say?"

I saw and understood that look on many white people who thought their power was being challenged. I knew it was going to be difficult for him to even *hear* what I was saying, so I needed to speak with the authority of a person who knew what I was talking about and was not going to back down.

Slowly and deliberately, I said, "Father, did you go to the Convention in Chicago last week?"

He looked at me and I could see he was puzzled. "No," he answered. He clearly was not happy to be questioned by the likes of me. It might've been the first time that someone challenged him about one of his sermons.

"Well, how would you know that the anti-war protestors were tough?" I got a little worked up, but was determined to stay calm, respecting the surroundings.

His fat white face turned as red as a Washington apple in midsummer.

"That's what I saw on TV all last week." The words tumbled out of his mouth, but his face did not return to its normal shade. In fact, it was glowing redder.

"What you saw was a riot started by police and the National Guard, not a riot started by peaceful protesters."

He backed up against the walnut-paneled wall like he thought I was going to hit him. The two Black altar boys who could've been ten or eleven years old stood there like they didn't know what to expect next. I wondered later that day, if I did move towards him, what side they would have been on.

I wasn't done saying my piece. "The protesters might have been the ones who went to jail, but they never rioted. The rioting, if that's what you want to call it, was only on the side of the Chicago Police and the National Guard."

It was clear I wasn't going to make a convert out of him. That is, if I can say convert when referring to a priest in a Catholic church. But I made my point. A member of his church stood up to him and wouldn't take his political biases.

It might not have come to him that day, but I'm pretty sure that sooner or later he would realize that he was the pastor of a mostly all-Black church and there were many people in his congregation who could think for themselves. In other words, he needed to stay in his lane. Religion was his game. Stay out of politics if you're white and want to pastor a church with a Black congregation.

In any case, I no longer felt welcome at that church, so I moved to Our Mother of Mercy, which wasn't too far away. The priest there was friendly. As a matter of fact, it was the church that I belonged to when I first met Senator Hank Grover and where the pastor suggested that I should contact its members to open accounts at Standard Savings when I was the branch manager there.

There were some lessons learned from the events at the Democratic National Convention. The first was that autocratic rule like Mayor Daley was known to enforce in Chicago was not one of the pillars of our democracy. Secondly, state and federal reinforcement of that autocratic rule in the name of public safety does not look good on national and international television. That might have been one of the contributing factors to the Republican win in November of that year.

That display of raw power was very similar to George Floyd dying under the knee of a uniformed police officer in May 2020. Public gassing of United States citizens and the public execution of an unarmed, handcuffed Black man in the streets doesn't make good international television.

Whether it's 1968 or 2020, neither of these events leave an impression on the world of our nation being a shining beacon of democracy.

THIRTEEN
THE TEXAS DEPARTMENT OF CORRECTIONS

The summer of 1968 turned out to be a busy summer for me. I received a call from a constituent who told me that her son, an inmate at the Huntsville Correctional Facility, was being abused. She was getting nowhere with the prison authorities and asked me if there was anything I could do to help. I agreed to investigate the situation.

The Texas State Penitentiary was in Huntsville, Texas. Its nickname is the "Walls Unit." The 54-acre facility is the oldest Texas state prison, opened in 1849. It's hard to believe, but originally the Huntsville unit was only used for white Texans. The only penalties available for Black Texans were whipping and hanging. There are many interesting facts about Huntsville. One is that during the Civil War, prisoners produced tents and uniforms for the Confederate forces in the prison's textile factory. After the Civil War was over, the Huntsville unit was the only prison in the former Confederate States to remain. It is still the site of the largest prison rodeo in the nation.

A few days after I received the call about inmate abuse, I made a call to Huntsville and asked to speak to the warden. After I explained that I was a member of the Texas House of Representatives, he was on the phone in short order.

I introduced myself and said that I would like to come up to visit with him for business that involved one of the inmates. He paused for a few seconds. "How about tomorrow?" he asked.

So far, so good. "What time works for you?"

"How about eleven? After our meeting we can have lunch," he replied.

"Sounds good to me," I answered.

I made the sixty-mile trip the next morning and at eleven I stood outside a twenty-foot high wall at a door of the Huntsville Penitentiary. I gave my name and was received quickly. I was escorted through guarded checkpoints, locked reinforced glass doors, and heavy metal doors. When that was over, I walked through a maze of offices to a large, dark, wooden door. My journey ended in the warden's reception office. I introduced myself to the receptionist and she touched the intercom and announced, "Dr. Beto, Representative Graves is here to see you."

He responded in a deep, low voice, "Bring him in."

She knocked lightly and opened the door. Seated behind a large dark mahogany desk in an oversized office was a tall balding man flashing a welcoming smile. Against the wall behind him was a matching mahogany bookcase filled with law books.

I had done my homework and knew that George Beto ng with being the director of the Texas Department of rrections, had a Ph.D. in criminal justice, taught at one of the cal universities, and was a Lutheran minister. The man had in pressive credentials.

He pointed to a big leather chair in front of his desk. "Please h ave a seat."

I sank into the well-upholstered chair. I learned later

that upholstering was one of the trades that was taught at the Penitentiary. That accounted for the beautiful furnishings in both the outer and inner offices.

"Dr. Beto," I said, looking directly at him. "I wanted to meet with you and talk about one of your inmates."

Still flashing that smile, he responded, "Can I get you some coffee?"

I smiled back. "That would be nice."

He pressed a button on his desk and the receptionist came on the speaker.

"Yes, sir?"

"Could you bring us two coffees, black?" He cupped the phone. "Black is alright for you?"

I nodded. "That's good for me."

After he got off the intercom, I mentioned the inmate again. For anonymity's sake, I'll call the inmate "Jim." I told Beto about the phone call from Jim's mother, who said that Jim was beaten by some guards. He seemed interested in getting to the bottom of any problem, so I asked to see the inmate and talk to him about the incident myself. Dr. Beto relaxed in his chair and agreed to arrange a visit. "But first, let me hear about you," he said.

I gave him the abridged version: I was from New Orleans and moved to Houston to go to college. He was familiar with the culture in New Orleans and told me stories about his appreciation of the good food he had enjoyed there while visiting. I made sure to explain what motivated me to run for office. I wanted him to understand that I wasn't there for any personal aggrandizement.

Before I knew what was going on, we finished our coffee and he was escorting me to lunch. In my mind, we bonded.

Before leaving his office, he stopped at his receptionist's desk and, in his low voice, left some instructions for her. I couldn't hear what he said, but the way she glanced at me made it clear I was the subject.

We walked down the long beige-colored hall with big locks on each of the cell doors we passed. "I have made arrangements for you to see the inmate after lunch," he said.

I thanked him. Turning the corner, we stood in front of a door, where we were greeted by a guard holding keys. He turned the key in a lock and nodded his head. "Sir," he said in a low voice.

We walked into a large dining hall filled with a few hundred inmates—white, Black, and brown. They seemed to have largely segregated themselves by race. They were seated at tables and benches that were fastened—hard-bolted—to the floor. At the other end of the large dining room was a small room with glass and bars where the guards ate. That room had moveable tables and chairs.

About halfway through the room Dr. Beto stopped, looked directly at me, and said, "You know, if I were to leave you here, they would take you hostage and we would have a big problem."

He was unaware that I remembered the incident in that facility in 1974. One inmate, a guy named Fred Gomez Carrasco, led his follow inmates on an eleven-day siege. In the siege Carrasco, who was a Texan and Mexican heroin kingpin, held several prison workers and four inmates hostage.

I met Beto's stare, making sure not to betray any emotion. I knew it was a gamble, but I needed to let him know that I was not a person who would be frightened easily.

"Leave me."

Beto looked at me and seemed to be gauging whether I was serious. I guess he decided that I was.

Without saying a word, he turned towards the guards' room and walked away.

I found a table with an empty seat and went over to sit. I introduced myself to the three Black inmates at the table and started a conversation about conditions in the joint.

From the corner of my eye, I could feel Dr. Beto's intense stare.

As he approached the guards' dining area, someone standing inside the half-reinforced glass door opened it to let him in. The men stood, but he waved his hand to let them know that it was alright for them to continue eating. The guard locked the door behind him.

I was on my own. I sat with the three inmates for ten or fifteen minutes just to let the warden know he was not going to frighten me. As I looked around, I could see guards standing around each of the walls watching the prisoners eat. After all, they did have forks and knives in their hands. They weren't metal, but they were still forks and knives. If someone wanted to start a fight, they could be used as makeshift weapons. None of the prisoners seemed to be on edge, but the guards remained vigilant.

Finally, I got up from the table and shook hands with each inmate at the table. After excusing myself, I slowly made my way to the guards' dining room. A number of inmates from different groups smiled at me as I walked to the end of the room. I nodded to several, even patted several on their backs.

At the door, I was let in and served lunch on a metal tray. I was also given a metal fork and knife. After lunch, we walked back towards Beto's office. I smiled as I passed his secretary.

Beto's demeanor had changed. He tested me and I could tell by his body language that I passed. I stuck to my convictions and would not allow myself to be intimidated by the situation. Moreover, I wasn't going to create any problems for him and might actually do some good. The respect Beto and I gained for each other that day lasted for many years and, as I look back on it now, might have saved lives.

As for the inmates, perhaps they realized that I was there to help them. Of course, it was quite possible that they didn't even know who I was.

Next, I was led to a room with dark wooden walls like that of a pricey law office or a very nice library. I sat alone for a short time before the door opened and a white guard led a large Black man with a shaved head in by the arm. He wasn't handcuffed and seemed to be fully compliant. The inmate wore a loose-fitting orange jumpsuit and sandals and looked very much like Michael Clarke Duncan, the actor in the film *The Green Mile*.

The guard left us alone and closed the door softly behind him. Jim flashed a half-smile and without saying a word, he started to take off his jumpsuit. He stood between me and the door. I couldn't help thinking of different ways to make an escape and get out of the situation. Perhaps I could pick up one of the chairs to fight him off like a lion in the circus.

Fueled by adrenaline, it's strange what goes through your mind.

After he completely stripped and was buck naked on the other side of the room, Jim turned around. "Look at me," he said.

I didn't know what he wanted me to look at, so I just stood there.

"See that I have no marks on my body." He turned all the way around before facing me again.

I still didn't know where this was going.

"The next time you see me, I might not look like this."

I can't imagine what my face must have looked like.

Without saying anything, he put his jumpsuit back on and crossed the room to sit at the table across from me.

Jim's strange behavior and his size made me very nervous, and I had no idea if my fear showed. His mother certainly gave no indication that her son was this huge, menacing looking guy who would scare the hell out of me.

And yet, he spoke softly. "I've been harassed ever since I

got here," he said. "But now that they know you've been here to see me, I'll really be in for it by the guards and their ass-kissing trustees."

We talked for more than an hour. I found him to be an intelligent, well-spoken person who, because of his size, was often picked on. It was at the point that he felt like he was going to lose his temper and do some serious things to get the harassment to stop. His bottom line was a very simple one: he didn't want any additional time added to his sentence.

In my estimation, it was a simple and completely understandable desire. I explained to him that I just met the warden and didn't yet know if he was a straight shooter. However, I told him that I would do my best to protect him from whatever harassment he was experiencing. I wouldn't try to contact him directly. We decided that we would use his mother as a middleman for our communication. I had her number and she had mine. She would let me know how things were going. She would call and let me know if his situation deteriorated.

The funny thing is that I'm not sure I ever knew what he was locked up for. It did not matter. He was a human being with a real problem and he and his mother were my constituents. That was all that *really* mattered. In a representative government, all you want from your elected representative is that they advocate for you.

I knocked on the door and told the guard that our meeting was over. He led Jim away from the room and another guard led me back to Beto's office.

I reported the entire meeting to Dr. Beto. I was later told by Jim's mother that that was the last of any harassment.

What really put an end to it? I'm not sure. Did my intervention convince Beto that he should protect Jim? As you'll see in other parts of my story, my friendship with Beto paid off big time for other inmates. I do remember an instance when intervention came too late and the inmate died. But in several other instances, the old Beto hookup was a real help.

Then there were the boys of Gatesville.

Early in 1969, I started receiving letters from parents of boys that were incarcerated in the Gatesville State School for Boys in Gatesville, Texas. The facility was a large 900-acre juvenile correctional prison that dated back to 1887. The Texas Legislature established the House of Correction and Reformatory not too long after the Civil War. It was the first such facility in the Southern United States. The facility was first operated by the Texas Prison System, opening in January of 1889 with 68 boys. These boys were previously detained at correctional institutions with adult felons.

The reformers who opened the facility intended for schooling and the farmwork in the dry climate to reform the juvenile delinquents. Robert Perkinson, author of *Texas Tough: The Rise of American's Prison Empire* said that the institution gained "a reputation for ruthlessness" as the decades passed.

Throughout the school's history, the state government did not appropriate sufficient funding and the dormitories became overcrowded. From the beginning, school officials complained about the influx of non-white children who they believed to be incapable of rehabilitation. Can you believe that they *openly said* that Black and brown boys were deemed incapable of rehabilitation?

Michael Jewell, a former Gatesville State School student in 1961, said that long periods in solitary confinement, stoop labor, fights between gangs, beatings perpetrated by staff members, and sexual assault frequently occurred at the facility.

The letters that I was receiving were not all from my district, but they were letters that got my attention. For the most part, they were from parents from across the state that felt that they did not know who to go to for relief for their children.

Then one day I received a call that *really* got me going. It was from a mother who said that she was getting letters from her son who was confined at Gatesville, and he was asking her to come to see him. She drove up to the facility and was told that she could not see her child. He was a sixteen-year-old boy and his mother was not allowed to visit with him. One of his letters included the phone number of a friend's mother, and he requested that his mother call her. She did and learned more then she wanted to hear. The friend's mother reported that her child was put in a dormitory that was known to house most of the homosexual Black boys. This was done as punishment for a fight he got into.

The mother also reported that many boys were beaten into signing papers saying that they were homosexual. The deeper I got into this, the more I thought that I needed to see if any of the legislative committees were interested in doing any oversight of the problems at the "Reform School."

The committee chairmen all thought that their roles were purely legislative and did not include oversight at all. I couldn't find anyone who would support me in exposing these atrocities at the hands of state employees. On top of all that, the legislature was continuously funding this facility year after year and there was no accountability.

At wit's end, I decided to take the matters up alone. That was risky and looked like I was grandstanding, but what else could I do? I started by calling to make an appointment to see one boy who was from my district. The facility said that I could see him if I came at the time assigned, so I made the over one hundred-mile drive to see this youngster. They allowed me to see him, but only in the presence of a guard.

Well, you know how that went. The boy didn't tell me a thing. However, I could see and feel the fear coming out of every pore of his skin. He didn't dare say anything that would have caused him harm. I said that his mother asked for me to see him since she was not allowed to visit with him herself.

I asked the facility about it, but they gave me no answer as to why his mother was not allowed a visit. I did everything I could think of to get some answers, but I was stonewalled me at every turn.

What else could I do? I decided to try to shine as much light on the facility's problems as I could. I decided to go public with the reported issues in the hopes that it might stop the abuse that was taking place. I thought that if a parent of a boy that was presently locked up said anything about conditions in the facility, they might come down on that boy so hard that his parent would be reluctant to say too much; I needed some parents of former inmates and present inmates.

At the time, I really didn't know how entrenched the problem was. Gatesville is rural Texas. The facility was, at the time, eighty years old and the only game in town. Fathers passed their jobs on to their sons for so many years that a culture evolved that had nothing to do with rehabilitation. The culture only made sure to keep the lid on the facility and draw a paycheck. It was the only industry and big paycheck in town, and that paycheck had to be protected. Eighty years had passed and the world around them changed, but the facility and its culture had not.

In desperation, I rented a meeting room at a local hotel and called a one-man unofficial hearing. I invited as many parents as possible, parents who would come and to tell their story. Some had boys in the facility and others had boys who'd made it out. Most importantly, the press had to be in the room to record and publish the parents' testimonies. That part was a success. A few newspapers and one TV station did send a reporter. But unfortunately, when the stories died in the press, nothing really changed.

What *did* happen is that I was invited to testify before the United States Senate Juvenile Delinquency subcommittee. I went to Washington, D.C. on July 11, 1969 and told the story, but nothing really happened to give relief to the more than 1,500 boys who were locked up. The 250 staff members kept doing whatever they wanted to do.

As fate would have it, in 1974, when I was out of the Legislature, a lawsuit was filed called *Morales v. Turman*. It was heard before the great East Texas Judge William Wayne Justice. The judge ruled that "the operations of the state schools consisted of cruel and unusual practices that violated the Eighth Amendment to the United States Constitution." In short, Judge Justice ordered that the Gatesville State School for Boys be closed and the state redesign the agency's juvenile corrections system.

I cannot say that I caused this change to occur, but I *can* say that if it were not for my shining some light on the problem, it probably would not have happened by 1974.

FOURTEEN

UNDER SURVEILLANCE

Late in the Johnson administration, I received an invitation from the Texas Young Democrats to give the keynote address at their annual convention in San Antonio. The convention was to be held at the University of St. Thomas, one of the private Catholic colleges in the city.

While writing the speech for the occasion, I decided that it was my time to come out against the Vietnam war. Personally it was a big step; I had never in my life said something publicly against the government of the United States. I was concerned about coming on too strong. After I finished the speech, I called Bob Eckhardt in his congressional office in D.C. to read it to him. After all he was my sounding board, and I knew I could count on him to tell me if I had gone too far.

Art Neville, the eldest of the Neville Brothers has a line in one of his songs: "We all have freedom of speech, as long as you don't say too much."

Eckhardt was my man to make sure I didn't say too much.

He was in his Washington D.C. office when I read the speech

235

to him. He listened carefully, finally saying that it sounded great to him.

What I did not know was that his congressional office phones were tapped by the FBI or some federal agency. As a result of that call, I too became a subject of domestic surveillance. From that moment forward, as I was to learn later, both my home and office phones were bugged. I was also followed by the FBI or their designee from time to time.

In fact, it had been going on for some time.

But at the time I did not know or suspect a thing. So the Saturday arrived for my keynote speech and I was ready. I was not told until I arrived that Congressman Henry B. Gonzales had been asked to introduce me. The University of St. Thomas was located in Gonzales' San Antonio Congressional district.

Henry and I had met several times and we knew each other. Still the Young Democrats gave him my resume so he knew better what to say about me.

As I walked on stage I noticed that among the several hundred attendees, there were a noticeable number of men that looked like they were not Young Democrats at all. Instead of being college age, they looked to be in their late twenties or early thirties. They all seemed to have crew cuts, not exactly the kind of hair cut that was in style among young people in the late sixties.

I also noticed that beside the podium mike for amplification, there was another wire. The wire went down the front of the podium. The fact that there was another cord taped to the floor with gray duck tape caught my attention. It went from a curtain back stage to somewhere inside the podium.

I noticed it but, like the unusual people in the audience, did not think that much of it at the time.

The time came for me to be introduced. Henry B. rose to do

his thing. His introduction was so generous that the audience gave me a standing ovation.

Congressman Gonzales caught a ride on Air Force One each Friday from Washington, DC to San Antonio. The President came home to the LBJ Ranch most weekends and the Lackland Air Force Base at San Antonio was the closest one to his property. I knew that Henry would also be with the President on that Monday morning return trip back to Washington.

So, pumped up by the standing ovation, I thanked my friend Henry for the over the top introduction and with a certain amount of cockiness I emphasized, "I think you should tell the boss what I have to say today."

I probably shouldn't have said that, but I said it. It was also highly unlikely that Congressman Gonzales would tell President Johnson anything. A smart politician like Henry was not going to say anything to Johnson that might get me--or him--in trouble.

But there I was, caught up in the moment and just young and arrogant enough to speak my mind.

However, there was a lot that I didn't realize. Years later I learned that a transcript of my remarks was being made by the FBI and it was delivered to the White House before the week was out.

I wish I had the foresight to save the speech but it is lost to history. However I know that it was seen by many people in the FBI, other federal agencies and in the White House. In essence, what I remember is that I condemned the war as being a crime against Humanity. I said that the only people who were profiting from this is assault against the people of Vietnam was the undertakers and defense contractors.

I think I spoke for about twenty minutes.

I do remember receiving a standing ovation. I was telling the Young Democrats of Texas what they wanted to hear. After all they were of draft age and they might be next to go.

• • •

I began to receive a lot more scrutiny than I deserved. I was informed that the FBI was told to get a story on me to destroy my career.

Then some months later, I received a call from the office of the Catholic Bishop John Morkovsky. He was then coadjutor bishop of the Diocese of Galveston-Houston. His secretary said that he needed to talk to me.

"When would he like for me to come?" I said.

"As soon as you can."

"How about tomorrow at 11:00?"

"The bishop will be waiting for you."

As I hung up the phone with great anxiety. I had seen the Bishop from a distance but I was never close enough to him to speak to him. The truth was that no bishop had ever called me for anything. What had I done? Was I about to be excommunicated? I didn't have an inkling what it was all about, but it didn't sound good.

The next day I was sitting in his outer office at 10:45 AM sharp. If I was going to the executioner, then I wanted it to be done with as soon as it could be.

His secretary picked up the phone and said in a real quiet voice, "Representative Graves is here to see you your Excellency."

"Send him in." I heard in response.

"The Bishop will see you now," she said with a worm smile.

I followed her through a door and "His Excellency", Bishop John Morkovsky was seated behind a large dark wooden desk wearing a big smile.

He jumped up and, to my great surprise, greeted me with a warm handshake and a smile. He was a short man about five foot six or seven. He looked to be about 60 years old. He had somewhat of a ruddy complexion and was dressed in a black suit, black shirt and Roman white collar. Under his coat coming from the left was a gold chain crossing his chest and down to somewhere on the right side of his coat-- a bishops cross was on the end of the chain, but I could not see it. He pointed to a sofa behind a coffee table that had a large over stuffed chair at one end.

"Please have a seat." he said pointing

He offered coffee or something else to drink. I declined.

I guess the guy could see that I was really uptight and did not know what was going to happen to me.

He barely whispered, "Let me get to the point of our visit to relieve your tension."

I guess he could see it all over my face.

"Yes, your Excellency."

I was thankful for my upbringing and knew how to address the bishop. After all, I was raised in a "High Catholic House." I was taught from an early age how to address priests, bishops, cardinals and for that matter the Pope, if I should ever encounter one.

More than his words, the tone of his voice indicated that he was going to tell me something that he did not want anyone else to know.

"An agent of the government who is Catholic, has come to me with some information that he wants me to share with you."

"Oh?" My immediate thought was that this was not about anything I had done. I could feel my tension easing a little.

"The agent has been told to get something on you to destroy your political career. They are following you and have bugs on your phones.

The agent did not think it was right, so he asked me to warn, you are a target."

I rolled my eyes in disbelief, but quickly realized the shit I might be in for.

The bishop had some advice for me. "Be careful where you go and with whom. They just want a story to take you down.

I really don't want that to happen. Do whatever you need to do so they will never have a story. Protect yourself as best you can without compromising your political positions."

"Without compromising your political positions," stuck in my head. He did not think I was going over the edge but just wanted me to think about what others might think.

I was married to Joanne Gordon by this time, and I thought to myself that anything that I said or did could be taken out of context to make me, or my family, look bad in the eyes of the public. I was quiet for a long moment. Then I said, "Your Excellency, I would like that cup of coffee now."

He reached over to the little end table between us and picked up the phone.

"Would you bring us two cups of coffee with cream and sugar please?"

I thought to myself, this man might be small but he commands respect..

"Be careful of any women you might be with. They might try to make something out of it."

I don't think that he thought I might have a problem with some other women in my life, But he was just warning me that this is the kind of thing that they might try to use against me.

As I drank my coffee and listened to my bishop I realized that the Gods must have smiled on me that day. I was lucky. What would have happened if it were not for an FBI agent, or whatever agent, who thought that it was not right? If it were not for the fact that the bishop had a heart and also was not a racist?

I thanked him, shook his hand and kissed his ring. After all, as a good Catholic I knew that is how you respond to a bishop. But this bishop was also really trying to save my political career. I should have kissed that ring at least twice. Well, today I think that a triple kiss would not have been too much.

I went home and relayed the story. As I grew comfortable

with the fact that I was under surveillance, I started to mess with anybody who was listening. I would call home and say mysterious sounding things that might get their attention. I just wanted to toy with them.

I did have trouble with my phone. The home phone would have a lot of static many days, so I would call the phone company. They came out one time and found a device on the telephone pole and told me about it.

We learned to live with it. That was the price I had to pay for being black, outspoken and in public life at the time.

Not too many months after that , word came out that many black politicians were being spied upon. I made a public statement about it and received a call from a staffer from the committee headed by Senator Sam Ervin III from North Carolina. This was early 1971 and he had not yet become famous nationwide. It was not until mid 1972 that he became a household name during the Watergate committee hearings. It was he, who chaired the committee that uncovered the scandals of President Richard Nixon.

Now he was chair of the Senate Subcommittee on Constitutional Rights. This was one of the Subcommittees of the Senate Judiciary Committee. He chaired many other committees but this was the one that was looking into the government surveillance of ordinary citizens.

Congressman Eckhardt called to tell me that he had written a letter to the Senator about what had happened to me. The letter was dated February 2, of 1971, and it said in part:

"I understand that your Subcommittee on Constitutional Rights will begin hearings at the end of this month on Military spying on civilians. . .I am enclosing an article from the Houston Chronicle on January 28, 1971 concerning a particularly serious series of espionage activities that took place in the Houston area. Two prominent black state legislators, Senator Barbara Jordan and Representative Curtis Graves, were among those reportedly under surveillance.

"Representative Graves has indicated to me that he is both willing and eager to testify before your Subcommittee to discuss this matter..."

Within days I received a call from one of the staffers of the committee saying I would be receiving a formal letter from Senator Ervin asking me to tell the committee what had happened to me.

The letter came and a few weeks later I made the trip to Washington and stayed with the Eckhardts. The hearing was to be held in one of the Senate office buildings. I reported to Senator Ewvin's offices to be briefed about the hearing which was to be held the next day. Within a few minutes, I was sitting in front of the Senator's desk waiting for him. I was told that he was on the floor of the senate casting a vote. His office was large and spacious, although there were too many chairs and other furniture in the room. The walls were crowded with plaques, pictures and other stuff. You could barely see any wall space. I sat there taking it all in when the door opened and he came bolting through the door thanking me for my time and testimony.

This guy was a North Carolina Democrat who had championed segregation for many of the years after his election to the Senate in 1954. Somewhere along the way he mounted another train and became the hero for his support of civil liberties. He was a heavy set man who seemed to have too much skin on his face. It sagged a little on both sides like a bull dog. He liked to call himself a "country lawyer."

I thought to myself that he might not be to kind to little old me a black man from Texas. However, I was wrong. He was a gracious as he could be.

After a few words of greeting and pleasantries, he got right to the point.

"Now, there are some things that you need to know."

"Like what?" I said.

"Well Senator Strom Thurmond is a member of the committee. He is very likely to be there. If he is there, he might be hostile. You know he has a long reputation for being a racist.

At that point I thought to myself that the man talking to me had a long reputation for being a racist. But at this point, the shoe seem to be on the other foot

"He just might try to give you a hard time. Don't let him get to you.

On top of that, he does not hear well. He may ask you to repeat everything you say."

I reassured him. "Senator, you know that I am a member of the Texas House. I have been coming up against his type for a long time."

"Additionally, I was born and raised in New Orleans. People like him can be found on every other corner in most cities in the South."

It also occurred to me that Thurmond, now a Republican, might try to protect the Nixon administration by discrediting my testimony.

His eyes grew large."I will do my best to see to it that he does not do anything if I can."

He then turned me over to his staff people. One of them whose name has been lost to the years from then to now was more then gracious as he and others helped me to walk through my testimony. They all kept telling me that I was going to do just fine. I was used to speaking before audiences, but this was a United States Senate Committee.

By the time of my and others testimony, the evidence that the agency of the government had indeed been spying on U.S. citizens was becoming more widely-known, mostly due to the publicity generated by Senator Erwin's "Subcommittee on Constitution Rights."

The *Houston Chronicle* published an article on January 28, 1971: *"Postman was Army Spy on Civilians in Houston:*

" A Houston postman says once he helped the Army spy on and keep files on such civilians as state Sen. Barbara Jordan , state Rep . Curtis Graves and boxer Muhammad Ali.

"Walter Birdwell, 28, says the spying took place while he was attached to Region IV of the 112th Military Intelligence Corps from 1965-1967, servicing in Austin, San Antonio, and Houston."

"Many of those allegedly spied on said they were angry, but had suspected as much.

"'I'm appalled, disturbed, but not surprised,' said Rep. Graves in Austin. He said he believed for the last four years he was followed and that his telephones were tapped by local police and others.

""I'm happy now that the public is able to understand the kind of pressure I and my family are under,' Graves said."

Journalist and former diplomat Carl Rowan published a piece under the headline, "Military Threatening U.S. Freedom."

The *Washington Star* followed with its own editorial, as did others.

My chance to testify came on February 25, 1971, Bob Eckhardt accompanied me to the Old Senate Office Building, Room 318.

We showed up a little early. The activities reminded me of T. S. Eliot's, "The Love Song of J. Alfred Prufrock:"

"In the rooms the women come and go talking of Michelangelo."

Many women and men seemed to be coming and going whispering in someone's ear. I didn't know that the senate and the committees had so much staff.

The dais was somewhat round but not quite a semicircle. The chairman set in the center and Republican members to his left and Democrats to his right. As I looked at the four or five senators seated, I did not recognize but two besides Senator Ervin. They were Senator Edward Kennedy on one side and Strom Thurmond, on the other. There were a number of reporters with cameras hanging on their necks.

Finally, I heard Senator Ervin asked the Committee Counsel to call the next witness.

"Sir, Our next witness is Curtis M. Graves a State Representative from Texas."

Senator Ervin looked up from his papers. "Mr. Graves, I am delighted to welcome you to the subcommittee. I am glad you could come to give us the benefit of your experience in the field."

At this point I had been asked to sit at a table with my name written on a cardboard sign in front of me.

He went on, "I would like to put in the record some information concerning you which has been sent to me by Congressman Bob Eckhardt."

I was at a table nearly fifteen feet from the dais.

I felt a little nervous but started, "Mr. Chairman I represent the 23rd Legislative District, which is identical to the Eighth Congressional District that Congressman Eckhardt represents. It is a good place, about a third of the city of Houston, Texas and the surrounding county.

"Mr. Chairman, it is indeed unpleasant for me to appear before this subcommittee this morning. It is unpleasant because of the fact that the things that have happened to me tend to make more people lose faith in the American system. When we think of our country, we like to think of freedom, tranquility, justice and liberty for all men. I can remember as a child thinking of Uncle Sam as a part of the family, because my family kept a close relationship with the Government and we talked about politics at the table.

"But now when I think of him, I think of repression and surveillance and miscarriages of justice –the cloak and dagger tactics which we used to see on the late, late show. I used to think the secret police and vast networks of spies checking on everyone were things which existed only in Communist countries.

"After what I have gone through in the last several years, I have come to the conclusion—and it is not a very happy conclusion—that the American dream is just that—a dream—-for it will never come true. The devious and repressive tactics which I attributed to the Communist and Fascist countries are not the sole properties of those countries, but rather they are used in the 'Land of the Free and Home of the Brave' extensively.

"The unpleasantry which brings me to Washington today is the fact that I have found the answers to a lot of questions which have plagued me for a long, long time. The answer is one of which I am not proud, because it literally destroys my faith in my country...

"...According to the information I have received, the U. S. Army Intelligence has had me under surveillance since about 1960...

"The agent farther told me that the files were kept on members of the Unitarian Church, the black Muslims and other people who were not public officials. They collected trivia like how many teeth they had extracted, or how many times they complained about back injury...

"... I also understand that local and State police divisions --- and I think this is and important part of my testimony - - -as well as the FBI collaborated on a weekly basis in Houston, Texas with the Army intelligence or with military intelligence to compare notes to exchange information.

"To give you a little history about myself, in 1960 I was involved in the sit-ins in Houston which eventually desegregated nearly all the public facilities and public accommodation facilities in that area. From 1960 until 1966 I had no idea that I was under surveillance by anybody. I did notice things but I guess you don't really pay attention to things like your phone making strange noises. . .

"... The phone taps were crude. I would hang up and the surveillance equipment would not hang up at the same time. I couldn't get another dial tone for several minutes. I assumed then that my phones were tapped and would pick up the phone and say things just to blow their minds from time to time.

"In 1966, I was first elected to the Texas House of Representatives. At that time I thought it could have been some political enemies of mine who could be out to get me in some kind of way. I really didn't think that it was Federal agents who were keeping this surveillance going on me.

"In January of 1967, I took office in Austin, Texas and within a very short time ---"

Senator Ervin interrupted me. "You mean by that , you took your seat as a member of the House of Representatives, State of Texas?"

"Right. At that particular time, I noticed very quickly that anything I said over my phone at my residence in Austin or my phone in the office in the Capitol, become public knowledge within 24 to 48 hours, or the word had gotten back to me in some way.

"In late 1967 or 1968, I noticed several times that too many microphones were on podiums where I was to speak. I can cite one case in point, which I think is particularly significant, I was saying something at a meeting which might have been of interest to the Army. I read the text of a speech I was going to give to the Young Democrats in San Antonio, Texas, to Congressman Eckhardt, my Congressman. I read it to him over the phone from my office to his office in Washington here, to get his opinion on the speech.

"It was a speech asking that we cease the war in Vietnam. I noticed a week later, when I appeared to make the speech in San Antonio, that on the podium where I was to speak there was a microphone taped—it was obviously a tape recorder microphone.

Senator, the microphone wire ran down the side of the podium and went into a locked box at the bottom of the podium.

"Congressman Henry Gonzalez from Texas was to appear on the same program that day also. At the time he was a frequent passenger every weekend on Air Force One. He used [ride with] the President [Johnson] every weekend and get a ride back to his district . . . thought possibly it was he they had under surveillance and not myself.

"I couldn't conceive of why a Federal agent would be checking on me. So at that time, I really thought it was not myself but rather Congressman Gonzalez.

"In 1969 I was a candidate for mayor of the city of Houston. Several times during that campaign, I gave speeches and noticed that several strange things happened. For instance, in many cases we would set up a meetings by phone. I set up a meeting one time in the Rice Hotel in Houston. It was a closed meeting of about 50 people. We were trying to raise a little money. These were people who could possibly contribute substantially to my mayor's campaign.

"I noticed when I walked up to the podium, that another microphone was taped to the podium. It was taped down with fresh duck tape. The wire ran down under the floor into the next room. It was a hotel and you know how they have those movable walls in hotels. So I tried to gain admission to the next room and couldn't do so.

"I had an idea that someone was in there with a set if phones and tape recorder. The things I said that night came back to me from sources that I knew were not there.

"I have come to the concussion that this kind of thing is done all the time to people like myself, who happen to be black, members of the Texas House of Representatives and members of State's legislatures, of public officials, and I am appalled by it.

"From 1969 until now, I can cite many instances where I have even seen people following me. For example, when I landed at an airport to make a speech, somebody was taking pictures of me. . . .

".. . .I have seen documents in many cases where things I have said over my telephone in my home in Houston, Texas, have become public knowledge in 48 hours.

"In summary, Senator, I must say that I literally have lost faith in this country as a result of the information that I have received from several sources. I have received call from other individuals who said to me, Graves, don't worry; there is nothing they have in those files that they could use to harm you in any way. It was just trivia that they collected and don't worry, nobody's going to get you. . .

"I seriously believe that our representative democracy is threatened by this surveillance and that if the Founding Fathers of this Nation knew how this democracy has diminished, they would be rolling over in their graves right now.

"I would like to thank you for giving me the opportunity to come up to Washington and give you this information. However, I must state again that I am not happy I had to do it. . . .I am very honored to be an elected public official in Texas. I am now quickly losing faith. I should not have to suffer this kind of indignity. Anything I say, anywhere, at any time, to anybody, should not suffer the scrutiny of somebody's computer bank.

"I thank you very much."

As I looked up I could see the Senator's staffer with a big smile on his face. Congressman Eckhardt was seated behind me so I could not read has face.

There was silence in the room. The silence seemed like an hour but it was less then thirty seconds.

It was the Erwin's turn to speak. After a quick question or two about the dates of my military service, he cleared his throat.

"Do you think it is a proper function of the military to exercise surveillance over the civilian segment of the population of this country?"

I looked straight at him "No Sir. I don't—especially that kind of surveillance on public officials.

The Senator when on, "Don't you agree with me that no branch of the government should exercise surveillance over civilians except the civilian branch of the government, and that even in that case surveillance should never be exercised unless information exists which reasonably justifies a conclusion that there is a clear and present danger that somebody might commit a crime?"

"Sir, I agree with you completely and I further think that the only way Federal authorities ought to be involved in any kind of surveillance is if they think there is a threat of treason of overthrow of the Government. . . We are concerned and so paranoid about everything said over our phones, I am now getting to the point that I go to a regular pay phone to conduct my business. I am afraid if I am seen in that pay phone too many times it is going to be tapped. . .Consequently, whenever a person stands up and starts to let somebody know that he is not to happy about the way things are going, that he would like to see us take another approach, that he would like to see some kind of change, and somebody is scrutinizing him, then we are not living under a representative democracy. We have some other form of government going on us here."

Senator Ervin broke me off a little smile, "I want to thank you very much for your appearance here and for the benefit of your testimony."

The Senator didn't look to his left. Senator Thurmond said, "Mr. Chairman, Mr. Chairman."

Senator Ervin never looked his way. " Call the next witness," he said.

Afterwards, I walked directly to Ervin's office with

Congressman Eckhardt and one of his staffers. As soon as I walked into the Senator's office, he shook my hand. and said, "How about that?"

With that he grabbed my hand and brought me in for a hug. He had protected me. The hug was indeed welcomed.

I went back to Eckhardt's office the same way we came in that morning. We caught an elevator marked members only and down to a sub-basement of the office building. There is a little train that runs into the Capitol building. We changed trains and caught another train that took us to the Longworth Building where Eckhardt's offices were located.

We both agreed that it was a good days work. After he finished some office work we went to Eckhardt house for several drinks and a great dinner.

Within two days after returning to Texas I got a call from the NBC *Today* Show. The producer said that they would like for me to come to New York to talk about my testimony with Barbara Walters. I agreed and that next Monday morning I called my mother and dad from a New York Hotel to wake them up so they could see me on NBC about 7:30 AM New Orleans time. The interview went well. My dad had gone to work but my mother watched. As mothers sometimes do, she commented on my suit, tie and how I looked in general, but little about the content.

I spent some time talking to the hosts, Barbara Walters and Hugh Downs off camera. It was not only my first time in a New York studio, but it was the iconic "30 Rock," Rockefeller Plaza.

As I observed several dozen people racing around, I was amazed at what it took to get the show on the air.

Senator Sam Ervin's "Subcommittee on Constitutional Rights" interviewed dozens of witnesses over eleven days of hearings along with hundreds of documents.

It seems quaint today, but one of the major concerns of the

committee was the proliferation of technology that could be used to violate U.S. citizen's constitutional freedoms.

Long before a time of personal computers. smart phones and social media, lawmakers were apprehensive about the growth of computers in the government. It was pointed put that over 5000 computers were already in use throughout various agencies, most notably in the military and law enforcement.

I did continue to be concerned about who I was with and where I went. However, I did not let the surveillance compromise my political direction. After all, I was not doing anything wrong. But with the Bishop's warnings, I realized that looking like something was wrong was just as bad as doing something wrong. It is a sad thing to say but perception is often more important than reality. And after all, the words that the bishop said were true. "They were only trying to get something on me to take me down."

In the more then 50 years since all this happened, I can think of several black public officials that were taken down by just a hint of impropriety. I did not want to be one of them.

But on the other hand, I still liked to have some fun messing with the folks who were keeping tabs on me. . I remember saying to one of my friends when I was on the way to his house, "Agent two, this is agent one. The package will arrive in a few."

I knew that some ears must have perked up when I dropped that one. But after all, when playing cat and mouse, a little provocation is always in order.

FIFTEEN

THE SECOND SESSION

My reelection to another term in Texas's House was easier than the first campaign. I ran unopposed in the June 1968 primary and in the general election in November. When it came time for me to be sworn in for the second time, I was a real veteran (or so I thought). After two years in elective office, I was sure, like many people are in their late twenties, that I knew where I was going and exactly how to get there.

The second session gave me and my office mate, Lauro Cruz, a little more office space. Even though the outer office stayed the same, they divided the inner office in half with a wall that made it impossible for me to see who might be on Lauro's side. The wall did not quite go to the ceiling so we could still hear each other's conversations, but it was a step up from the previous arrangement. Now each of us had our own space.

I had been lucky to find Mike Arnold, an exceptional young man, to serve as page for my first session. It would be hard to replace him, but the same Houston friend who ultimately helped me find my secretary, Dr. Theodore Youngblood, had told me that he had a son that might be able to serve if things were right. I called Dr. Youngblood in the week before the session and asked if his son was still interested in being a House Page. I knew his grandparents lived in Austin. Perhaps he could live with them from January to May.

Dr. Youngblood was enthusiastic. "Let me make a call to my parents to see if it's okay for him to stay with them for the session," he said.

Within a few minutes, he called me back with a positive answer. His son, Kneeland Youngblood, could move to Austin to stay with Dr. Youngblood's parents for the entire session.

Kneeland served me and the House well and he credits this experience with giving him an incentive to do great things with his life. He became a medical doctor and a venture capitalist and to this day he remains a successful businessman.

I had heard during the primary that a woman was running for office. I was intrigued. In my first session, the only female serving in the Texas House or Senate was Barbara Jordan. As the new session unfolded, I thought I might need to mentor two newly elected assembly members. One was Frances "Sissy" Farenthold and the other was Zan Holmes. In actuality, neither of them needed any mentoring.

Sissy, from Corpus Christi, was a very accomplished attorney who knew her way around the conservative white male majority. Zan, on the other hand, was a seasoned member of the Dallas clergy. He may not have served in elective office before, but he knew just how to navigate through the craziness that was metropolitan Dallas politics in 1969. Both being a little older than me, it was clear they could hold their own.

In their own way, each of them showed me how carefully applied moderation might help me get more done. Sissy's intellectual and quiet way was often much better than my brash approach. Zan's ministerial style was a way of getting things done that I had not seen or understood. From time to time, I would go out of my way to draw fire. Zan, on the other hand, would work though the back door to get the job done. In the end, he needed me to rattle the beads and I needed him to make the close. Within a month, we had it down to a science.

A few years back, Zan reminded me of something that I had forgotten. It was on the first day of the new session. He came over to introduce himself on the floor of the House. Apparently I shooed him off, saying, "We shouldn't stand together on the floor. If we do, they might be able to kill both of us with one shot." I had to admit, it *did* sound like something I might say.

Both Sissy and Zan, in different ways, gave me new energy and direction. Sissy started to put together coalitions that were more effective than my approach of going it alone.

A new Speaker was in the Chair that session. He was Gus Franklin Mutscher from Brenham, Texas, a rural area a little west of Houston. Cash payments swirled around many politicians like John Connally and Ben Barnes (the Lieutenant Governor at that time), at least by rumor. Mutscher wasn't that clever. Instead of taking cash like many Texas politicians had done for years, Mutscher allegedly took stock. It was his downfall.

As I look back on it now, I can say without question that my second session was more on-target. Zan and Sissy were helping me to see that there were many ways to get the job done that did not involve grandstanding, a skill that I had mastered the first session. Grandstanding gets the word out and pumps up your base, but in too many cases it turns off as many as it attracts.

As a result of this new way, many of the things I did that session got accomplished without lots of fanfare. Because of Representative Tom Bass, I had several local bills that got introduced, moved through committee, and passed without objection. As leader of the Harris County delegation, Tom gave

Rev. Zan Homes and Curtis working magic on the House floor

each of us from Harris County a bill or two that was only of interest
to the people of our county and city. For instance, I introduced
a bill that changed the pension process for the Houston Police
Department. I had several Houston policemen come up and
testify for the changes in the process and the bill sailed through
without a hitch. I carried a bill or two for the police department
each session. Unlike now, where partisan politics seems to rule
the day, the House and Senate were both largely Democratic, so
things got done differently.

The bill that caused much difficulty was one that focused
on the minimum wage. We had no minimum wage laws in the
state at the time. The recently activated Farm Workers Union
and the labor movement as a whole wanted a Texas minimum
wage passed. I made several speeches in Austin and across the
state to pass a minimum wage. It was a cause I believed in and
had been working for since before my first day in office. It's still
an important issue today. If people don't make a living wage,
they are relegated to second-class economic citizenship. The

businesses that see the light turn out to be more successful. The others suffer turnover and retraining expenses that they don't factor in when making a decision about a living wage for their employees.

Don Horn from the Houston AFL-CIO had briefed me on strategies that we might use to get the bill passed. Each of us who wanted to speak on the issue had a part of the story to tell in our speeches. We coordinated our remarks and delivered them from the microphone in front of the House. As I remember it, I asked to speak last. We had the gallery filled with members of several unions. The Speaker needed to call for order many times during the speeches. As I think back on it now, I think the Speaker's team didn't know if they had all the votes they needed to defeat the bill. As the electronic vote was called, the Speaker's team was running around the floor pressing buttons on desks where members were not seated. They were yelling "Kill it, kill it!"

As you would expect, they killed it.

However, another big thing that came up that session was the subject of liquor by the drink. In many states, including Texas, liquor could not be served by the drink. Several states were nearly dry. Other states had laws that said that you could bring a bottle into a bar, but someone had to pour the drink for you out of your own bottle. In Texas you could buy a set-up; you could bring in your own bottle and buy the glass, ice, and mixers, and pour your own drink. You could buy beer in any bar, but hard liquor had to be bought at a liquor store and paper-bagged in for your own consumption.

To make matters chaotic, each county in the state could set hours of consumption and vote wet or dry. The state's hotel and hospitality industry badly wanted to fix these crazy laws, which would enable a person to get a drink anywhere they wanted and at a later hour.

I was in favor of the bill, but it wasn't the most important thing on my agenda. The word on the floor was that the vote was going to be close. As a matter of fact, it was likely the bill would be defeated if only one or two votes went against. I was already counted on as a "yes" vote. Several members close to the Speaker had come to me to confirm my "yes."

The day came on the legislative calendar for the bill to be considered. When other matters had been finished, the Speaker called up the bill and it was read by the House clerk. I called over to one of the members of the press who was seated at the press table near me and said, "I'm taking my voting machine key into the bathroom to get a shoe shine. I will not come out until I get assurance that some of my bills that are stuck in the rules committee will be released."

They were all local bills, non-confrontational local matters that were slow-rolled just because I was the sponsor. I knew that all of them would be gaveled through on a voice vote if they were allowed to come out and be considered.

I knew that I had a pressure point and I also knew that my one vote was needed for liquor to be served by the drink in the great state of Texas. I invited in a press photographer to document my shoe shine, holding up my voting machine key. (I have hunted for that picture and I cannot find it.)

A very nice Black man operated the shoeshine stand in the men's room. His stand was just to the right of the bathroom's swinging doors. He and I were having a pleasant conversation when, after we were only five minutes into my shoe shine, the doors flung open. It was none other then His Highness Speaker Gus Mutscher coming to get me and my vote.

"I thought you were going to vote with me on this bill!" Mutscher exclaimed. His face was red and his eyes were on fire. I could see that I had gotten his attention. He was *pissed,* which was exactly what I wanted.

"I've taken financial commitments to pass this bill today," he said angrily.

Now *that* was an interesting admission from a sitting Speaker, or any politician for that matter. But I didn't flinch. I knew I had him by the short hairs.

"Mr. Speaker, I have two local bills stuck in the rules committee," I responded slowly. "They will be passed without objection, but I cannot get them on the calendar for a vote."

I paused for dramatic effect.

"Can you help me with that?" I enunciated each word.

He looked at me with a fire intensifying on his face. A Black man had hit him and he could not hit back.

"You'll get a vote next week."

I could see by his face that pushing my bills out of the rules committee was unpleasant to him. However, my objective was not to make him feel good, but rather to get my bills passed.

"Can I get you to finish this up?" I asked the elderly shoeshiner. He nodded and smiled as I got up from his chair.

I followed the Speaker to the floor. He was walking quickly, like a man on a mission. I, on the other hand, did my slow walk with my voting key dangling in front of me. The smile on my face told the story to most of the House members who knew exactly what I was doing.

I voted for the bill and it passed by only two votes.

The next Monday, I was sitting in my office when I received my daily calendar of bills to be considered that day. Both of my bills were listed. They were passed that day without objection.

Sometime later, I had my second major encounter with the Texas Department of Corrections. I got a call from a woman who had just been notified that her husband had died of a heart attack at the Huntsville facility. Almost simultaneously, she got calls from two relatives of inmates that had witnessed her husband's death. According to them, there was a prison guard sitting on his chest when he died.

According to the inmate witnesses, the woman's husband had gotten into an argument with another inmate in the lunch line. The guards came in to break up the argument and took her husband down to the floor. One overweight guard sat on his chest to restrain him. He had a heart attack and died because of the chest compression.

I called my new friend Dr. Beto. I relayed the story to him and said that I wanted to see the man's body before he was moved. He said that he would call me back with some information within an hour. Well, in less than an hour I got a call from the warden informing me that the local coroner had released the body to a local Black funeral home. He gave me the funeral home's phone number and, without putting down the receiver, I immediately called the funeral home.

I reached the funeral director and he said that he had just gotten back from the penitentiary with the man's body. He was going to embalm him that afternoon. I asked him if he could hold off until I got there and he agreed.

I quickly jumped into the car and drove to the funeral home in Huntsville. In Texas at the time, the county coroner was an elected position. The person running for coroner was not required to have a medical degree, or, for that matter, *any* degree. He was just a person who could win a county election.

The coroner looked at the body and, without an official autopsy, determined that the man's cause of death was "natural causes." The funeral director allowed me to check out the body myself. The only thing that we could see was a dark mark on the deceased's face. The two of us could not determine the cause of his death.

I made a few calls to the Harris County Coroner's office and convinced them that this man, who was a citizen of Harris

County, should be autopsied by them. They picked up his body and determined that his chest was cracked. His heart stopped because it did not have any room to beat.

Without any press or other public notification, I called Dr. Beto and sent him the autopsy report. He looked into the matter and called me back in a week. The two guards involved in the incident had been relieved of their duties.

I relayed this information to the man's wife. She was very thankful that at least *something* was done about her husband's death. Sometimes a quiet resolution of a problem is the best for all concerned. This seemed to be one of those times. If the wife would have demanded compensation for the death, or if I would have gotten pushback from the Texas Department of Corrections, things might have been different. In today's litigious environment, there probably would have been a lawsuit to compensate the family for the loss. At the time, his family didn't push it and I didn't think of it.

There was one other thing that was memorable about that session. Taxes needed to be raised to balance the state budget. After many stories in the press and much debate among House members, a bill was crafted to quietly make up the shortfall by raising the tax on food from grocery stores.

A tax like this would hit poor people more than anyone else because it would apply to the food that they had to buy in stores to cook dinner. No matter how little money you make, you have to eat. It was as regressive a tax as you can conceive of and the poorer you were, the higher the percentage of your income you had to pay just to eat.

This was my kind of issue. The labor unions were solidly against it and they had gotten people from all over the state to come to Austin to lobby against the bill. The bill was to come up about 11 AM. for debate and a vote.

A few minutes before the clock struck 11, a bomb threat was

called into the Capitol. Capitol guards came to each office and made everyone leave the building. It took nearly an hour for the building to be emptied. Then the bomb squad came in and swept the building from top to bottom. The entire process took more than three hours.

Well, what do you think a number of members did during that time? They went to a restaurant or bar for an extended lunch and got drunk. When we were allowed back into the building around 3 PM. and called back into session, there were some wasted white boys among us. Tempers were flaring and it seemed certain that shit was going to happen if things didn't go their way.

During our time away from the Capitol, we had someone from the unions go out and buy as many loaves of bread in their plastic wrappers as they could find. They were passed out to the union members as they entered the building to fill the galleries.

It was a scene. The Texas House of Representatives gallery filled with people holding loaves of bread over the railing. This was my kind of demonstration. Bill Heatly was the chair of the Appropriations Committee. He and I had never spoken to each other in the more than two years I'd held office. To say the least, he was not my kind of person, and he was the lead person to defend the bill.

I, along with several other liberal members, had drafted several amendments to the bill that would eliminate the tax of food, among other things. I stood at the back microphone and addressed the Speaker. "Mr. Speaker, would the gentleman yield for a question?" I asked.

The Speaker asked Heatly if he would yield. Much to my surprise, he agreed for me to ask my question. As I began to speak, I pointed to the gallery with the people hanging their loaves of bread over the railing. Just then, I heard someone behind me yell, "Stop the nigger from speaking!"

As I turned around halfway, I could see arms flying from

the corner of my eye. One House member was hitting another member. I quickly thought that I was about to get my ass kicked by some drunk white boys.

What should I do? This was the question running through my entire body. Then I heard someone shout, "Take that mic from that nigger!"

It was at this point that I knew I just might get my ass kicked for real. When faced with so few alternatives, I decided to take the high road. I jumped up on the press table just in front of me, microphone still in hand. On my right side the Sergeant at Arms was trying to get me off the table. On my left was R.C. "Nick" Nichols, ready to hit anyone who laid a hand on me. Nick was a steelworker from right outside of Houston who looked like a Klansman out of his robes.

Absolutely nobody wanted to get in Nick's way, so I felt like I was home free of any ass-kicking. I knew that Nick had my back. It was a contentious moment. My boys from Harris County were behind me. Rex Braun from Harris County was behind me. Edward Harris from Galveston County was backing him up and big Dave Allred was holding up the back wall. Other members were rolling on the floor fighting.

Now I had to get down from the table. I sure wasn't going to get off on the same end that I got on, so I walked gingerly between the members of the press to the other end to get down. It might not have been artful, but I had avoided any confrontation. I had also stopped the bill from going anywhere that day.

Let me paint the picture for you. At the front of the House chamber, the Speaker was slamming the gavel down like a blacksmith making horseshoes. At the same time, he was yelling, "Order! Order in the House! Order in the House!"

Just in front of him was Bill Heatly, standing there like the referee at a tennis match. Stuff was going on all around him and he just did not know what to do. The press table was in the center of the room and members were scattering to keep from getting hit. I was making my way off the front of the table. Behind the table was the podium for questions that I had abandoned. The mic was still in my hand.

Behind that, a few drunken members were on the floor in a brawl. Nick was standing guard beside the table, keeping any one of those fools from getting to me. The Sergeant-at-Arms and his people were trying to break up the fights. On top of all of that, there was a gallery full of people waving loaves of bread. It might have been a first for all-around chaos in the Texas House of Representatives. The Speaker, left with few real alternatives, adjourned the House for the day. It was an infamous day in the great state of Texas.

The bill was brought up a few days later and it barely passed.

Two weeks later, I arrived on the House floor early. I strolled to my desk and was greeted by my own mugshot. It was just sitting there, looking up at me. I looked around at the other members' desks and noticed that each desk had the same photo.

I walked over to the press table to find a friendly face that might give me some insight as to who did this. One of the good guys in the press said that Rep. Heatly had gotten them made and distributed to each desk.

I looked around to see if Heatly was at his desk, but he was not. I sat for a few minutes to collect my thoughts and to decide what I was going to do. I came up with a good comeback, so I just waited until he showed up at his desk. I took my mugshot in hand and headed to the back of the chamber to confront him.

Bill Heatly was a big man with a round face, like a mean sheriff of a county somewhere in the southern part of the United States. He saw me coming and I could see the color red overtake his face. When I slammed the picture on his desk, I could almost see blood oozing through his pores. He looked like he thought I might hit him.

I looked him dead in his bloodshot eyes and said, "This proves that I went to jail for my people. Can you tell me one good thing that you have ever done for yours?"

He looked at me as if I was lighting a match to his coattails.

I thought I needed to hit one more time so I added one more salvo. "You can't come up with one, can you?"

It was a standoff. He stared at me, waiting for me to make the next move, and I stared back at him, waiting to see if he was going to self-immolate. Well, he did not, so I walked away.

Nearly fifty House members came over to my desk to ask about the photo. I told each of them about my encounter with the rattlesnake and most of them said something to the effect of not letting this get to me. It really didn't. It made me stronger. I knew that I could take whatever they threw my way.

There were lighter times during that session, too. One of those was when I took Gretchen, my oldest daughter, and Christopher, my son, to the House floor. They were so proud to sit with me at my desk, but the truth was that I was so proud to have them sitting with me. Many representatives came over to visit with them.

In time, the session ended and we all went back home. I was home only a few days when I got a call from a stranger from Baton Rouge, Louisiana. He identified himself as Joseph Delpit. I recognized the Delpit name because his family owned a restaurant in Baton Rouge called The Chicken Shack. "I'm thinking of running for the Louisiana State House of Representatives and I really don't know what I'm doing," he shared with me.

It was reminiscent of the call that I had made to Georgia Representative Ben Brown when I was thinking about running for the Texas State House. Delpit wanted to know if I would come to Baton Rouge to help him with his campaign. Without hesitation, I answered, "Yes."

"When are you available?" he inquired.

"In two weeks, I'm nearly open all the time."

"How much time do you think you can spend?"

"How about a week?" I asked.

"That sounds wonderful." Then he asked the important question. "How much will this cost me?"

"A plane ticket and hotel."

Graves Press table stand against taxes on food

"Are you serious?"

"Yes, but you need to hear me out. Several years ago, I made the same call you're making to me now. I called Georgia Representative Ben Brown," I shared. "He agreed to help me, and now I am paying it forward. In several years you may get a call, and you need to help the next person."

"I understand," Delpit said.

Within a few weeks, I arrived in Baton Rouge and Delpit met me at the airport. He made sure I understood that I would not need a car because he or one of his people would take me wherever I needed to go. I helped him set up his office and went with him to several campaign meetings. I critiqued his speech and helped him sharpen his message.

Before the end of the week, Delpit said that he had made contact with the governor and he would like to have me for dinner.

Gretchen and Chris sitting with Curtis on the House floor

The governor at the time was John McKeithen, who served from 1964 to 1972. I was dropped off at the front door of the governor's mansion and brought in by a butler. MeKeithen came in and introduced himself. He said that he thought very highly of Joe Delpit and he thought that because I was a Texas State official he should have me for dinner as a thanks for helping Joe with his campaign.

We sat in a big dining room with Governor McKeithen sitting at the end of a long table while dinner was placed in front of us.

McKeithen talked about an education bill that was being introduced by one of the really conservative members of the Louisiana House. Because of the racist intent of the bill, he did not make any remarks about the bill to keep the House member from attacking him. If the bill passed he planned to sign it. However, he had already called his friends on the Louisiana Supreme Court to have it ruled unconstitutional. "If I were to openly oppose the bill, he would use that to run against me in the next election," he explained. "I would rather kill it without showing my hand."

In politics, sometimes it's better to choose what fights you want to have. The bottom line might not be what fight you wage, but what you can do for people with the tools and conditions you're living with. In other words, play the cards you have and not the ones you *wish* you had.

SIXTEEN

THE RACE FOR MAYOR OF HOUSTON

N ot too long after the session was over, I decided to make a run for mayor of Houston. A guy named Louie Welch was mayor at the time, and he had a police chief named Herman Short. The two of them were hated in Black Houston. There was a story in the press and on TV nearly every week about some atrocity against a Black person at the hands of the police or some other part of the city government. With that as a backdrop, I decided that a run for mayor might change things for the community.

As I analyzed the pros and cons of joining the race, I decided that I could run without giving up my House seat. 1969 was not a year that I needed to run for reelection and the mayoral race would keep me busy along while simultaneously doing something for the people of Houston. What I didn't know was that running for mayor would be the most dangerous thing that I had ever done.

Exposing facts about the Welch administration and its malpractices was something that would drive the crazies out of their holes. Who knew that in 1969, racism was still deep and strong, just lurking below the surface? Who knew that a Black man trying to expose some of the out-and-out vestiges of the long-gone Confederacy would cause so much pain in the greater Houston community?

As time unfolded, I was soon to find out. My candidacy announcement went well but before the week was done, I started getting letters and telephone calls telling me that my children were not going to see adulthood. Some of the callers used such terrible language that I would hang up after three words were spoken. By this time, I had two phone lines installed in the house. One night, just after the 10:30 news was over, I received a call. "Is this Curtis Graves?" the person asked.

"Yes it is,"

"I mean Curtis Graves the nigger?"

Without hesitation, I said, "Yes, sir, it is."

"Nigger, you have 10 minutes to live," he said.

At that moment, the second line rang. "Sir, would you mind holding on for me to answer the other line?" I asked.

Without his agreement, I switched to the second line. Someone asked, "Is this Curtis Graves?"

"Yes it is," I said.

This time the person didn't want to make sure he had the right Curtis Graves. He just yelled, "You're going to die!"

"Thanks for the warning," I said.

I pressed the button to go back to the first caller, but he was gone. I just might be the only person who ever put a bomber on hold.

Nothing happened and I moved on. My thoughts at the time were that if they were really going to kill me, I wouldn't get a warning. Well, that turned out to be a fairly good thought. I'm here telling the story. If it had gone down the other way, I would not be.

Within a week of my announcement, the man who owned

the service station where I bought gas asked me if he could help with my campaign. His name was John Cherry and he had been very friendly with me for several years. "What do you have in mind?"

"I would like to provide security for you," he said. "I have a friend that might be willing to help, too."

After the several threatening calls I had received as well as letters talking about castrating my children, I thought security might be a good idea. The friend he had in mind was a guy named James Forman. The two of them had guns and were comfortable carrying them to protect me.

From that day at the service station until Election Day, Cherry and Forman rolled with me wherever I went. Several Black Houston police officers also said that they would look out for me, and they did, but my main guys were Cherry and Forman. After a few weeks of having them drive me everywhere in Cherry's black Cadillac, I began to relax about the possibility of someone hurting me or my family.

The calls and letters followed a pattern. If I was on the nightly news, I would receive a few calls. The same would happen with the letters. Many were as anti-Semitic as they were anti-Black. It was common for the letters to have statements like, "The Jews put you up to this."

I really wasn't concerned until one person slipped a letter through my car window. Because of the Texas heat, it was common practice to leave the car window cracked open an inch or two when you parked just to let some air in to keep the windows from cracking. One day, after spending some time at the federal building in downtown Houston, I returned to my car and found a letter on my seat. It gave me pause and I turned it in to the FBI. I never heard anything back from them, but they weren't exactly on my side at the time, either.

The race was heated. I put up some billboards with a United

States flag in the background only to receive a letter saying that I couldn't use the flag in that way. Now I think of President Trump wrapping his arms around the flag and how no one said a word.

Within a few weeks I got a call from John de Menil, the wealthy Houston oilman who gave us the check that saved the Martin Luther King fundraiser. He wanted me to come out to talk to him. I agreed and we set a date for me to visit him at his house in River Oaks, the ritzy part of Houston.

The day came, and I arrived at this house that just blew me away. There must have been three or more Picasso paintings hung up in the house. One really struck me as I walked into the foyer. It nearly took my breath away.

A maid let me in and said that Mr. de Menil would be with me shortly. As I looked around, it seemed like most of the art in the house was African. There were so many pieces that I could not believe that any museum might have more than de Menil had right there in his home.

De Menil was a small man with a warm, quick smile. He ordered coffee and we sat to discuss my race for mayor. He said that he would like to help.

"Mr. de Menil, I would love your help," I said graciously. Truth be told, I could remember the big check he sent my way a few years before. I could see from his house that he could help without putting a dent into his family wealth.

In a quiet voice, he asked, "Can you take off a few days to go with me to New York to meet some people that I think very highly of?"

"When would you like to go?" I asked.

"How about next week?" he responded. "Give me a day and I'll make all the arrangements for us to fly up and you can meet my people."

I agreed and it was on. We flew first class to New York and were met by his New York chauffeur. He drove us to de

Menil's Park Avenue apartment that was adorned with as much artwork as his house in Houston. I slept in a bedroom with one wall covered by an Andy Warhol painting of Mr. de Menil's wife, Dominique.

The next morning, we had guests that were coming in from about 10 AM on. One of these guests was Ron Hobbs. He was a Black man who must have been at least 6'5" and very slim. He was an art agent in New York and Mr. de Menil believed in him. There were several other people in the advertising world that we talked to, but what I got from the meetings was that Ron Hobbs was my man.

Mr. de Minel said that if I needed anything, I should call Ron. He would get the best buy and format for billboards, TV ads, radio commercials, or newspaper ads. If Ron thought it was a good thing and we agreed on how it looked, he would pay for it. As a result of these meetings, I really don't know how much money the de Minel put into my race. This was before all the reporting requirements, so I didn't keep track, but it might have been as much as $50,000. I was on the radio and TV every day for weeks. The week before the election, I had thirty-second commercials on each of the three channels at 10:30 each night.

One night, after a rally that Mr. de Minel attended, he confided in me about his real motivation for being so active in my race. After Dr. King's assassination, de Minel decided to do something in his memory. He commissioned a sculpture by Barnett Newman called *Broken Obelisk*. He wanted it put up in one of the Houston parks with an inscription that read, "Dedicated to Dr. Martin Luther King."

The city refused the offer of the monument and inscription on any public facility in Houston, so de Minel decided to get some land from St. Thomas University in Houston and build an interfaith chapel. He wanted *Broken Obelisk* and the inscription to be there forever. Today the chapel is used for all kinds of events. It is a true addition to the Houston community.

The Broken Obelisk sits outside a chapel funded by the De Minels that has been used for many years. (courtesy Rothko Chapel)

I have heard many stories of things that happened to people during the election. One story was about Rodney Ellis, a former Texas state senator and now a Harris County Commissioner. Rodney then was in a predominantly white junior high school and had one of my "Graves For Mayor" buttons that he was wearing to class. The button was about two and a half inches in diameter. To say the least, it was a *big* button. Rodney proudly wore the button as one of my supporters. A teacher called Rodney to her desk and asked him not to wear the button in her class. He refused to take it off, so she sent him to the principal's office. The principal told him that he couldn't wear that button in school.

"If the students who were wearing the George Wallace [running as a third-party candidate for president] buttons take their buttons off, I will take mine off," Rodney responded.

Well, both the principal and teacher backed down because they weren't going to make students take off their Wallace buttons. Now I must admit that the "Wallace for President" buttons were only about an inch and a half in diameter. Mine was twice that big. Even so, Rodney got to keep his button and the issue went away.

Many people told me that they were stopped in their cars because they had "Graves For Mayor" bumper stickers. One person shared that the policeman said to her, "Don't you know that he is a member of the Communist Party?"

"I thought he was a Democrat," she said in reply.

He gave her a ticket and went away. She was sure that she wouldn't have gotten the ticket if it weren't for the bumper sticker. Even so, she told me that she wouldn't take the sticker off. She'd rather just pay the ticket and rub it in their faces.

Several people came in to help with my campaign. Richard Hatcher, mayor of Gary, Indiana, came in to speak at a rally several days before the election.

We also had several entertainers make appearances on behalf of my campaign. One of them was George Kirby.

I ran a good, hard campaign, promising to make the streets safe for all Houston citizens and to add 1500 police officers to the force. At the same time I questioned the unequal justice both perpetrators and victims receive from white-controlled courts.

Shortly before the election, in a bit of bravado that I truly

don't remember, I was quoted by *Jet* magazine as saying that I "was the man to beat in the race."

I was hoping to draw 25,000 white voters to go along with my base of Black and Hispanics. We never had a debate. Even without one, the race did one thing for Houston that had never been done before: it woke up the white electorate. More than 30,000 people who had never voted in a city election before came out to vote. Problem was, they were voting against me for the most part.

I placed second among six candidates. I had some success splitting the white vote but in the end Louie Welch and his police chief, Herman Short, were reelected.

Two days later, a reporter from The *New York Times* came to interview me. Among other things, I told him that Houston would rather elect a crook than a nigger. As you can guess, that made the lead in the story.

Even though I lost, the experience was a good one for me. The Black community came together to support me like they had not done before in any race. I was also able to raise money for the campaign from the professional and business communities like no Black person had ever done before. In the back of my mind I was thinking that if I wanted to run for anything else, I could use the citywide exposure I had garnered. At twenty-nine, my political future was bright.

The only real downside was that my campaign stirred up some people who had never manifested real hatred to come out from under whatever rock they were hiding. The possibility of the election of a Black mayor was just too much for some folks.

It would be nearly three decades before the people of Houston finally elected Lee P. Brown, former chief of police, as its first Black mayor.

SEVENTEEN

THE SANDRA SMITH STORY

Sandra Smith was a beautiful Black woman who lived in Houston. Her life of 67 years took many twists and turns as chronicled in *The Blessing of Movement*, a book by her younger sister, Deborah Konrad.

Sandra's parents were good people who had done everything they could to keep her out of trouble, but children choose their own road, and sometimes it's not the best one. By 1970, Sandra had already been arrested twice on forgery and burglary charges. On July 24 of that year, she was sentenced to five years in the Texas Department of Corrections. However, her lawyer was able to keep her out of the penitentiary on bail for a time.

On Saturday, August 22, Sandra was shot at a party and taken to a Houston hospital. As a result of the gunshot, Sandra was close to death. It took all the skills of the Ben Taub Hospital staff to save her. As Deborah wrote:

"Ben Taub was one of only a handful of hospitals in the United States that had a shock room. This is where those that are

277

technically close to leaving this world are brought back to life. It was one of the best in the world for this. Sandra was lucky to live in Houston. The doctor says she will live... but she will never walk again."

This prognosis hung over her family like a truck full of concrete. They were not ready for what the doctors called "a quadriplegic." Paralyzed from the chest down, Sandra couldn't walk or even feed herself. This, as her sister wrote, meant "complete and total dependence. I would ask my mother why God had not left her with the use of her hands. It just seemed like overkill to make her helpless."

Through all of this, Sandra's brain was still sharp. She had almost completed all of her college work to get a degree in chemistry. She may have become a quadriplegic, but she still could speak for herself. Sandra wanted the best care but also wanted to return home to be with her family. But first, she needed to spend some time in a rehabilitation facility. Her family visited her every day for three months until she was able to come home.

Some thought that Sandra might walk again at some point, but her family made plans for her permanent care. Sandra's hospital bed was placed in the den of their home and all the equipment required to keep her alive and comfortable was placed in the house. Everyone had assigned jobs to care for her, including cleaning the urinary care equipment needed to irrigate her bladder.

Throughout all of this, the issue of Sandra's prior arrest had never been resolved. She had been sentenced before she was shot and the sentencing and resolution of her case had not been adjudicated. She was meant to serve three years for one charge and five years for another, but the issue of her serving time had never been considered by the family.

On a holiday weekend in 1971, the state of Texas decided to pick up Sandra Faye Smith to have her pay her "debt to society."

Two officers showed up at the house to take her to the state penitentiary to serve her time. According to Deborah, the officers saw the wheelchair, hospital bed, and all the medical equipment necessary to keep Sandra alive. They saw *everything* and none of it made a difference. They picked Sandra up and placed her in a police cruiser.

The officers must have realized that Sandra couldn't keep herself upright in a regular car. Without being tilted back and secured with a belt or some other means in a car, she would just fall forward; she didn't have any control of her upper body. Sandra's mother, Rosie, saw the officers tie her daughter up with a rope for her to make the seventy-mile trip to the Goree State Farm for Women, a prison facility just outside of Huntsville, Texas.

Rosie knew that Sandra needed various medications as well as special medical care just to stay alive. Something as simple as the ride to Huntsville without proper support could be detrimental to her health and might just kill her.

The first thing that Rosie thought of was to call State Senator Barbara Jordan. After all, she was a Black Houstonian, the daughter of a minister, and she gave the appearance of addressing community needs. At this point, Rosie was a desperate woman. "She would have called the president if she had his number," Deborah said.

Deborah explains what happened:

"[Barbara Jordan] was well-known and well-connected. Mama was sure she could and would do something. After all, she was a Texan, African American, and a woman. She would certainly intercede on the behalf of logic and mercy."

"Mama obtained the number to Ms. Jordan's office and, surprisingly, spoke directly to her. She explained that Sandra had gotten into trouble, but since her trouble, she had become paralyzed from the neck down. There was no reason for her to be in prison, and her life was at stake. She pleaded with Ms.

Jordan to intercede to get her child home. She had already been punished for her actions. At this point, her health was the issue. She should be cared for by her family at home."

"Ms. Jordan, in perfect diction and a deep, barreling voice said, 'If she did it, then she should serve her time. There is nothing I can do!'"

Rosie was beside herself. She felt no empathy, no apology, and no humanity from Senator Jordan. She started thinking about what alternatives were at her disposal. She talked to a friend who suggested that she call me.

Sure enough, I received a call from a hysterically crying lady who I did not know. Between the tears and her hysteria, she explained that she had talked to Senator Jordan and she was treated in a way that made her wonder if she was the same person who had made those great speeches that she had heard for years. She told me that I was her last resort. Between her sobs, she said that she didn't know where else to turn or who else to turn to.

It didn't take me very long to realize that her daughter might not live if she stayed in the custody of the Texas Department of Corrections (TDC). "Mrs. Smith," I told her, "the Lord has sentenced your daughter and there wasn't anything that the TDC could do but let her die in their custody."

Upon reflection, I know that those words might have been too harsh for a mother to hear from someone that she didn't know, but that's what came out of me at the time. I couldn't take it back.

It was a holiday weekend, but it was not yet 5 PM and I thought that I might be able to get Dr. Beto on the phone. I told Rosie that I would try to make something happen as quickly as I could. I didn't know what I could do, if anything, but I was going to give it a real try. I said that I would call her back shortly. She thanked me and I was off to see what could be done.

I call Dr Beto's office using the card he had given me.

Explaining who I was, I asked to speak with him, but he was already gone for the day.

I wasn't going to give up that easily.

"Are you the lady I met when I was up to visit with Dr. Beto?" I said to the woman who answered.

"Yes I am," she answered.

"I am so glad I that I got you." Lowering my voice, I said, "You know, I really need to get to him if possible." I paused. "It just might be a matter of life or death."

"Oh Representative Graves, let me see what I can do," she promised.

Now this was before the days of cell phones, but I knew that she had a way to reach him in an emergency. After all, this *was* the state penitentiary. Anything could happen at any time.

"I really thank you for whatever you can do for me," I told her.

"I will get back to you," she assured me.

I hung up. Less than fifteen minutes later, the phone rang. I recognized the voice on the other end after he had said just one word. It was Dr. Beto himself. I knew he could work magic if magic was available.

"Doc, I am so sorry to call you like this on a holiday weekend, but we have a problem," I said, hoping he could detect the urgency in my voice. I also wanted to make him feel like we were in this together.

He sounded very concerned. "What's happening?"

"Your people have just taken possession of a young lady who is a complete quadriplegic. She needs to be fed, medicated, diapers changed, catheter sterilized, turned every few hours, and all that goes along with watching her all night long. She can't even sit up in a chair without being tied or tilted backwards," I explained.

"She was convicted of a non-violent crime, but the Lord

has given her a sentence a lot greater than you can in your penitentiary." To really drive the message home, I added, "Doc, she will die in less than a week if you keep her."

I wanted him to consider me as part of the solution. "We don't want that on our watch," I said.

Dr. Beto was quiet, making me wonder which way he was going to turn. In the back of my mind, I thought he might say, "Well, what do you want me to do?" Hoping for the best, I was nevertheless ready for whatever might come.

"This is a holiday weekend. Monday everything will be closed in Austin." He was thinking out loud, I was sure.

"Yes," I answered anyway.

"Tuesday morning I can be sitting in the Governor's office with the paperwork to get her out of Goree," he said.

He understood the gravity of the situation. I sighed in relief.

"If she is not turned regularly or is left in her own waste," I added, "It could be fatal."

I punched each word to make sure that he got the message, like I felt when talking to Rosie. "Man, she is labor intensive. She'll require more help then you can provide in your hospital facility," I suggested.

"I got it. The ball is in my court. I think I can work it out and have her delivered to her parents before dark on Tuesday," he assured me.

I thanked him profusely. "I knew if anyone could make the impossible possible, you were the man."

As I hung up the phone, I thought to myself that I had gotten the magic I was hoping for. But my hand did not come off the receiver. I immediately dialed the Smiths' number to give Rosie the good news.

As you can imagine, she was beside herself. She thanked me many times. She told me about the family's plan to visit her the next day. As I learned from her sister's book, they did just that;

they drove to Huntsville to see their daughter at the Goree facility. Visiting their paralyzed child in a state prison facility was not in any way for the faint-hearted.

When they arrived to see Sandra, she was brought out on a stretcher covered in white blankets. Again quoting from Deborah Smith Konrad's book:

"Not one to complain, she seemed content and able to withstand the next three days in Goree. In later years, I asked her how she managed a smile during this ordeal. Once again, she said that she knew she had to be strong for us. She also made a point to say that her fellow inmates looked out for her better than the matrons. ... She never, ever forgot those women that, in her mind, took care of her while she was there."

And I'll never ever forget how much it meant to me that I was able to get her released. If it were not for the personal friendship I established with the warden, Dr. Beto, if I was not able to reach him in an emergency, and if he had not also seen the gravity of the situation, who knows what would have happened to Sandra Faye Smith? How many days more could she have survived in that prison hospital?

On Tuesday, the first business day of the week, I got a call from Dr. Beto. It was about 1 PM when he reached me. He said that he had talked to the governor and had gotten the papers signed to have her on her way to her family that evening.

Just like Dr. Beto promised, Sandra was returned to the loving care of her family in Houston before dark. I am told that they rolled her into the house on a stretcher and transferred her to her own bed.

Despite getting to come home, Sandra's story was not over. She needed to be pardoned for all of her crimes against the state. It took three years, but because of my and Dr. Beto's efforts, the Texas Board of Pardons and Paroles gave Sandra a full pardon. It was signed by Governor Dolph Briscoe and dated December 16, 1974.

I was already out of office by this time, but even when the

wheels of justice grind exceedingly slowly, they keep grinding in the right direction. In Sandra's case a full pardon was the right direction. Again, the Lord had sentenced her to much more then the state could ever do to her.

Can you believe that despite all that had happened to her, this young woman completed college at Texas Southern University? She reconnected with her teachers and, with the help of her parents and many others, was able to get to classes in a wheelchair, not a very easy task in those days.

Sandra also got married, and she got to spend 35 years together with her husband, Charles Taylor. In most cases, quadriplegics often don't live that many years, but Sandra actually outlived her husband. None of this would have happened if she had stayed just *two weeks* at Goree, where even a simple infection might have killed her.

I've reflected on this true and sad story for many years. I've thought about Senator Barbara Jordan and what she told Sandra's mother. I must admit that I had somewhat of an inside track at getting something done for her, but I just can't imagine someone not at least willing to give it a try.

In the end, I think I learned a lot about myself and, for that matter, Barbara Jordan. I learned that it just might be better to feel good about the person who is looking back at you in the mirror each morning than to do that which is expedient. I learned that if you use all the skills at your disposal and turn over every rock, sometimes it pays off. I learned that compassion is something that comes from within. In many cases, you can't learn it. It just has to be an innate part of who you are. I learned that the human spirit is resilient. Even when life has dealt you a bad hand, you must pick up your cards and play anyway. You just might have more strength in you than you knew you had.

EIGHTEEN

THE HOT SPECIAL SESSION

S pecial sessions of the Texas Legislature are relatively rare. Since my first regular session had ended, this was my first time attending one.

If you're a legislator, you receive a letter from the governor that invites you to be in Austin for a thirty-day, special session on a given date and time and a particular subject, known as "The Call." Members can only introduce and consider legislation that is within that subject.

In early 1968, Governor John Connally called a special session to raise revenue. That meant that the only legislation that could be introduced were bills that raised revenue in any kind of way. However, everyone knew that if the governor increased the Call, whatever he specified could pretty much be included. This was a way for The Call to be enlarged and whatever he put in the expanded Call could be introduced and considered.

Many felt that these special sessions were just a license to

285

steal. The governor would meet with lobbyists and The Call would be inflated to satisfy one group or another.

By this time, I had developed my own legislative agenda. Of particular interest was slowing down the purchase of firearms in the state. I thought this might be the perfect time to introduce a bill that would do so. I just needed a way to tie it to revenue. I also knew that to take on all firearms at once might be a little much, so I settled on trying to limit the sale of handguns. At the time, assault rifles weren't as much of a problem, nor were high-capacity magazines for handguns and rifles.

With a little research, I found out that at that time, you could visit a pawn shop in Texas and buy a gun for as little as $25. For one dollar more, you could have them load the gun for you. In many locations in the state, alcohol and guns were sold in the same store. I believed then, and I still believe now, that this was a recipe for disaster. There were stories of pawn shops being robbed by a person who had just bought a gun and then had the store owner load it for him. A drunk person with a loaded gun in his hand robbing the store where he was drinking sounds like something that needs to be rethought.

The biggest hurdle was making a gun control bill into a revenue-generating bill. I needed to charge some fee that would bring in some revenue for the state. Something nominal would work, like a registration fee. If I could get a bill drafted that would charge a fee for the registration of a handgun, then people who wanted one might have a cooling-off period instead of coming back into their house with an easily bought gun and shooting their spouse. Furthermore, it might stop people who had been convicted of a felony from owning a legal handgun. I even might be able to slip something in that would stop anyone who had severe mental problems from acquiring a handgun, too.

I settled on a bill that would do it all. For the grand sum of $5, you would be able to register to buy a gun, or for that matter, as many handguns as you liked. I had not considered how much money this might raise for the state, but with the brisk sale of guns in Texas, it might be significant.

However, there was a little kicker in my bill. You would have to give your name, address, age, and then check a box that said that you were not a felon and had not been adjudicated insane. If you were a felon or insane, as determined by a court, you could not get the permit. Permits would be sold at the county courthouse in each Texas county. The bill really didn't limit the sale of handguns, it just slowed down the sale and gave the state a way to see who owned guns. If they said that they were a law-abiding citizen and not insane, firearm possession wasn't a problem.

Now any reasonable person could see that this bill was only a matter of public safety. Who wouldn't want to prevent a person who admitted that they had been convicted of a felony from purchasing a handgun? This bill also wasn't an attempt to take guns away from the majority of people in the state. It's intent was merely to prevent those who are felons or those who are mentally ill from walking into a pawn shop or gun store and purchase a handgun that could do harm to all of us sane and law-abiding folks.

Judging from the mail I received, which picked up tenfold after the introduction of my bill, I guess that Texas didn't have many reasonable people. I wasn't trying to change the way of life in the United States, but you couldn't tell that from the return addresses on the mail I started receiving. Would you believe that I received mail from people as far away as the Commonwealth of Australia? The National Rifle Association had made my little bill into a cause to rally against. I was now on the radar of people who would not and could not be affected by this little bill designed to raise some money and slow down the weapons sales in Texas.

I found out what committee my bill was referred to, asked

for a hearing, and was granted one. I knew just as well as everyone else that this bill was not going to get out of committee, so I needed to make a splash. But what was I to do? I talked to some people in Houston and some Texas House members that understood what I was trying to do. The state was never going to pass my bill; I just wanted to educate the public of the dangers of the wide-open sale of handguns.

After a lot of thought I decided to go to Travis County, the county where Austin is located, and borrow a few handguns that were used in crimes that had already been tried in court. They loaned me three. I think that all the guns were .22 caliber pistols. In Texas at the time, this kind of gun was called a "Saturday Night Special," a type of gun was used in most crimes because it was so cheap. I also had my .38 caliber Police Special that the Houston Police Union had gifted me. I then went to a local gun store in Houston and bought some blanks for my .38. My plan was to wear my revolver into the Chamber and let it be seen under my suit coat. I knew a shoemaker in Houston and he fashioned a left-handed shoulder holster for me.

I showed up for the session wearing my shoulder holster and gun loaded with blanks. I had a white shirt on that day and I never buttoned my coat during the session. I could tell by the looks I received that a number of the members saw that I was packing. One of my Mexican American friends came up to me and reported that he overheard some members saying in the members lounge, "That nigger is wearing a gun."

At the time, there were known security arrangements in the State Capitol. Anyone could walk in with anything and the Capitol Police would not stop them. I had laid the premise. Now I needed a show for the evening news. I warned several friendly members of the press that they should be present for my gun hearing that afternoon.

After the daily session and everyone had dinner, an evening

hearing was held. The hearing was gaveled to order by the chairman and announced that this was a hearing for my bill. The room was full, not only of committee members, but also of many people opposing my bill. Because of the amount of attendees, the hearing was moved to the House floor. Since we were using the House chamber, I stood at the podium that was at the end of the press table during regular sessions. For committee hearings, the committee members sat at the press table and the public could sit in members' chairs and in the gallery.

The stage was set. I started to defend by bill. I talked about

Curtis holding each of the borrowed handguns for the public to see.

the dangers of too many handguns in the hands of people who might not use them for the right reasons. I talked about the ease of purchase in every part of the state. I talked about the proliferation of cheap "Saturday Night Specials." I talked about the fact that these cheap .22 caliber revolver handguns were not even made anywhere in the United States.

I waved around the three borrowed pistols and talked about how and where they were used. I gave as much of their history as I could. I carefully put each back in a brown paper bag and then, with a flourish, reached inside my coat and pulled out my own .38 Police Special. By now, the room was silent. I had everyone's attention.

"Mr. Chairman, one of us could say something on the floor of this House that might anger someone sitting in that gallery right up there," I said, gesturing to the gallery with my left hand holding the gun. "They could walk out the front door of this building and go into a pawn shop three blocks from here. They could, for the small sum of twenty-five dollars, buy a handgun just like the ones that I have shown you. For one dollar more, they could have the pawn shop owner load that newly acquired gun. That same person could then come back to this building, enter the gallery and—"

At that moment, I fired off the first blank at the ceiling. I looked around and the room was clearing. People jammed themselves through the doors. The committee members at the press table cowered underneath it. The people seated in members' seats were hiding under the chairs and desks.

I paused for a few more seconds to let it sink into all who were gathered. I wanted to make sure that I had everyone's attention.

Then I fired off the second blank.

I leaned into the mic and said loudly, "—you would be dead."

I calmly re-holstered my gun and waited for the smoke to clear. It was nearly a minute before the chairman came out from under the table where he was hiding and started pounding his gavel. That minute seemed like a week. The room was dead silent and nearly no faces could be seen.

"Order, order, the committee will come to order!" The chairman said as he pounded his gavel. He and I were the only two people standing.

As they say in the Western movies, "I stood my ground." I did not offer an explanation for my actions. I made my point and I was going to see it out. It took several minutes for things to settle down.

Slowly, people started coming back into the room or peeping out from behind where they were hiding. It was a sight! The chairman quickly gaveled the committee to end.

Neither my bill nor anything else was considered further that evening. The chairman adjourned the committee and things were over that night. Several members of the press came up to me after we had adjourned to ask if I had fired off blanks. They needed that to finish their stories.

A few days later, I was told that the bill was not voted out of committee. I already knew that my bill had less of a chance of getting out of committee than a $100 bill lasting more than a minute on a New York City sidewalk. But that was not the purpose of it, anyway. The purpose was to point out the danger of selling handguns to anyone who walked up and had a few bucks.

Now here we are, more than fifty years later. The price of a handgun is at least several hundred dollars. Cheap "Saturday Night Specials" are not for sale at your nearest pawn shop.

Some states have indeed limited magazine capacity and the Federal government has background checks, but anyone who has the money, regardless of his or her mental capacity or age, regardless of his or her status as a felon, can somehow get their hands on a pistol, rifle, or shotgun.

News outlets are filled with stories of people going into schools, churches, mosques, temples, or synagogues and killing untold numbers of people. We see nightly on the news that people drive up beside someone on the freeway and shoot into their vehicles. In too many cases, they kill people that they do not even know.

Several days after my mock shoot-out, my little story with pictures made every paper in the great state of Texas as well as several national publications. Now, things have escalated to the point that my same attention-grabbing tactics might not even have made the papers. Real stories of mayhem don't even make the daily news. There are so many that we can't even remember who did what to whom and where they did it.

NINETEEN

MY LAST SESSION

In 1970, I again I ran for re-election unopposed, but I campaigned like I was in a difficult race. We passed out many bumper stickers and yard signs and I spoke at as many churches with Lauro Cruz and Bob Eckhardt as we did the first time we ran. It helped that the three of us liked to hang together and campaigning was fun. We went to all the candidate forums and enjoyed meeting many supporters.

By this time I knew my way around and was respected like a senior member of the House. Even so, many members still walked around me. When I'd come down the hall they would avert their eyes so as to not have to engage me in conversation. However, I made a point of always acknowledging them and called out to them by name.

The third session opened with a bang. It was announced that the Securities and Exchange Commission (SEC)filed suit against a number of defendants for stock fraud. Before long House

Speaker Gus Mutscher's name surfaced and he and his allies tried to prevent it from diminishing his control over the House.

In response, Sissy, I and others formed a group that came to be known as the "Dirty Thirty." It was made up of liberal Democrats and a handful of like-minded Republicans.

The Democrats were politically divided all across the political spectrum. If you could get thirty votes to go in the same direction, that just might make a real difference.

As things evolved, the Republicans voted with us more times than we expected. Their motivation for voting with us was, in most cases, different, but the bottom line was if they didn't vote with the conservative majority, it was a vote for our side. You might not be able to get much passed, but you could stop almost anything. In this way we managed to stymie most of the Mutscher's legislative agenda.

To put the speaker on notice, I introduced an resolution that a plague and picture of Mutscher be removed from the meeting room where it had been placed and given to him at the close of the session. No serving member in the government had ever had a room dedicated in this way. Of course, the resoluton went nowhere.

The Sharpstown scandal dominated the session. There were stories in the paper every day about some aspect of the scandal Not only did it consume the Speaker and his people, it upended Texas politics.

Later Mutscher was convicted and sentenced to five years' probation for accepting bribes. He was later cleared on appeal.

Governor Preston Smith was tainted with the scandal as well, but was never indicted.

Later, I was introduced to a couple in Houston who was trying to adopt a child. In the course of our conversation, I learned that there were many minority children that were up for adoption that could not be placed in permanent homes. It was similar to what was happening to handicapped children. I thought that if there was some kind of incentive, more families would consider adoption. I went to my contact in the Legislative Council and discussed the problem. After a few meetings, we came up with a concept that just might work.

We drew up a bill that stated a family would receive the sum of $50.00 per month for five years if they adopted a handicapped child. I then defined the term "handicapped" to be a child who is a member of a minority group and/or had a physical or mental disability.

Being one of only two Black members of the House, I knew that it would be a long shot to pass such a bill with just our support. I needed someone to front it for me that might be sympathetic to the cause. I remembered that a very conservative representative from East Texas had a handicapped child. I had seen the child at the Easter egg hunt at the governor's mansion during the last session.

I knew this representative would not be seen with me on the floor of the House. I needed a strategy to pitch my idea and have him to run with it.

I had the bill drafted for introduction and packaged nicely. I called his office one morning about a half hour before the opening gavel. He was in and willing to meet me in his office. I assumed he preferred to meet this way so we would not be seen together.

I explained that I wanted to talk to him about a subject that might be of interest to him. "I've found that we have a problem in Texas that just came to my attention, I said in a voicelittle more than a whisper. "There are many handicapped children in foster homes and other places who are never going to be adopted because of their handicap. I thought that if the state offered some incentive to adopt, they might be taken in by loving families and not live lonely lives in foster homes or some other institutions."

I had his attention. I didn't mention that I knew he had a handicapped child, nor did I mention that I had a little twist in the definition of handicapped in the bill that included black and brown children in addition to the physically or mentally handicapped.

I explained that I didn't want to be seen as the originator of the bill. "I would like to give you this bill because I thought you might have an interest in it," I said. I could tell his curiosity was piqued.

"It would pay a family fifty dollars a month for five years if they adopted such a child. It might be the incentive a family

Curtis giving testimony on the clean restroom bill

*Cartoon by Neil
Caldwell. Caption
reads: "What about the
dirty restrooms?"*

needs to seek out such a child and bring them into their home.
Now this bill is yours."

I handed him the proposed bill. "If you want to get co-sign-
ers for the bill, I would be willing to sign somewhere down the
line. It's something that *should* be done and so far as I'm concerned, it is your bill."

John placed the bill in a nice new folder. I thanked him for
seeing me and went on my way.

Within a week, the representative came to my desk after a
session and asked if I would sign the adoption bill. I told him
I would be happy to join him and, in fact, many members had
already signed. Before a month was up, it was passed in both the
House and the Senate and the governor had signed it into law.

I really don't know if John ever appreciated the reality that
this might help Black and brown kids even more than the dis-
abled. Maybe he realized the benefits for all Texas children in

need. My dad used to say there are many ways to skin a cat. Here was a good example, and many kids were helped by it.

During the first month of the session, a young man came to my office and asked to see me. His concern was that there were no standards for what you could call a bathroom in a public place. Of course, the better restaurants and bars all had nice clean restrooms, but there were many others that were not so pleasant and had very little in the way of public facilities, if anything at all. I had once gone to a bar in West Texas that just had a half wall around a tin sheet of metal where men could relieve themselves. I guess women had to hold it until they got home. There were no sinks, no toilets, no nothing.

The fellow had a bill drafted that would address this problem. It set out minimum standards for restrooms in places that served the public. It would require that if an establishment had a license to sell alcohol or food, then they would be required to have restrooms for both men and women with a flushing toilet, a sink with soap, and paper to wipe your hands.

After he had explained the problem to me, I thought I would adopt his bill. I thanked the young man and introduced the bill in a matter of days. It was assigned to a committee and a hearing was requested.

The bill passed through the committee in record time. One day, a very sharp, quick-witted representative from East Texas named Neil Caldwell came up to my desk and leaned over to whisper in my ear. "How did you come up with this clean crapper bill?" he asked.

If anyone could put a funny spin on something, it was Neil. He was also a great artist who loved to draw cartoons. He pushed the bill with me and it was passed and became law.

The decennial census had been taken in 1970 and now, in 1971, it was time for redistricting. Committees were set up in both the House and Senate to draw districts for not only the State House and Senate, but also the congressional districts. I decided that a good move for me in the future was to run for the State Senate. It would be the next step up the ladder.

Word on the street was that Barbara Jordan was going to draw herself a congressional district where she could easily win a seat in the U.S. House of Representatives. I really had no problem with that. Because she was the chair of the redistricting committee in the Senate, I was sure she would leave her district lines in place and I had a great chance to win that seat.

The House passed the Senate bill leaving the lines in place in Harris County, but there were some modifications in other parts of the state. The Senate passed the House bill again with little modifications for other districts elsewhere in the state.

The House and Senate appointed a conference committee to resolve any differences. Lauro Cruz, my suite mate and campaign buddy, was one of the House conferees. One day, the committee was meeting near the end of the session when Lauro rushed into our office. He was quite angry. "You will not believe what just happened!"

"What just happened?" I asked.

"The bitch just fixed it so you can't run for the Senate."

"What?"

"We had these maps on the table that showed all of Harris County," he began to explain.

I sat there, a little numb, wondering what he was going to say next.

"She asked me, and I quote, 'Where is Curtis's house located?' I thought she was trying to protect you." His brown face was turning red.

"I showed her your house location," Lauro continued. "She had a big magic marker in her hand and she drew the line down from River Oaks to pick up your house."

Former President Lyndon Johnson and Curtis on the House floor.

"Tell me that again," I asked in disbelief.

"She drew something like a finger extending the River Oaks senatorial district down to include your house," he repeated.

"Damn! Damn! She burned me!" I yelled out.

Needless to say, through this redistricting move, Barbara Jordan made it impossible for me to run for State Senate and win. She also made it impossible for *any* Black person to represent Harris County in the Texas Senate for ten years. She divided up her senatorial district in a way that no single minority candidate could get a majority of the vote. It would have to wait until the next redistricting.

That pill was hard for me to swallow. Within two weeks, I announced and filed to run for the U.S. Congress. That might not have been my best political move and, in hindsight, I can say definitively that it was not. I could have run for my same State House seat, easily been re-elected, and served until Jordan retired or sought a different office. Then I would have had a good shot at being elected to Congress. But, as they say, hindsight is always 20/20.

Before the session ended, former President Lyndon Johnson came over from his ranch to meet members of the State House. He looked pretty good in the months before his health troubles caught up with him.

So, the session ended and I went home to Houston to make a run for the United States Congress in 1972.

TWENTY

A CONGRESSIONAL RACE

To make a serious run for the U.S. Congress, I would need help. I asked a dentist friend of mine, Dr. Arthur Higgs, to head up a group of supporters that would raise the money, frame the issues, and start me in the right direction.

Arthur and I had done some business together promoting closed-circuit boxing broadcasts in several Louisiana and Texas cities. They featured Muhammad Ali as the main fight on top of the undercard matches.

Arthur had been with me since my first race for the Texas State House and I thought he would be the perfect fit to lead my campaign, so I was pleased when he accepted the job as chairman. He put together a group of supporters who were committed to help me win, drawing mostly from the Black community.

We rented a building that was once a car showroom on Scott Street near both Texas Southern and the University of Houston. The dealer had moved out and it was available at the right price.

We printed materials, staked out our positions, and we were off to the races.

Just a few days after I qualified to run, Barbara Jordan filed for the same 8th Congressional District. What I didn't know at the time (and didn't learn until after I was out of office) was that Jordan had already cut deals to put her in solid position to take the seat. Former President Lyndon B. Johnson had agreed to help with her race and she also had the support of Lieutenant Governor Ben Barnes, a powerful post in Texas politics and a man I had considered a good friend. There were others.

I was told by a few people that Barnes let it be known that he and others did not want me in Congress under any conditions. Many years later, I had a long talk with Congressman Charlie Wilson at Bob Eckhardt's house. He confirmed the story. I guess the higher-ups that ran Texas at the time did not want someone like me, who they knew they could not control, in the House of Representatives.

For now I had a Democratic primary for Congress to win. Early in the month, before the election, there was a reception held at the Rice Hotel to raise money for Jordan's campaign. President Johnson was in attendance. There was a picture taken with the former President kissing Jordan on the cheek. The picture ran not only in every paper in Texas, but in nearly every major newspaper in the nation. I was told that they raised a lot of money.

I didn't have a chance to absorb the information, so it didn't hit me right away. But by the next morning, I realized that I was most likely not going to Congress in January.

Barbara and I spoke at many events one after the other. I remember a friend who was a union organizer coming up to me after one of these events.

He said, "Curtis, you are saying something. You have done more for the people of your district then she has in hers. Keep saying what you are saying. She is not addressing the issues and you are. She is depending on her oratorical stile, and you are speaking to the needs of the people."

I remembered every word of that and did just what he said. But sometimes stile wins over substance.

Even so, I soldiered on. I raised enough money to run a decent race and be competitive. I actually carried the majority of the Black vote. Still, the deck was stacked against me. The district as drawn was about 50% white, 40% Black, and 10% Latino. I was able to carry most of the Black vote and split the Latino vote, but I lost the white vote by ten points or more.

Sometimes you just have to follow your gut. I knew that I was doing the right thing for me by running, but it turned out that my best intentions would not win a congressional seat that year. I was pretty sure that this was the end of my political career, at least in elective office.

I remember my dad consoling me that night, telling me I had waged a good fight and that I was true to myself. "But the hard truth is son, sometime you don't win."

A hard truth, indeed. I did not win a seat in Congress but it changed the course of my life, and I came out with my integrity intact. Today, I can look back and see that it just was not meant to be. I changed directions but I still came out the other end feeling good about my life so far.

TWENTY-ONE

THE GEORGE McGOVERN CAMPAIGN

Within a few weeks of the primary, I received a call from a friend at the National Democratic Committee. He was leaving the committee to work for George McGovern's presidential campaign and asked if I would be interested in working on the campaign, too. At this point I needed a job, so I quickly said yes.

Senator McGovern had emerged as the front-runner for the nomination over former vice president and 1968 presidential nominee Hubert Humphrey and others including Shirley Chisholm, the first Black woman elected to Congress, and Alabama Governor George Wallace, who had been paralyzed in an attempted assassination weeks earlier in Maryland.

After some negotiation about money and where I could do the most good, they decided to sent me to San Diego, California. It was a winner-take-all primary. If McGovern lost, it would make it more difficult to gain the Democratic nomination outright on the first ballot.

305

It was a good assignment. I covered the entire area south of Los Angeles to the Mexican border. I set up offices in downtown San Diego, staying more than a month at the Hotel del Coronado. It turns out that a big donor to the campaign was high up in "The Del's" management.

The historic hotel was one of the premier locations in the county and right on the beach. I enjoyed every minute of my stay there. I arranged for people like actor Leonard Nimoy, Captain Spock in *Star Trek*, to come in. Jesse Jackson came in for a rally. I even had Senator McGovern himself come in for a campaign rally and speak at several gatherings. I remember bringing Senator McGovern to the Hotel del Coronado for one event. Soon after he arrived, we were waiting to bring him in to meet the people assembled to see him when he whispered to me, "Where is the bathroom?"

"Follow me," I said. I led him to the bathroom, we went, and just a minute later we walked out to greet the people. He made his remarks and as we were leaving the hotel, we passed another men's room. Again, he said, "Lets stop in here."

We did, and when we were washing our hands, he said, "When you're campaigning, never pass up a bathroom. You never know when you're going to see another one. It's better to go before you need to than need to when you can't find one."

You know, I never forgot those words. I didn't know then that I had run my last campaign, but those were valuable words nonetheless. It really is strange, the things you hear from people that stick with you forever.

Back in those days, everything was done in cash. It was a little over a week before the primary soldiered, so I made a run to Los Angeles one day to pick up money to pay all the poll workers. It was $25,000 in cash. More precisely, it was $25,000 in twenties. Can you believe that would be more than $160,000 in today's money? But back then it was just $25,000 and it was my job to make the bag run to the Los Angeles headquarters to pick up the cash.

That morning, I caught an early flight carrying a briefcase and was to come back clandestine-style with the money that afternoon. LA political activist Bob Farrell picked me up from the airport and took me to the McGovern campaign's California headquarters in downtown LA, an office abuzz with famous Hollywood types and other wannabes. I again ran into Leonard Nimoy and he introduced me to Nichelle Nichols, Lieutenant Uhura of *Star Trek* fame. *That* was something to remember. She was a household name in Black America in those days. I had a chance to meet several other famous celebrities, but running into both Spock and Uhura that day stuck in my mind.

After the hobnobbing was done, I received my money and Bob was to drive me back to the airport to catch a flight back to San Diego. Instead of going through with the trip as planned, Farrell asked me, "Why don't you catch a later flight and roll with me to the preview of a film at MGM Studios?"

The flight back to San Diego was a shuttle that you could catch nearly every hour. I really didn't have anything to do but eat and go to bed when I got back, so why not visit a film studio?

The cast of the film would be there and I would get a chance to meet many other folks from the Hollywood community. What did I know about studios and movie previews. That sounded like something that a New Orleans boy who had transplanted to Texas would enjoy.

I agreed and we were off to the preview at MGM. When we were on the freeway driving 70 miles per hour, Bob said that he was feeling badly.

"How bad?"

"I think you should drive," he said. "We're just a few miles from the gates of the studio."

He pulled over and I got out to switch to the driver's seat. I didn't have a clue where to go, so I had to depend on him for directions. In the back of my mind, I was aware of the fact that if he couldn't tell me where to go, I would be lost.

I restarted the car and then asked, "What seems to be the problem?"

Bob looked worried. "I'm lightheaded and my fingers and feet are numb."

The good news was that he was able to give me directions. We pulled up to the main gate of the studio in just a few minutes. Trying to convey a sense of urgency, I said to the guard, "I think my friend is having a heart attack or something."

"Just a minute," the guard said.

Just like in the movies, before you could wink an eye a medic showed up on a golf cart. He checked Bob's pulse, then reached into his medical bag and pulled out some pills. "Have him put one of these under his tongue," the medic said. "It's faster for you to take him to the nearest hospital."

As I remembered from when my grandfather died, the pill was nitroglycerin. It's designed to relax the blood vessels to the heart and slow down a heart attack. As I turned the car around, I remembered my last encounter with the drug. I hoped to myself that this time the results would be better.

"Bob, do you know where the nearest hospital is located?"

He shook his head. "I need to go to Kaiser. That's where I'm a member." He had put the pill under his tongue but he still looked distressed and his breathing was labored. "There's one close to here."

He gave me directions and within a few minutes, we were pulling up to the emergency room door. I jumped out of the car and ran in to get him a wheelchair.

When I returned to the car, a guard was standing there insisting that I could not park there.

"My friend is having a heart attack and I need to get him inside," I explained.

Without saying a word, the guard turned his back. I retrieved my briefcase with the money, put Bob in the chair, and wheeled him into the emergency room. I pushed him up to the desk and said, "I think my friend is having a heart attack. He needs to be seen right away."

A large nurse who looked like she could have been a drill sergeant gave me the once over. "Push him right over there and give me his name and date of birth. We'll get to him *soon*."

She looked like a person you didn't question, so I did as she suggested. At this point I really did not know what to do. Bob needed someone to stay with him. I needed to move the car to a parking lot or someone would tow it away. I was carrying a sack full of money and this was not my town. I had to make a command decision.

"Bob, I am going to park the car and be right back," I said, depositing the chair in the place the nurse suggested.

With the money in one hand, I rushed out. I found a parking spot in a parking deck next to the hospital. When I returned, Bob looked worse than before. I ran up to the front desk. "He needs help now!" I punched every word with as much as I could in that setting.

The nurse looked over her glasses. "I will get to you soon."

"Soon" might not be soon enough. Bob looked like he going to check out. I was convinced that Robert Farrell was going to die right in front of me and I had not done what I needed to do to help him.

Just then the drill sergeant nurse yelled out, "Farrell! Farrell!"

I pushed him up to the desk. "Yes ma'am, Farrell."

By this time, Bob was slumped over in the chair.

She looked at me and pointed, "See that red line on the floor?"

"Yes."

"Well, follow it and it will take you to the cardiac unit. I have sent Mr. Farrell's records to them and they will treat him."

I thanked the nurse-sergeant and, without wasting another second, I followed the trail marked by the red line. As fate would have it, there were many turns in the hallway before we reached out destination.

Now, you need to have a good picture of this. I was trying to carry the briefcase full of money, listen to what Bob is saying, and push a wheelchair down a hallway following a red line on the floor. To make my trip more complicated, there was also a yellow line and a blue line on the floor. But the real problem was, at this point, Bob is sure he is going to die. I was not a doctor, but he had me convinced.

As I'm pushing his wheelchair, Bob starts giving me his last dying instructions. "Tell my wife that the strong box is under the bed with the papers in it," he begins.

Then he starts telling me more stuff than I really wanted to know. I am still holding my briefcase of money while pushing and trying to remember everything he is telling me. He tells me some phone numbers and I had to stop to write them down. A third and fourth hand would have been helpful at the time. All the while, I am staying focused on that red line on the floor that marked the route.

We arrive at the cardiac unit just in time. He hadn't died on me yet. I identified him and they took him away, telling me to sit and wait.

With all I had on my plate, telephone numbers written in my hand and on paper, waiting was not at the top of my agenda.

The first thing I needed to do was find a payphone to make the calls with the bad news, starting with Bob's wife. I found a phone and reached in my pocket for a quarter to make the call. I had two nickels and three or four pennies. I pulled out my money clip and I didn't have any small bills, only a few twenties, and of course, I also had a briefcase with $25,000 in twenties. All that money wasn't doing me any good at the moment.

I stood there for a second, then decided to go back to the admitting desk and get some change. I follow the red line and made the return trip without getting lost. Again I encountered the same nurse, and her attitude hadn't improved. However, I could see that she did not want any part of me at this time. I mustered as much kindness as I could. "Excuse me, but would you have change for a twenty?"

She looked up over her glasses. "Do I look like a bank?"

"I'm just trying to get a quarter to call Mr. Farrell's wife to tell her that we're here."

She pointed to the door and said, "You go out that door and turn right. In two blocks, you'll find a Walgreens. They can change your twenty."

To say that I was in an advanced state of pissed off would be an understatement.

There was a Black man to my right with a mop in his hand. He looked at me, eyeing the situation. "How many quarters you need?" he asked.

I held up two fingers. It was hard for me to get words out at this point.

He reached into his pocket and fished out two quarters. I pulled out my money clip and grabbed a twenty.

"No, that's alright," he said.

I smiled, pressed the twenty into his hand, and went to find that payphone.

Down the red line I went. When I reached the cardiac unit, a doctor was waiting for me. "He is going to be okay," she said calmly. "He was just hyperventilating."

"*Hyperventilating?*"

Hyperventilating my ass!

"You can go in to see him," the doctor said.

When I entered the room, it was a different Bob Farrell. He was sitting up on the bed with a big smile. "Well, you had quite an ordeal," he said.

"I was just about to make a call to your wife to tell her where to pick up the body," I replied.

He began laughing heartily. "Now I am really going to take you to the airport."

"Man, I don't think I can take any more excitement," I said.

What I *really* wanted to say was that I needed a stiff drink to get myself together. But me and my sack full of money were off to the Los Angeles airport as soon as he was released. I never did get my tour of the movie studio.

A few days after my ordeal in LA, McGovern won the primary. I had done everything I was supposed to do. The money got to the right people and I was happy that I had played a role in the whole thing.

I went home for a few days, then I got a call asking if I would pack my bags again and go to Pittsburgh, Pennsylvania. With the Democratic nomination secured, I was to work Pittsburgh for the general election. They found me an apartment and set me up to help coordinate the complex local democratic machine to pull for McGovern. It was hard work, but unlike local elections I had been involved with, there was enough money to help the precinct captains get out the vote. I was an outsider but I had enough high-placed insiders around to make it work for me. Because Pittsburgh was a party machine town, everyone knew who he or she reported to and what was expected of them.

One of the highlights of the Pittsburgh tour of duty was that I got to bring in vice presidential candidate Sargent Shriver. By this time, Secret Service was assigned to all of the candidates and it was a mess to work them and the candidate's staff to pull off a downtown hotel rally. I remember riding in the back of a limo with Shriver and his wife, Eunice Kennedy Shriver. Secret Service agents were driving the motorcycles and trying to control traffic and it was a mess. I can remember the driver just slowing down and the Secret Service guy in the front seat jumping out to stop traffic as we made a left turn on a red light. I just sat with my mouth open and things went on.

The Shrivers were very nice to me. Mrs. Shriver said to give her a call when I was in D.C. I put her card in my pocket, thinking that I would never use it.

We did what we needed to do and after all was said and done, McGovern may have done all right in Pittsburgh but he lost the state of Pennsylvania by twenty points and the general election in a massive defeat. No matter the result, I had done my part to carry everything forward as I had been assigned.

Was it even possible for anyone to win against the incumbent Richard Nixon? Now, that was the year of the Watergate Scandal began. His people broke into the Democratic headquarters in the Watergate Apartments for whatever reason. I don't think that Senator McGovern ever had a chance. He ran a good campaign, but the defeat was more than anyone could have imagined.

I have often thought to myself just how different the nation would have been if Nixon had lost the 1972 election. The nation would not have gone through the Watergate ordeal. Gerald Ford would never have been president. Jimmy Carter most likely would never have been president.

One can play the what-if game forever, but history is what it is. We have to live with the way it is and not the way we wanted it to be. So I moved on from McGovern's loss and tried to make a life for me and my family.

TWENTY-TWO
AFTER POLITICS

Inow needed a job. After the election dust had settled, I hit the ground in Houston to see what I was going to do with the rest of my life. Before long, I realized that many potential opportunities were not coming my way. Perhaps Barbara Jordan, now in the U.S. Congress, did not want a potential rival back in Houston or maybe something else was in play.

It didn't really matter because the truth was that I had a family to feed, especially my three young children who needed a dad who had a regular paycheck.

So, I cast a wider net beyond Houston and Texas. I looked to Washington, D. C. I reached out to a friend from Shreveport, Louisiana, Gerald Wallette, who now headed up an agency called the Leadership Institute for Community Development that provided services to local agency poverty programs.

When I called he was receptive and suggested that I should come up the next week to see if I liked the organization and how I could be of service to them. I made the trip to D.C. and right away it seemed like a good fit. I stayed with the Eckhardts on that trip but when I started work, I moved in with Wallette for a brief time while I looked for a new home.

The children were in school in Houston, and it was better for me to find a job, a place to live and my way around town before I moved the family. Things were moving fast but that suited me. It was now a few days before Thanksgiving and I needed some income quickly. My state pay for serving in the House would run out on the first of January.

I found a rental house in Bethesda, Maryland located very near a good Catholic school so the children could start in January. Then I returned to Houston to begin the move. My plan was to start driving a few days before Christmas. spend Christmas day in New Orleans with my parents and finish the trip in time to meet the movers when they arrived.

Our relocation went well and before the next year was out, we were able to buy a house in the District and within another year or so I was recruited by the National Aeronautics and Space Administration (NASA).

Washington was a great place for us to live and to raise three children. It was also an exciting time to work at NASA.

My main focus was education. We ran special briefings for educators at the Kennedy Space Center and elsewhere and trainings along with materials for thousands of teachers at every level.

I encouraged NASA initiatives to provide minority teachers and students with internships and career opportunities with a particular emphasis on science and math. I felt the future of NASA depended on it.

By 1988, I was Deputy Director of Civil Affairs. In recognition of my work, I was honored to receive the Frank G. Brewer Trophy, given annually for "significant contributions of enduring value to aerospace education in the United States."

The ceremony was held in November 1989 at the Smithsonian's Air and Space Museum where I was presented with a trophy.

My name was inscribed on the original trophy which is on permanent display at the Museum.

Administered by the National Aeronautics Association, the award had been given since 1943. It turns out that I was the second African American to receive the honor, the first being, Charles Alfred "Chief" Anderson, considered the father of Black Aviation.

At a time when people questioned whether Negros had the ability to fly, Chief Anderson famously took Eleanor Roosevelt for a flight, lending support of training Black pilots for the military. When World War II started, the Army chose him as Tuskegee's Ground Commander and Chief Instructor for aviation cadets of the 99th Pursuit Squadron, America's first all-black fighter squadron.

It was a genuine honor for me to personally present the Brewer Trophy to Anderson in 1985.

You would think that the accomplishments of Chief Anderson would be well-known and held up proudly by the Black community and Americans at large. Yet beyond a few political leaders and some sport figures and musicians, you had to dig to find the stories of the many Black Americans who inspired others. While working at NASA I noticed the need for children, especially Black children, to be exposed to these incredible individuals. Yet in the 1980s this need remained mostly unfilled.

I began to collect names of individuals whose life stories would benefit the young people who learned about them.

I knew an educator that I had collaborated with, Jane Hodges, who worked with NASA and together we tackled this problem. Jane had created a series of childhood activities and skills development that we applied to a list of people that we chose. I supplied the biographies.

And so, *Famous Black Americans: Folder Games for the Classrooms* was born. Published in 1986; by 1989 it had gone through three printings. It was most useful for late elementary or middle school students, Later we saw a need for something to reach earlier ages and published a version to reach those ages with most of the detailed activities in a separate teacher guide.

Some of the personalities contained were obvious selections, like Martin Luther King, Jr. or Frederick Douglas or Sojourner Truth. Others were less-known but pioneers in their chosen field. We tried to encompass many disciplines like science, mathematics, education, literature, civil rights and politics.

We began with the early days of the United States with Benjamin Banneker, who helped survey Washington D.C. and gave a taste of the black experience and history in America for young people.

I have known a small number of them but that certain wasn't a requirement, nor was it even possible. Of course since the book was published, many more names could be added. As my friend Fred Gregory, astronaunt and Space Shuttle pilot—himself one of the entries—wrote in his Foreword for *Famous Black Americans*: "The selected sample in this book bears evidence that Blacks have invented and explored and discovered. Each new contribution makes us aware of the depth and uniqueness of the Black experience in contemporary American culture. Each new experience tantalizes us with a vision of what is yet to come."

Choosing the entries was not easy. Should it be the most famous included? The most impactful? Remember it was not now, but over thirty-five years ago.

One person I struggled about including in the book was Mohammed Ali. He certainly was famous enough. In fact, I wondered if there were any young children who did not know of him. Instead I chose another boxer, Joe Louis who was a hero to most Black Americans, and almost universally admired in my parents' day. His two matches with the German, Max Schmeling, captivated our nation amidst ominous international tensions with the Nazis.

I first met Ali when he refused entry in the Army as a Conscientious Objector, the beginning of his three year battle with the U.S. government. He was not only sentenced to prison but stripped of his heavyweight title.

In 1970, he returned to the ring and the following March he fought Joe Frazier. It was his first professional loss. In July, Ali fought Jimmy Ellis in Houston and was scheduled to fight at the Astrodome again in November.

One afternoon I was at the Astrodome when he got through with his workout and training. He was done for the day and he was looking to relax and kill a little time. I didn't have much to offer, only a trip to pick up my kids from school. To my surprise Mohammed asked to join me.

Driving along he began to sing. His voice was pleasant enough, but I didn't recognize the tune. I knew that he had once recorded an album with a cover of his friend Sam Cooke's single "Stand by Me."

What I didn't know is that in 1969 he had been featured in a Broadway musical. He was always looking for way to earn money while he was out of boxing. *Buck White* had a Black empowerment theme, with music and lyrics by jazz stylist Oscar Brown, Jr., who I had met years earlier when he had performed in Houston.

Despite decent reviews, *Buck White* didn't last a week. The cast, including Ali, appeared on the "Ed Sullivan Show" singing "We came in Chains." One interesting note: He used Cassius Clay as kind of a stage name with "a/k/a Mohammed Ali" in very small type.

Gizelle the youngest of our children was too young for school, so we first stopped at the Catholic school where Gretchen was in kindergarten. She was waiting outside with her class when I drove up. She jumped in the back seat and I introduced her to Ali. She said hi, and went on singing some song she had learned at school. Mohammed Ali did not mean anything to her. At five hears old Scooby Doo might have impressed her, but Ali sitting in the front seat couldn't compete. Next we picked up Christopher who was at the Libratory School or pre-school at

Mohammed Ali with Gretchen and Christopher

Texas Southern University All three of us when in to fetch him. Gretchen had attended this pre-school the year before, so she was glad to skip along to see some of her teachers and friends. As everywhere, Ali caused a buzz.

Outside, again people gathered around. Someone had a Polaroid camera and wanted to snap a few pictures. Ali, ever gracious, agreed.

While I would see Ali every now and again, I cherish most the memories of those rare everyday times with him.

After 30 years with NASA, I retired and moved to Tucker, Georgia, where I am now living with my current wife Kay Bryant.

With the encouragement of Kay, I became more serious about my love of photography. I have enjoyed taking pictures all over the world and many are now hanging in museums, galleries, and private homes. My photography of the Louisiana plantations where my family was enslaved has appeared in several gallery shows, I still do consulting work and serve on several boards.

My three children all are in the middle of successful lives. Now I also have six grandchildren—two boys and four girls—who all seem to be moving in the right direction. I am extremely proud and very blessed in my life.

As they make their own way, I have tried to convey to them something that I was taught at a young age; in order to really know who you are, you need to understand where you come from. Telling my story here is one attempt to offer a little insight into what should be a lifetime pursuit of wisdom, not just for them but for anyone and everyone who is interested.

It is a journey that does not end. I recently had an opportunity to learn more about my ancestor, Marie Celeste Becnel Haydel. I wrote about her in Chapter Two, but previously unknown documents which needed to be translated from French have emerged.

Known as Celeste, she was born a slave on what is now the Whitney Plantation but was then known as Habitat Haydel.

She was the daughter of Francoise, a slave and Florestan

Gretchen Graves, Christopher Graves and Gizelle Graves Bryant.

Becnel, the Master of the neighboring Evergreen Plantation, and the brother-in-law of Azelie Haydel, wife of Marcellin, Master of Habitat Haydel.

Celeste was either donated or sold to Florestan Becnel her father. What we have found is that when Josephine Haydel (the legitimate wife of Florestan) died in 1844, Celeste was one of the slaves listed in the inventory of the Evergreen, their plantation

Florestan had eight children with Francoise and he allowed all of them to carry his last name of Becnel.

With that many children, we can probably assume that Florestan's white family, with Josephine Haydel Becnel, living in the big house on the Evergreen, knew about the black family on the Whitney just next door.

In 1854 Celeste was bought by her white half-brother Leo Becnel for about $600, after the death of his father. She was described at the sale as a Creole Mulatto aged 17.

She was not married in the Church until 1871 according to the records of St. John the Baptist Catholic Church. By that time Celeste already had five children with Victor Haydel, starting in 1858. Victor was the son of Anna, a slave girl bought by Marcellin Haydel in New Orleans when she was about 3 or 4 years old. Marcellin and Azelie, were second or third cousins. They had no children, so she raised Anna in the big house on the Whitney Plantation. When Anna was about 13 or 14 years old, she had a child with Antoine Haydel, who was Azelie's brother and an overseer on the plantation. It was not a consensual relationship. Anna hated him and never married.

Azelie, however, was a devout Catholic and demanded that her brother take Victor, his child with Anna, to St. John the Baptist Church on River Road to have him baptized. On the baptismal record, he claims Victor as his son and Anna as the child's mother.

In 1858 Victor Haydel Jr., the first of ten children, was born. We really don't know where Celeste was living at the time but in

1859, she had the second child, Theophile. We do know that Celeste was a servant in the household of Leo Becnel her half-brother. He must have cared for her and recognized her as his sister because even though he had paid $600 to acquire her, he freed her in 1862. So Celeste was the first freed member of our family. Her husband Victor was not freed until emancipation. According to the 1870 census records, neither Celeste or Victor could read or write.

Victor and Celeste continued to work for Leo in his household. In 1881, they had saved the grand sum of $700.00 to put down on a plantation of their own. Leo carved off the south or down river end which was the last 183 front feet of his plantation 89 acres and sold it to his half-sister and her husband for the sum of $1,400. They signed a note to pay the remaining $700 in three installments. They did so in a year.

The property was a little strange because it was 183 feet wide and 4 miles deep, Celeste, Victor and their sons leased additional land to create a working plantation which the family owned and worked until 1926. Facing the present-day Highway 18 or River Road on the west bank of the Mississippi, it is very near where the St. John the Baptist Parish library is located now.

This amazing woman who died when she was only 41 or 42, was the matriarch of my family. The descendants of Celeste and Victor, two former slaves, include a mayor of New Orleans, medical doctors, a first lady of New Orleans, lawyers, people with advanced degrees, college professors, a state legislator, business people of all kinds and just great citizens of all stripes. We live in nearly all the states of the Union and in many places around the world..

I think it's a quintessential American story.